THE TRADING EDGE

THE TRADING EDGE

A Learner's Guide to Ace the Stock Market

VIVEK BAJAJ

HARPER
BUSINESS

An Imprint of HarperCollins *Publishers*

First published in India by Harper Business 2026
An imprint of HarperCollins *Publishers*
HarperCollins *Publishers* India, Cyber City,
Building 10-A, Gurugram, Haryana – 122002, India
www.harpercollins.co.in

2 4 6 8 10 9 7 5 3 1

P-ISBN: 978-93-7307-723-9
E-ISBN: 978-93-7307-094-0

Typeset in 11/14.4 Aldine401 BT
by HarperCollins *Publishers* India Pvt. Ltd

Printed and bound at
Magic International Pvt. Ltd., Greater Noida, India

HarperCollins *Publishers*, Macken House, 39/40 Mayor Street Upper,
Dublin 1, D01 C9W8, Ireland

Additional Disclaimer

This book is intended solely for educational and informational purposes. The views, strategies, methods and opinions expressed herein are those of the Author. They do not constitute financial, investment, legal or professional advice. Readers are advised to consult with a certified finance professional before making any investment or trading decisions.

Trading and investing in securities and financial markets involves substantial risk and may not be suitable for all individuals. Past performance, whether actual or indicated by historical tests of strategies, is no guarantee of future results. The author and the publisher expressly disclaim any liability for any direct or indirect loss or damage incurred by readers acting upon the information contained in this book.

All references to companies, data, markets and instruments are included for illustrative purposes only and do not imply any recommendation or endorsement. The author and publisher do not guarantee the accuracy, completeness or timeliness of any data or information provided.

By reading this book, the reader acknowledges that they understand and accept the risks involved in financial markets and agree that the responsibility for any investment decision lies solely with them.

The detailed notes pertaining to this book are available on the HarperCollins *Publishers* India website. Scan this QR code to access the same.

Acknowledgements

This book is not just a piece of writing—it is a reflection of my journey, my learnings, and the people who have shaped me along the way.

First and foremost, I bow my head to god, whose invisible hand has always guided me. Every success, every lesson and every challenge has unfolded under his grace. I owe my deepest gratitude to my parents, who built the foundation of who I am. Their values, discipline and faith have been my biggest strength. To my brothers and family, who have stood by me at every step—thank you for your constant support, trust and companionship. To my wife, Etee, and my children, Aishani, Ishaan and Vivaan—you are my world. Your love, patience and belief in me have been the quiet force behind all my pursuits. You give meaning to my ambition and balance to my madness. I am equally grateful to my business partners and my team, both past and present. Each of you, directly or indirectly, has played a role in shaping my thoughts and my learning journey. Your hard work, ideas and belief in the vision have made this possible.

A special word of thanks to Annapurna Chowdhury (co-author) and Nidhi Somani, who worked tirelessly to give this book its final shape. Your dedication, attention to detail and emotional connection with the subject made this book come alive.

Finally, to every person who has been a part of my journey—my mentors, colleagues, students and friends—thank you for adding your energy to my evolution. This book is not just mine. It belongs to everyone who has walked with me, and taught and inspired me.

Contents

Preface

This book was conceptualized during the early days of the pandemic—a time when the world slowed down, routines were disrupted and reflection became unavoidable. In that pause, I met Annapurna, a young professional—curious, eager to learn, yet uncertain about what to do with her savings. Like millions of others in that period, she felt drawn to the stock market, influenced by the growing conversations surrounding it.

Her questions were simple, honest and deeply familiar. They echoed the same doubts and confusion that every beginner faces when stepping into the world of trading. That's when a thought struck me: What if I could distill my 2 decades of trading experience into conversations that would feel relatable, practical and unintimidating? That thought led to the birth of the Learn2Trade series on my *YouTube* channel.

I began recording sessions with Annapurna, where her curiosity became the voice of thousands of aspiring traders—people who wanted to learn but didn't know where to begin. What started as a passion project soon grew into something far bigger. Session by session, step by step, the series reached learners across the country and eventually crossed 100 million views.

Under structured guidance and disciplined learning, Annapurna began trading with a small amount of capital. Over time, she evolved into a far more confident and independent market participant—an outcome that reaffirmed my belief that trading, when taught correctly, can be understood by anyone willing to put in the effort.

As the video series expanded, we realized there was another audience—those who prefer learning through reading, reflection, and revisiting ideas at their own pace. That insight led us to extend this journey into a book. Written in simple, accessible English, this book is designed to make trading approachable for every curious beginner. Annapurna joined me as a co-author, ensuring that the book addresses the very doubts, hesitations, and questions she once had—and that every new trader still does.

I'm glad we chose to take this step. This book has emerged as a practical masterclass on how I developed my edge in trading. For anyone exploring trading—whether part-time or full-time—this book aims to be a complete, reliable companion on that journey.

Note: We have elucidated the concepts in this book through tables and figures. However, given the print-layout limitations and for clarity, please refer to them on my website vivekbajaj.com.

1

Getting Started

Why should you read this book? What makes it worth your time and effort? How will it deliver differently from other trading books?

Well, if you are browsing and still making your mind up, I encourage you to trust your gut feeling; you are headed in the right direction.

Before I tell you why this book is a great pick, I want you to write down the top 3 reasons you want to be a trader.

1. ______________________________
2. ______________________________
3. ______________________________

The market is a great teacher, but you need to be a willing student.

I feel that financial markets are crucial to our lives—irrespective of whether you are a trader or not. Here are some reasons why I believe this:

1. The financial market is not just one industry, it's an aggregation of multiple industries. Knowledge about the markets gives you insights into multiple businesses. If you are part of the market ecosystem, you essentially are exposing yourself to the entire economic scenario of your country and the whole world too.

2. Trading is an essential part of human evolution. What we are today is because of our early understanding of the art of speculation.
3. The financial market is an abyss with profound applications and opportunities. Along the journey, one discovers his/her skills that help him/her sustain and grow in the market and otherwise.
4. As we grow professionally, our life will need help from the market in some form. Considering that investments are a crucial part of building financial wealth. Investing in any form of equity would eventually become more of a need than a want. Hence, starting early is advisable.

A successful trader is someone who can beat the markets over a longer period of time through consistent practice and is able to keep their calm when everyone else is in panic mode. There is a saying in the market that if you stay here long enough, you will be rewarded. *You have to put in that extra effort to stay. Even if you lose money, don't lose hope.*

This is a learning through my own share of failures and successes. I will share my journey with you—its turning points, successes, failures and hard decisions—to give you insights into the world of trading.

With my Bloomberg Terminal in 2007

With Bloomberg in 2026

Failure in life can be a stepping stone or a setback. It is all about how you deal with it.

It has been 25 years since my first big failure. I failed my CA Final Group-1 in 2001. This failure became one of the most important turning points in my life.

I had distinction in 3 out of 4 papers in that group. So I had to appear for only one paper in the next term. The fact that I failed in that *one* subject was a setback as I missed my all-India rank. I decided to move to Mumbai for a job after giving the exam. I wished to join a financial services company and get some holistic exposure. I landed a job as a management trainee in the sales division of JM Mutual Fund.

I owe a lot to my boss at the time, Prabal Nag, and my super boss, Krishnamurthy Vijayan, for helping me transform from a boy to a man. Mutually, we tried our best to work in synergy, but I soon realized that the job was not for me. I came back to Kolkata, my hometown, and started my own mutual fund distribution business. The business failed. I treated it as a good failure, yet again to rise stronger.

In the meantime, derivatives trading was properly launched in India. I was fortunate to have access to a trading terminal because of my family's business background and connections in the market. My father and elder brothers were already members of the Calcutta Stock Exchange and gradually became members of the National Stock Exchange. I got a chance to experiment there. I still remember my first big profit was in trading ITC Options where I made money because someone made a mistake. A clerical error that cost the counter party Rs 5,00,000 became my gain. Mixed emotions clouded me but I also realized this is part of the process.

While I was happy trading, the entrepreneur inside me was getting restless. I realized I was never meant to be just a trader. I believed in building an enterprise around my passion. This encouraged me to do an MBA. I appeared for GMAT but scored poorly—the third setback on my growth curve—but then got through IIM Indore. The next 2 years were the most defining and amazing years of my life.

I joined the emerging commodities market right after with the conviction that *new markets will always offer better opportunities*. I shifted to Mumbai in May 2005 and was the first employee at JM Financial Commtrade, and as a commodity analyst, I analysed gold, silver and crude oil. I was quite successful in predicting their movements which fuelled me to come back to Kolkata and trade for myself. This was on 9 January 2006.

The first 6 months in this new phase were full of dramatic highs, emotional lows and intense action—much like a Bollywood movie. I had a love–hate relationship with the main characters—the commodity contracts on NCDEX and MCX. I had set myself a budget—Rs 10,00,000—and promised that if I lost it all, I would return to Mumbai for a job. The pressure was immense. I was highly qualified—CA, CS, MBA and MCom—but had chosen a field that was not respected and was almost considered gambling back in the day. The regard was so low that it also impacted marriage proposals. I had a lot to prove—to myself and to society. My conviction that what worked globally would ultimately be accepted in India kept me going.

I lost 25% of my risk capital in the first 6 months. My confidence took a greater hit than my bank account. However, I convinced myself this was the 'learning fee' for the market, and I kept going sincerely and upheld my integrity. I kept repeating to myself that I should not worry about the loss.

My breakthrough came with a trade in natural gas. My confidence was restored, and I earned Rs 25,00,000 in a single trade. I learnt '*Apna Time Aayega*' is a mantra that always comes through for people who believe in themselves.

I invested the money in a Bloomberg terminal. It cost Rs 1,50,000 a month to have access to every minute detail in the financial market. It was a very bold decision to make. I am grateful to my elder brothers who supported me so early on in my career.

The Bloomberg terminal was costly. I wanted to derive maximum out of this investment and for this, I started recruiting people to smoothen my journey. The 2007–2008 crash, which was perilous for most market participants, turned out to be profitable for me. I capitalized on the falling market and the introduction of the currency market. I became a scalper and spread trader in the currency segment of NSE, MCX-SX and later BSE.

In 2009, a revolutionary change occurred in India with the introduction of co-location facilities by exchanges, allowing traders to host servers onsite. We were among the first to apply, but I lacked technical knowledge to develop an algo-trading software. I partnered with like-minded individuals in Mumbai, and we developed a software for our use, which significantly grew the firm large. *I truly believe that to realize one's shortcomings and to partner with experts for those is key to growth.*

From 2006 to 2013, between 9 a.m. and midnight every day, I was busy building the foundation for what I am today. However, in 2013, several significant events occurred at the same time:

- Commodities Transaction Tax (CTT) was introduced, making commodities trading unviable
- Raghuram Rajan's measures in the currency market reduced volatility, making currency trading infeasible[1]
- I was blessed with twin boys

My wife Etee then suggested that I rethink my working lifestyle. It was the crucial phase of life for my 3 children (I have an elder daughter) growing up. I agreed and began searching for a way to transition from active trading to passive trading. It was a stressful journey, akin to a midlife crisis, as I consciously made efforts to change my mindset from watching screens all day to a more passive approach. I took it up as a challenge, and I credit the transformative journey of Inner Engineering with Isha Foundation for my spiritual training.

> 'It is not the strongest of the species that survives, nor the most intelligent; it is the one most adaptable to change.'
>
> —Leon C. Megginson[2]

During my research, I discovered the concept of relative strength, and in 2014, began my journey as a swing trader. The reader in me picked up *Bloomberg* by Michael Bloomberg as a flight read. It left me highly inspired and drove me to the next phase of my life. With like-minded partners I went on to build Elearnmarkets, now India's foremost financial e-learning platform aimed at empowering people. Then came StockEdge, a data-driven analytics tool, StockEdge Club, a community for serious stock market participants, and other initiatives. Today we are relentlessly working on building the StockEdge ecosystem to empower the retail investors of India—just as Michael Bloomberg empowered institutions.

My Evolution as a Market Participant

Each market strategy needs you to have or build certain characteristics. In my 20 years of trading, I've practised different strategies during different stages and each of them required me to adopt different kinds of characteristics. It has been an exciting journey of growth and evolution. The following table will help you understand the different types of trades and identify which is close to your personality and risk appetite.

Strategy	What Is It	Characteristic Needed
Scalping	Tick-by-tick trading with a very short interval and price action. Mostly driven by short-term market breadth (top 5 buyers and sellers) and 3-minute price action of dependent variables.	Young, active and looking to be there in the market from open to close. Extremely proactive in judging the cause-and-effect relationships in the market.
Spread Trading	Trading the difference between 2 different instruments. Spread prediction is all about estimating the outperformance of one instrument vis-a-vis other. Classic spread trading is a calendar spread in different instruments of same underlying and pair trading between 2 different underlyings.	Analytical mindset with an understanding of the concept of mean reversal. Willing to spend more time on data analysis as this is a low frequency trading style.
Options Trading	Application of trading strategies using options via delta, gamma, theta and vega.	Highly analytical mindset with ability to do multiple scenario analysis using data.

Swing Trading	Identification of stock swings and participating from low to high and also from high to higher in a shorter time frame.	Ability to identify the origin, maintenance and termination of swing using technical analysis. The most important aspect of skill requirement here is patience and practice.
Momentum Investing	Longer tenure swings to capture much larger movements supported by fundamental justifications like earning, growth, etc.	Ability to understand new emerging business themes and connect the same with price action. The ability to eliminate noise related to narratives around an opportunity. Just like swing trading, patience and practice holds the key to momentum investing.
Value Investing	Investing in businesses for long term.	Ability to understand how businesses work. The most important skill set in this category is networking.

I have been through all these phases in my journey till now. My journey is not just about my personal success but also about embracing change, whether it's forced or voluntary, as circumstances shift.

In the stock market, you get what you deserve, not necessarily what you want.

I was an active trader till 2013. I became a passive trader from 2014. I did swing trading till 2020. Today, I see myself as a perfect momentum investor and am now looking to evolve to become a full circle investor.

Over the years, I have also come to realize that *society rewards anyone who gives back.*

I was privileged to have been exposed to quality education and resources at an early age in my life, and I felt the need to give it back to society. Education has been my major source of motivation and inspiration. To help everyone around learn the art and science of investing and trading, I became an active knowledge contributor. In 2008, we started an offline centre for financial education in Kolkata: Kredent Academy (kredentacademy.com). To overcome the physical barrier of education, we shifted our education initiative from offline to online via elearnmarkets.com in 2013.

The introduction and rapid adoption of social media, especially YouTube, made education more accessible to the masses, and I felt the need to reach out to every knowledge seeker who is online. We started working on creating varied content online with the sole objective of spreading the knowledge from the right people.

We initiated the #Face2Face podcast, which has become one of the largest finance podcasts in India. I then recorded my own trading series, #Learn2Trade, which is the most comprehensive trading education series available online. I am still recording the series #Learn2Invest, which is relevant for anyone and everyone interested in investing. I strive to keep sharing such content on both YouTube and elearnmarkets.com and to spread financial education for the benefit of India+Bharat, the urban and rural population alike. This book is another avenue for me to impart knowledge.

I hope my journey inspires you, motivates you and provides valuable lessons, helping you chart your path in the stock market. *I strongly believe that if I can do it, anyone can.*

How to Use This Book

This book expects you to have a level 1 (out of level 10) knowledge about financial markets. If you are at level 0, please use the QR code mentioned on my website vivekbajaj.com/thetradingedge and get free access to a basic course on the market before processing further.

Additionally, I would request you to spend time on the important concepts to ensure you understand it well, and also practice all the exercises that we've added. These exercises are part of your foundation building and extremely important if you want to truly start trading. Some chapters have been added because, I feel, as a market participant, it's important to have holistic knowledge of certain concepts. However, you can choose to move forward with those at a fast pace. I will mark the time you should be spending on these chapters.

This book has been divided into 5 major parts after this introduction. It is easy to finish each section in a day. But unlike a leisure read, the point is not to *finish* the book, but to understand the concepts well and apply them as you move forward in your trading journey. I highly recommended that you dedicate at least 1 week to each section, to grasp the concept well before moving on to the complexities. I have mentioned on my website a rough schedule that you may follow. All you need to do is just dedicate 2 to 3 hours each day to really work your way through the materials so you come out prepared to take the plunge in trading.

Eventually, I would want you to be the turtle in the race. Slow, steady, consistent and ultimately a winner. *The turtle mindset* is a term I coined inspired by the story of the turtle.

Let's recall 'The Turtle and the Rabbit'. A simple race between a fast-paced animal and a slow-paced reptile. At the onset, it feels obvious who would win; but the turtle surprises us. Did it win because of the speed? No, it won because of its mindset, and that's what matters the most in the end—having the winning mindset, or the turtle mindset.

Turtles represent longevity and wisdom that comes with age and experience. They are symbols of patience, endurance and resilience. They're known to be process-oriented through their slow, steady movements. It serves as a reminder for us to drive our life at our own pace and trust the process.

On that note, let us delve into this book—learn tricks, pick up tips and slowly but steadily start making money in the market.

Parallel Learning

There is a dedicated section on my website vivekbajaj.com where I have given a proper learning map for every serious learner. It included links to my topic-wise Hindi videos, quizzes and some fun games to understand trading better. Please note that the content of this book and the videos are not exact, but the core concepts remain the same.

I suggest, while you read this book chapter by chapter, do consider parallel reference on the website for clear image outputs and 360 degree learnings. The QR code is here:

2

Building the Foundation

'With the great guidance and inspiration I received from you, I have finally become an independent swing trader. I left my job one year ago, and this year, I more than doubled my corpus. From having zero knowledge of the financial market to gaining a solid understanding, my journey has been transformative. I've transitioned from a dependent job to becoming an independent investor and trader. I feel very happy and proud of myself. Thank you for all your support. I know many Indians are achieving success like me, but I wanted to share my story and gratitude with you.'

—Raj Sharma, Learn2Trade student

In this chapter, we talk about everything you need to know before you begin trading. But first, I need you to know the difference between trading and investing.

Trading Is Not the Same as Investing

Often people confuse the 2 terms. Let us understand the fundamental differences:

	Trading	Investing
Time Period	Short-term	Long-term
Objective	Aims at short-term profits due to price fluctuations	Aims to gain profits with asset appreciation and dividends over time
Risk	Riskier and associated with frequent transactions and dependence on market volatility	Less risky and associated with company mismanagement, economic downturns and market corrections
Analysis Needed	Technical analysis: Study of stock charts for price and volume to predict movement in the near future	Fundamental analysis: Study of the company and its financials to judge the intrinsic value through financial statements and the management. It questions the current market price.

Table 2.1

Having understood the differences, let's be clear that this book is about trading. Trading is for everyone who has an analytical bent of mind and some risk appetite.

How Can You Introduce Trading to Your Life?

Trading can be as big a part of your income as you would like it to be. You can choose to start small and then see where the journey leads you. You can be a

- part-time trader: who spends limited time in a day tracking the markets as a means of additional income;
- full-time trader: who has no other source of primary income and spends most of his or her time in the day trading; or
- pro trader: who alongside their own money also uses other people's money to trade in the market for a commission.

Trading has the flexibility of being anywhere and still being at work. In my experience of 17 years as a trainer, a lot of my students have made the switch from being part-time traders to trading full-time since they were performing exceedingly well and they enjoyed the flexibility it brought.

Let's Start!

To trade, you need:

1. a demat and trading account with a broker
2. charting software (I use TradingView)
3. a stock analytics tool for stock selection and analysis (I use StockEdge)

Please note that for all the charts we analyse and in all the examples, we use these 2 software. While you can use any, for ease of following the book, I recommend starting with them.

The 2 Types of Trading

- Intraday Trading: Intraday trades are those made during the day. That is, where you buy in the morning and square (or sell) it off by the end of the day at market close, and take back home the profit or loss incurred during the day.
- Swing Trading: Positional/swing trades are created for a defined time frame. That is, for 2-20 days, 21-60 days or 60-180 days, depending on the analysis of the trader.

Must-Knows of Technical Analysis

Technical analysis is trying to predict the future of a stock by looking at its past behaviour. It involves studying charts that show how the stock's price has moved over time and examining the volume of shares traded. By analysing these patterns and using special tools called indicators, one can make informed decisions about when to buy or sell a stock.

Instead of focusing on a company's earnings or the economy, technical analysis helps make sense of price movements and volume to guide trading choices. The entire discipline and all patterns, indicators and concepts are derived from these 2 basic data points.

Price and Volume

Figure 2.1 represents the price chart of the State Bank of India. The time frame of the chart is 1 day or daily implying that the price is plotted at the end of every day to make it into a graph. The scrip code—a symbol defined by the exchange—of the State Bank of India is SBIN.

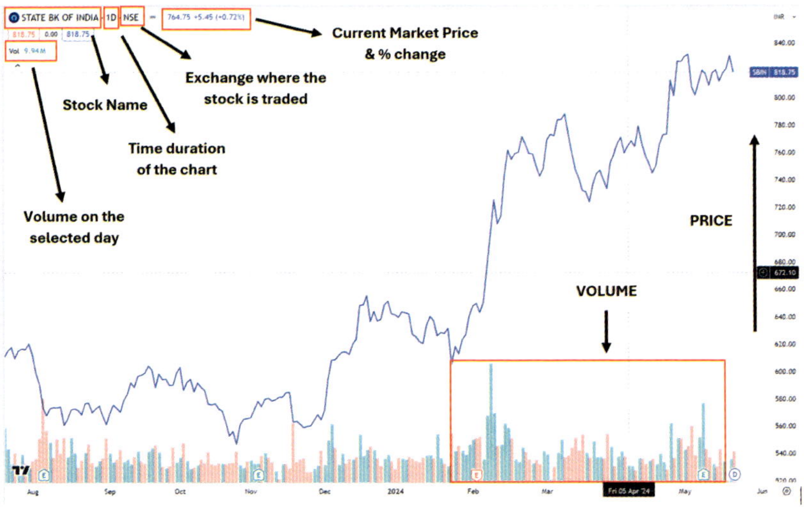

Figure 2.1 Daily chart of State Bank of India

Price of a stock changes as per the demand and supply in the market. The stock market, like any other commodity, also plays by the rule of economics—higher the demand, higher the price, lower the demand, lower the price.

At the bottom of the chart on Figure 2.1, there are certain multiple towers or bars that reflect the volume traded in a stock on that particular day. Traded volume is the quantity of shares or securities transacted. The higher the tower the higher the quantity of shares that was transacted on that day at that price. The colour of the volume bar corresponds with the colour of the candle formed on the same day. This will be evident when we change the chart type to candlestick chart. We will cover candlesticks later in the book.

When a price movement is supported by high volumes, it is a sign of great conviction for the traders that the stock is more likely to continue moving in the same direction, be it up or down. Similarly, if a price movement is complemented by a low volume bar, then there is no conviction in the move irrespective of its direction.

For example: if price rises with a volume of 100 shares and if the price rises with a volume of 1,000 shares, then the price rise with a volume of 1,000 shares is more relevant for traders and depicts that more people are buying at the increased prices, giving conviction of the upward movement of the stock. In Figure 2.1, the red box indicates high volume. If you observe, the price rise was also highly incremental along with high volumes, sustaining the trend.

TREND	VOLUME	INTERPRETATION
Up	High	Uptrend may go a greater distance
Up	Low	Lack of Conviction in uptrend, may retrace
Down	High	Downtrend may go a greater distance
Down	Low	Lack of Conviction in downtrend, may reverse

Table 2.2 Interpretation of volume

Support and Resistance

There are buyers and sellers available at every price point in a stock. At a few price points, the number of buyers is greater than the number of sellers, making it the demand zone. The presence of a high demand on these levels makes the price bounce back up whenever it touches this demand zone. These price points are called *support*.

Similarly, there are more sellers than buyers available at a few price points, making it the Supply Zone. The presence of a high supply on these levels makes the price go back down whenever it touches this supply zone. These price points are called *resistance*.

This is the simple law of economics which suggests that if supply is more than demand, the price will go down and if the demand is more than supply, the price will go up. The same theory works for financial markets as well. Thus, as a trader, one needs to identify the demand zone and the supply zone, i.e., the support and resistance of a stock.

Figure 2.2 Daily line chart of Axis Bank

Let's take Axis Bank's example. In Figure 2.2, you can see that whenever the price goes up and touches around 811 to 823 level, sellers step in, dragging the price downwards, making it a supply zone. Similarly, observe how the price bounces back up as soon as it comes near the 633 to 650 level. There were multiple attempts made to drive the price further down from this level, but the buyers were active at this level preventing the price from going down further, making it the demand zone. It's important to note that the demand and supply zones are not one specific price point but a small range where the buyers and sellers are very active. For example, the support points were between the 633 to 650 level and not just at one specific level.

Breakouts and False Breakouts

When the price moves above the supply zone it is called a *breakout*. In Figure 2.2, the breakout point is at 824. It implies that there has been higher demand than the supply at that particular price point, dragging the price up indicating that the stock is ready for a rally. It is important to note that with each new breakout the former supply zone becomes the new demand zone. For example, if we look at the chart in Figure 2.2, the 811 to 823 resistance level became the new support level post giving a breakout.

Not all breakouts are genuine. For example, observe how in Figure 2.2, the stock did attempt to give a breakout above the 823 level but failed to sustain above those levels. This is a typical case of trapping the retail investors called *false breakouts*, as a lot of traders look for such breakouts to enter the market, presuming that the stock will give another rally. Always look for volumes as a way of breakout confirmations. If the breakout is not supported by high volumes, then there's a good chance it will give a reversal.

These zones are extremely crucial for traders to mark as it helps in navigating the markets, deciding the entry points, retracement points and assessing the risk-reward ratio. We will dive deeper into each concept in the following chapters.

LET'S PRACTICE

Use a pen/pencil to mark the demand and supply zones in the following charts:

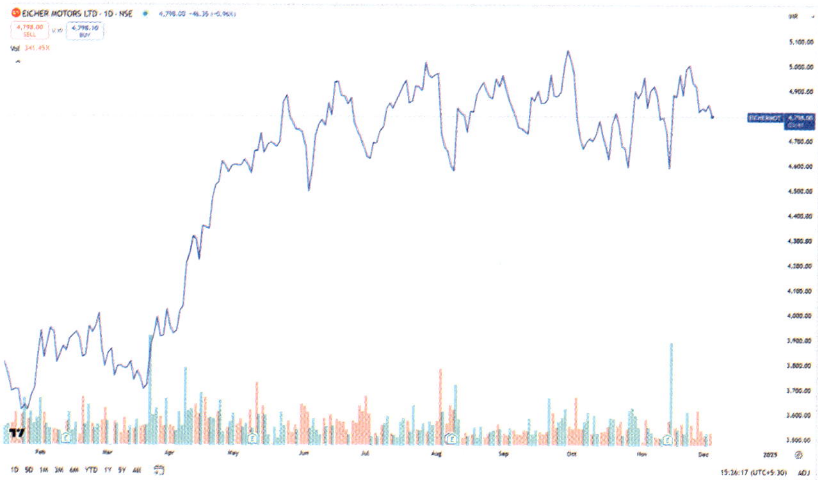

Figure 2.3

Figure 2.4

Figure 2.5

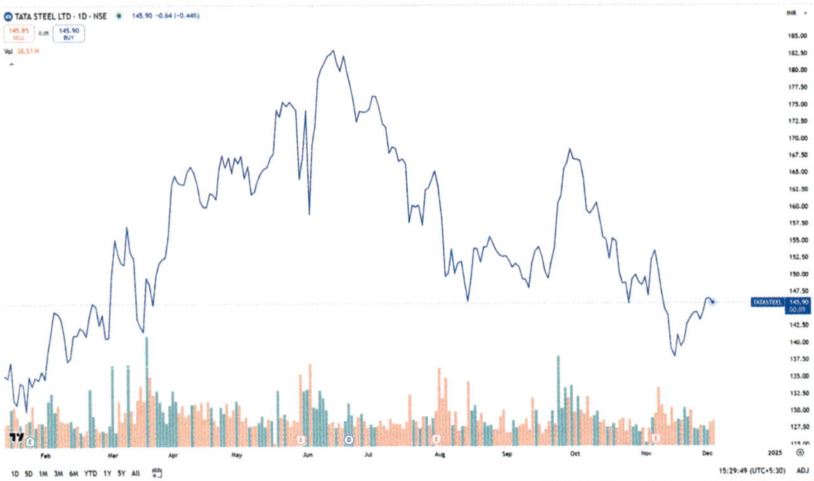

Figure 2.6

Figure 2.7

You can keep practising more on TradingView. I would highly recommend you identify the demand and supply zones for at least 10 stocks every day to get into the habit of it.

Stock Trends

Stock prices always move in trends. A price trend is a continuous or a directional price movement. We call them an uptrend if in the upward direction and downtrend if in the downward direction. If we look at price action in the market through charts, we will find that no price movement happens in a straight line.

Trends can broadly be of 3 categories:

- uptrend
- downtrend
- consolidation

Figure 2.8 Daily chart of ITC

Theoretically speaking, when a stock is making higher highs and higher lows in a sequence, with each new swing (refer to Figure 2.8), the stock is in uptrend. In Figure 2.8, the stock started making higher highs and higher lows from April onwards and thus is in an uptrend or in a bullish trend.

Note: A *swing* refers to the movement of a stock's price between high and low points within a trend. It represents the natural oscillations in the price as it moves up or down.

To understand this better, observe Figure 2.9. Three distinct points—A, C and E—have been marked to show higher highs, and points B, D and F are making higher lows, indicating an uptrend. Thus, the stock is bullish.

Similarly, when a stock is making lower lows and lower highs in a sequence, with each new swing, the stock is said to be in a downtrend. In Figure 2.10, the stock started making lower lows and lower highs from January onwards, indicating a *downtrend* or *bearish trend*.

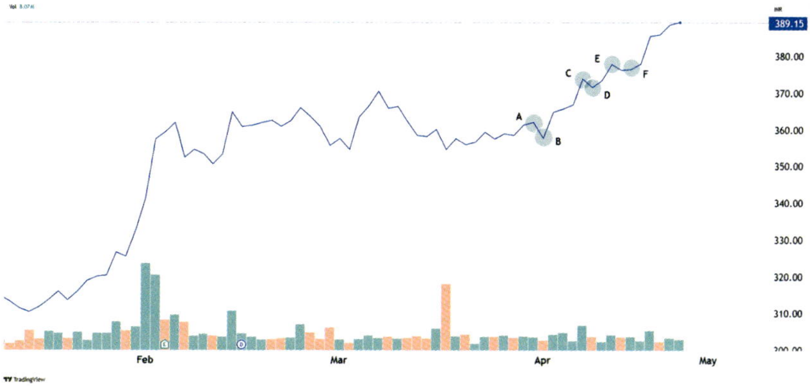

Figure 2.9 Daily chart of ITC Ltd

Figure 2.10 Daily chart of Infosys Ltd

To understand this better, observe Figure 2.11. Two distinct points—A and C—have been marked to show lower highs, and points B and D are making lower lows, indicating a downtrend. Thus, the stock is bearish.

Figure 2.11 Daily chart of Infosys Ltd

The 3rd movement is when the market moves sideways. It's known as market consolidation or a range-bound market. During this period the market only moves in a range without giving a big upmove or downmove. Upmove and downmove are terms we use colloquially to mean uptrend and downtrend in stocks. You will see these words throughout the book.

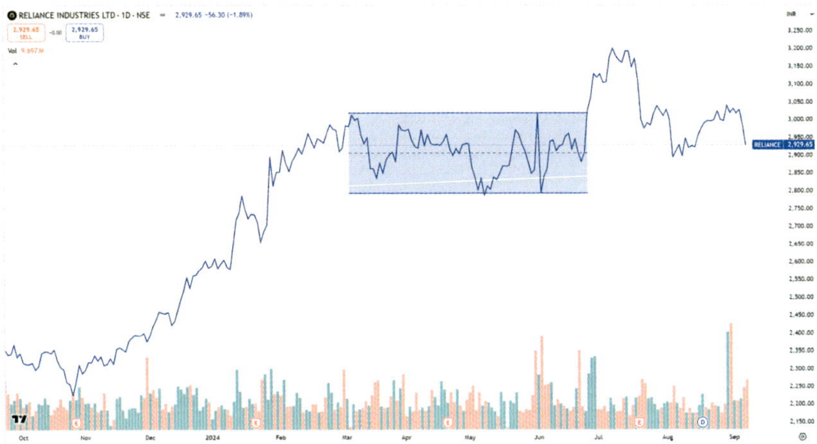

Figure 2.12 Daily chart of Reliance Industries Ltd

In Figure 2.12, observe how the stock was moving between 2,800 level to 3,000 level for a while between March and June 2024. This is the period of *consolidation* in the stock.

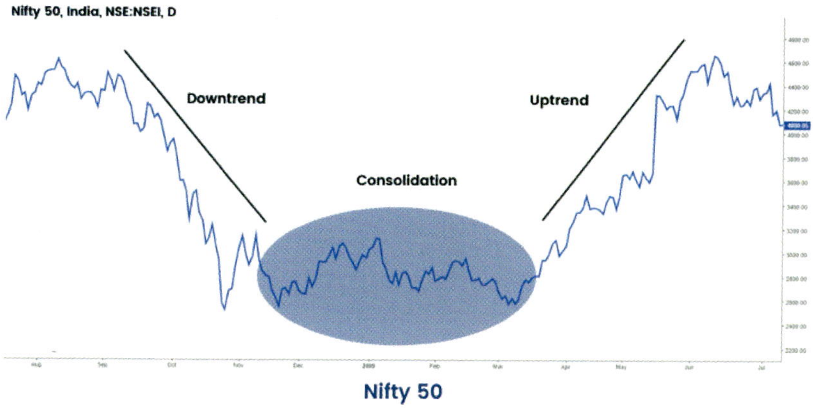

Figure 2.13 Daily chart of Nifty50

In Figure 2.13, we can see all the different movements of a market mapped in the chart of Nifty50.

How Is the Time Window Relevant to the Trend We See?

Trends may vary as per the time frame. A stock may be in uptrend on a weekly chart but in downtrend on an hourly chart. For example, observe Figure 2.14. As per the daily price chart of JIOFIN, the stock is looking to be in downtrend, but in the 5 min chart in Figure 2.15, the stock is in uptrend. Should you have a bullish or a bearish view of the stock?

Figure 2.14 Daily price chart of Jio Financial Services

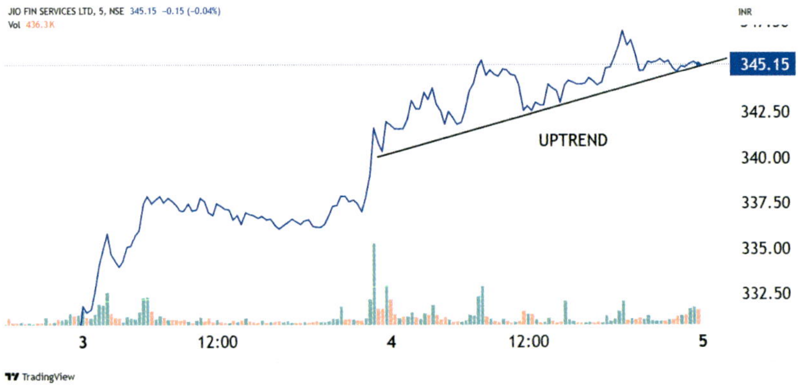

Figure 2.15 5-minute price chart of Jio Financial Services

It depends on your trading tenure. If you want to take small time-frame trades, enter and exit within a small period of time, then you consider the small time-frame charts, and for longer tenure trades, you consider the longer time-frame charts to make a view of the stock.

In the above example, to take a 1-day trade, we will form an opinion looking at the 5-minute chart and have a bullish view of the stock, whereas for a longer tenure trade, say 2–10 days, we will look at the daily chart and form a bearish view of the stock.

Your Trading Tenure Defines Your Trading Time Frame

Charts of multiple time frames are available—for example, hourly charts and daily charts—and the right time frame to follow or analyse depends on your objective. A smaller time-frame chart shall reveal any price or trend change earlier than a longer time frame because smaller time frames reflect first-hand information faster.

Recall that earlier in the chapter, we talked about the different types of trading—intraday trading and swing trading. While intraday is buying and selling on the same day, swing trading, also known as positional trading, is buying and holding the stock for more than 1 day. For intraday trading, you can use a 75-minute chart, 15-minute chart or even 5-minute chart. For swing trading, you can use a 2-hourly, daily, weekly or monthly chart. It will depend on your trading tenure. For short swings, 2-hourly or daily is good; for longer swings, you might want to track weekly or monthly.

Hence, the most important first step is deciding the tenure of your trade. You need to decide whether you wish to take many trades in a small time frame or take lesser but effective trades on a larger time frame. This will help you track the right time-frame chart.

Which Timeline Should You Follow?

If you're a beginner, it's best to start with swing trading, and I would recommend that you track the daily time frame, get comfortable with the charts, identify the support, resistance and trends before you move on to more active trading.

Bearish Trend in Bullish Trend? Understanding Retracement and Correction

Retracement is a very powerful concept in technical analysis. It is a temporary reversal in the direction of a stock or asset's price, which is still part of an overall longer term trend. It is not possible for a stock to just keep going up in a linear manner; it always comes down a bit before making a higher high and maintaining its uptrend. In other words, during a retracement, the price pulls back or 'retraces' some of its recent gains or losses before continuing in the original direction of the trend. It's a short-term pause or dip in a bigger price movement, often seen as a healthy part of an uptrend or downtrend. It is also commonly referred to as a pullback.

Imagine a bouncing ball. It keeps going up and down on different levels with every bounce. Similarly, stock prices also move in a bouncing motion whichever trend it is in, and each new bounce is a retracement.

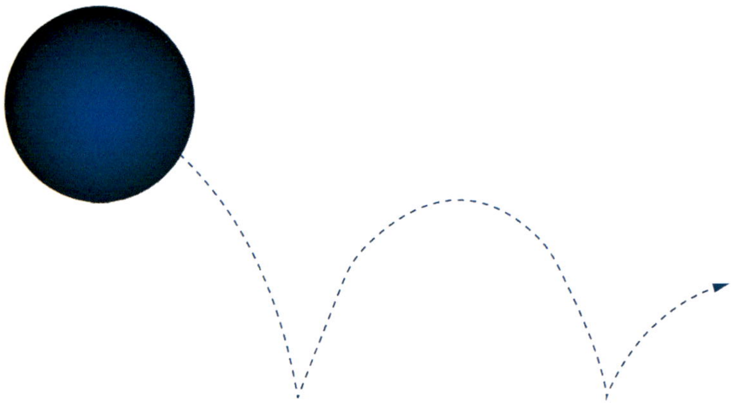

Figure 2.16 Motion of a bouncing ball

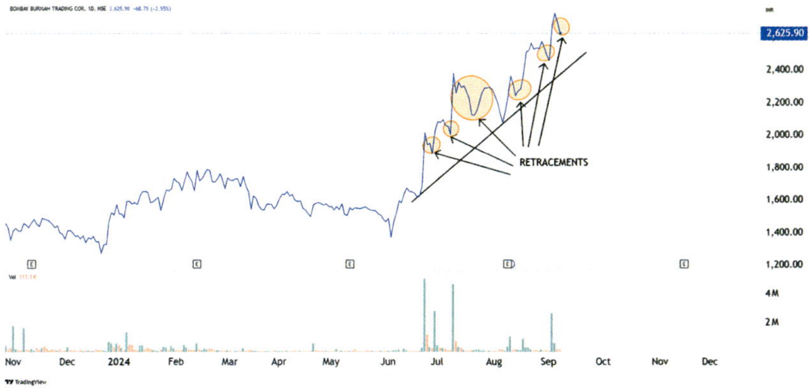

Figure 2.17 Daily chart of Bombay Burmah Trading Corporation (BBTC)

In Figure 2.17, observe how the stock keeps retracting after every breakout, maintaining its uptrend, just like the bounce of a ball.

Similar to retracement, a correction refers to a more significant and longer term price decline (usually 10% or more) from a recent high, and it suggests a broader adjustment in the price trend. Corrections can occur in both uptrends and downtrends, and indicate a deeper movement in the market.

Figure 2.18 Daily chart of Bajaj Auto

In Figure 2.18, the stock came down significantly before moving up again and maintaining its uptrend.

Does This Mean That the Stock Is Bearish?

The terms bearish and bullish need to be used very selectively. In Figure 2.18, the stock maintained its bullish trend even after facing correction. A correction does not imply a change in trend. This is merely a price adjustment, which can be a buying opportunity for retail investors to enter the trade. To determine the trend of the chart, you need to focus on the larger trend.

You need to analyse charts and try to identify the stock trends to actually progress. To become a good trader, you need to be comfortable with the charts, and the more time you spend with them, the better you get at reading them.

LET'S PRACTICE IDENTIFYING TRENDS IN THE STOCK

Use a pen/pencil to draw the trendline in the following charts:

Figure 2.19

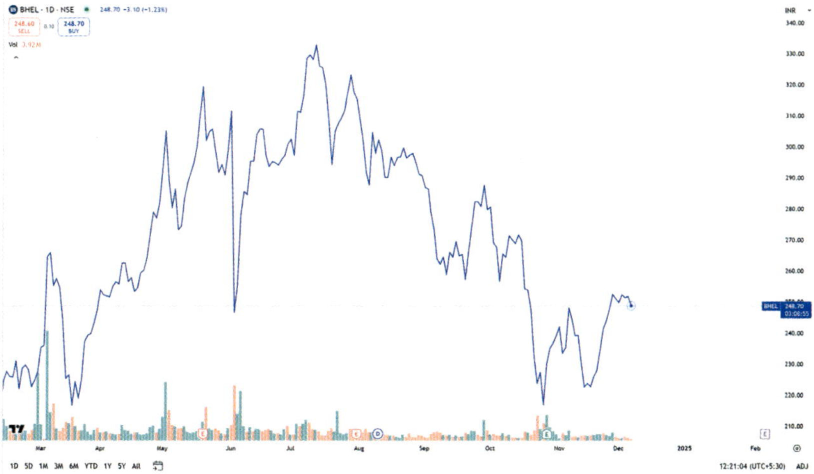

Figure 2.20

Figure 2.21

Figure 2.22

Figure 2.23

You can keep practicing more in TradingView. I would highly recommend you to draw trendlines for at least 10 stocks every day to get into the habit of it.

SUMMARY

- Demand zone is the price point from where the stock keeps bouncing back up indicating the presence of buyers at that price point.
- Supply zone is the price point from where the stock retraces indicating the presence of sellers at that price point.
- As a trader, the first thing is to identify demand and supply zones in any chart.
- Uptrend is when a stock is making higher highs and higher lows.
- Downtrend is when a stock is making lower highs and lower lows.
- Consolidation is when the stock moves sideways in a range.
- When the price moves above the supply zone, it is called a breakout. The stock is more likely to stay in an uptrend post it breaks out.
- For a shorter period of trade, use the smaller time-frame chart. For longer periods of trade, use the longer time-frame chart.
- Price does not move in one straight line; it moves in a swing-like motion.
- Retracement is a temporary reversal when a stock bounces after making a high without any change to the primary trend.
- Correction is a deeper decline (usually more than 10%) from the recent swing high without any change to the primary trend.

LEARNER'S CORNER

Which broker should I open the account with?

There are 2 types of brokers:

Neighbourhood Brokers

They can be a friend of your father who might be a broker or a sub-broker, or may be one of your friends who might have started brokerage. You can open an account with any of them. This type of brokers will give you access to a trading terminal.

Online Tech–Oriented Brokers

They are also known as discount brokers or 100% tech-enabled brokers. All services, including account opening and relationship management, are provided online by them. It has its own advantages as the transaction cost is low, but there are some disadvantages as well, such as customer support service might not be very helpful. For example, Zerodha, Groww and Angel One, as well as bank-based brokers like Kotak Securities.

The choice is entirely yours. Both serve the purpose of giving you access to trading.

Should I do intraday trading or swing trading?

Each individual has a different temperament and risk appetite. Before you decide which trading style to follow, it's important to understand the traits needed to nail each trading style, and then decide which one would be more suited for you. If you're a complete beginner, it's highly recommended to start with swing trading so that you can get comfortable with technical analysis. You can always move to intraday trading a bit later.

Should I be tracking the news for any updates in stocks?

Tracking news is something that one should do for general knowledge and to be updated with current affairs, but taking positions based on news is not a wise thing to do. I will cover this more deeply later in the book.

Does the financial performance of a company matter when I'm trading?

Yes, it does matter, but that will reflect in the price action. So, as a trader, all you must do is only follow price action to make a judgement.

How much capital do I need to start trading?

I hope you have started trading by using the concepts we have discussed so far. To begin with, my suggestion is to start with a minimum capital of Rs 5 lakh. However, even if you have a smaller corpus, you can start and experiment with the markets.

Should-Knows of Technical Analysis

'अपने मरे बिन स्वर्ग नहीं मिलता।'

This is one of my favourite idioms which implies that one cannot get anything without effort. Before you proceed with this chapter, I hope that you've been sincere with your practice suggested in the previous chapter. If you've completed all the exercises mentioned, I would still suggest you keep practising drawing the support, resistance and trendlines for whichever chart you come across.

Before you play a sport, you warm up, prep your muscles and then get into the game and get better with time. Similarly, identifying the support, resistance and trends helps in building the muscle memory for when you actively start trading.

With this in mind, let's move into something very crucial to trading—liquidity.

Liquidity and Its Importance

The number of buyer orders and seller orders that exist at a particular price level in the open market in a stock gives us a measure of the market breadth in that stock. The higher the number of buyers and sellers at a price point, the greater is the market breadth. The greater the market breadth, the higher the liquidity in a stock. As a trader, you would always want to trade in stocks which are highly liquid. If there are few people buying and selling a stock, the chance of manipulation gets higher.

A higher participation with higher volume reflects a genuine market. There is a theory called efficient market hypothesis,[1] which states that wider market participation leads to genuine entry and exit in a stock.

Would you want to deal in a stock with high chances of manipulation? Absolutely not. You would want to enter and exit when and as you want, and that is only possible if the liquidity is high in a stock. If you have to spend more time in a trade because of lack of liquidity, then the chance of loss is higher. This concept is known as impact cost. It measures the difference between the price you want to execute a trade at (the market price) and the price you actually get when the order is executed, especially for larger trades. In simple terms, impact cost reflects the *price slippage* caused by the trade itself. When an order, particularly a large one, is placed, it can move the market price against the trader.

Impact cost is high in securities that are less liquid, where larger trades move the price significantly, and low in highly liquid securities, where large trades can be executed without much price movement. Imagine you want to buy 1,000 shares of a stock trading at ₹100. If the stock is highly liquid, you can buy all 1,000 shares at or near ₹100, resulting in a low impact cost. However, in a less liquid stock, your buy order might push the price up, meaning that as you buy more shares, the price might increase to ₹101 or ₹102.

The difference between the expected price and the actual price paid is the impact cost.

Hence, you need to select stocks that have:

- good breadth
- high liquidity
- low impact costs

To begin, let us keep it simple. There is an index called NSE 500 in NSE which comprises 500 stocks. Mostly, these stocks are liquid. The only criteria that you can now have is whether the stock belongs to NSE 500 or not, to track and trade. BSE is another exchange where most of these are listed but NSE has a wider market participation and thus higher liquidity, so I recommend sticking to it for large quantities in trading.

There are roughly 5,000+ stocks listed in the market with roughly 700 being highly active. This acts as a filtering mechanism and helps you to focus only on quality trades where there is a higher probability of upside.

Different Ways of Participating in the Market

There are 2 ways to participate in the market—go with the flow or go against the flow.

Trade with the Trend

Going with the trend implies that if the stock is in uptrend, you intend to go long or buy the stock at the current market price (CMP) to sell at an anticipated higher price. If the stock is in downtrend, you intend to go short on the stock or sell the stock at CMP to buy at an anticipated lower price. It implies that you're not questioning the trend, you believe that if the stock is in uptrend, then it is going to stay uptrend, and vice versa.

Shorting the stock is currently available in the derivatives market or if you're doing intraday trading. Swing trading is generally on long side unless you get to borrow and go short the stock in SLBM segment, which is not active right now. Considering the entire book is based on swing trading as intraday trading is more nuanced and not suggested for someone who is beginning to trade, all the discussions henceforth will be based on going long.

Contrarian Trade

The next type of participation is being a contrarian trader. Contrarian is when you question the trend and you anticipate a trend reversal, going short in an uptrend, and going long in a downtrend.

You can choose to participate either way, although I must warn you that trading contrary is like putting your head between a double-edged sword.

Trends are not created by people like us, the retail participants. They are created by market participants who have a large investment corpus—the fund managers, HNIs, FIIs, etc. They are called *operators*.

Operators take big positions in the market and have the capacity to make the market move according to them.

As retail participants, we do not have the power to bet against an operator in terms of money. Hence, we would always want to follow the operator. When the operator is going long, we go long. The best way to identify the operator's intent is in the charts. If the stock is in uptrend, that's because the operator is betting on the stock. It is highly recommended to follow the footsteps of the operators and trade with trends.

This is something that needs to be muscle memory and is a stepping stone to build the turtle mindset. Turtles have the ability to camouflage themselves or blend in the surroundings and stay still if they sense danger around them. Similarly, it's important to blend into the market's trend and stay patient. By moving with the market and not forcing trades, you align yourself with the trend, just as the turtle aligns with its surroundings, staying quiet and steady until the opportune moment.

I will cover how one can identify the operator's intent in detail a little later.

Stop Loss

In the stock market, we must have some threshold to hold a stock. That's the concept of stop loss.

I will share my own experience with you to help you understand this concept. Like I've mentioned before, I failed my Chartered Accountancy foundation exam, and was very sad. I went to my father, who is a CA, and he said, 'So what, CA means Come Again.' So, I gave another attempt, and this time I passed with a rank. But during that time, I had decided that I would attempt this exam 3 more times, and if I still don't clear, I will quit CA. Thc limit of 3 attempts in CA was my approach to stop loss so I do not waste more time. I thought that if I couldn't do it in 3 attempts, I won't be able to do it all, and I could use the time and effort somewhere else. Similarly, we do not want to lose money in a trade that is not reviving but rather use it elsewhere.

It's difficult to accept that we can incur a loss. Hence, we hesitate while booking losses. Loss aversion is one of our cognitive biases[2] and a very common trait among human beings, as it can be emotionally draining.

However, accepting a loss can be the best gift that you give to yourself. We need to understand that we cannot be right all the time. By accepting this, you're more prepared in facing a loss. Being prepared helps you to limit your losses.

In my opinion, stop loss is a blessing that forces us to book losses, and stop them from compounding further. You need to have a stop loss for every trade you take to limit your loss in case it goes wrong. If you wish to become a successful trader, the most important thing is to respect stop loss, and no one can teach you that but yourself.

You need to be disciplined and respect your stop loss.

One of the crucial rules of money management is that the stop loss should be small and take-profit (the profit anticipated in a trade) should be high for you to make money. There are different methods of putting stop loss. I'm going to share all the methods that can work later in the book.

Someone who adopts the stop loss at the early stages of trading takes a step closer to building that turtle mindset. Did you know that turtles dig burrows for self-protection and take shelter from heat, cold and predators? Similarly, your stop loss is a tool for self-protection that protects your profits—it's that safety zone that gives a shelter to you if the market moves against you.

Risk and Reward

Observing Figure 2.24, we see the stock continuously making higher highs and higher lows indicating an uptrend, and the Current Market Price (CMP) of Glenmark Pharma is 1160. Would it be the right price point to enter the stock? The answer lies in evaluating the risk and reward.

Risk is the measure of the degree of the fall that the stock may take, also known as downside, while reward is the degree of the upside that the stock may face. Estimations of downside and upside can be done by drawing support and resistance.

Figure 2.24 Daily Chart of Glenmark Pharmaceuticals

Case Study: Glenmark Pharmaceuticals

The best price to buy would be around 1079–1059, or 1026 levels as the possibility of loss at this level is low considering it's a support zone, where demand is high. Stock market is all about probabilities. You cannot enter at any price and expect it to offer you a big reward. As a trader, you would prefer to enter at a price where the risk is low, and the probability of success is high.

If you enter around 1079 to 1059, the risk and reward are likely to be more favourable as there was a resistance earlier at this price level, which could be the new demand zone. Even if the stock falls from 1079–1059 to 1026, the downside is only of Rs 53 to Rs 33, whereas the upside would be till 1180 level, that's almost Rs 100 to 120. The risk-to-reward ratio in this case would be almost 2:1 (53:100).

Please be mindful that when we say that risk-reward is 2:1, we mean that reward is 2, while risk is 1.

Assessing the risk and the reward is the definition of a good trader. Technical analysis as a science is so powerful that it provides the skill set required to measure the risks and rewards. To master this science, it's important for you to track the charts very closely and regularly to be comfortable with it. This is the foundation of becoming a quality trader.

How to Learn This

Well, it's like learning a language. Learning the alphabet is easy but the real learning starts when you speak that language, regularly. Make this part of your trading habit: Review at least 50 charts a day. Let your subconscious mind understand the language of charts and your conscious mind learn to make sound judgements.

Before we move on to the next part of technical analysis, it's important to know the different kinds of charts.

Different Types of Charts

There are different types of charts and before we proceed, it is important to understand these.

1. The first is a line chart, which is drawn as a simple line plotting the close prices of the stock. It is the one that we've been using till now.
2. The second is a candlestick chart, which simultaneously considers the open, low, high and close of a given time frame. It will be green if the stock has closed above the open price and will be red if the stock has closed below the open price. The bars and the lines, known as wicks, represent the movement throughout the day. The 2 extreme ends are the high price and low price for the time period selected. Candlesticks are the most

popular chart pattern in technical analysis. We will cover this in depth in the next section.

Figure 2.25 Daily candlestick chart of ICICI Bank

3. Next is a bar chart which is similar to a candlestick chart in the sense that it also depicts the open, high, low and close of a stock at a particular time frame, but the colour depth inside the bar is not visible.

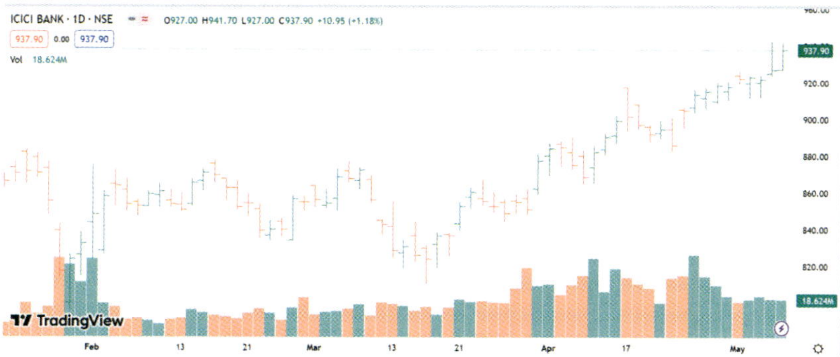

Figure 2.26 Daily bar chart of ICICI Bank

Thus, every chart has a different format, and each chart type tries to tell us a story. It's best to choose to follow only one type of chart when tracking the markets since it is difficult to follow each of them and one can get lost.

Candlesticks

Candlesticks are the oldest type of trading technique and one of the most efficient ways to analyse the change in the prices of an asset. It depicts the trader's psychology with utmost clarity, in comparison to other forms of charting. In the 1700s, the candlestick charts were used to predict rice prices. In 1750, Munehisa Homma, a Japanese merchant, started using his candlestick analysis for trading at the Rice exchange at Sakata.[3] Since then, it has evolved and is now very widely used by traders across the world on various financial securities.

There are different candles formed in the markets and each candle represents something unique. Each new candle formed tries to indicate something, and as traders, we need to take these into account while trading.

Candlestick covers open, high, low and close prices of a stock. To explain it better, we'll take the help of an Excel. We'll input numbers and create candles and play with the numbers to see how the candle changes.

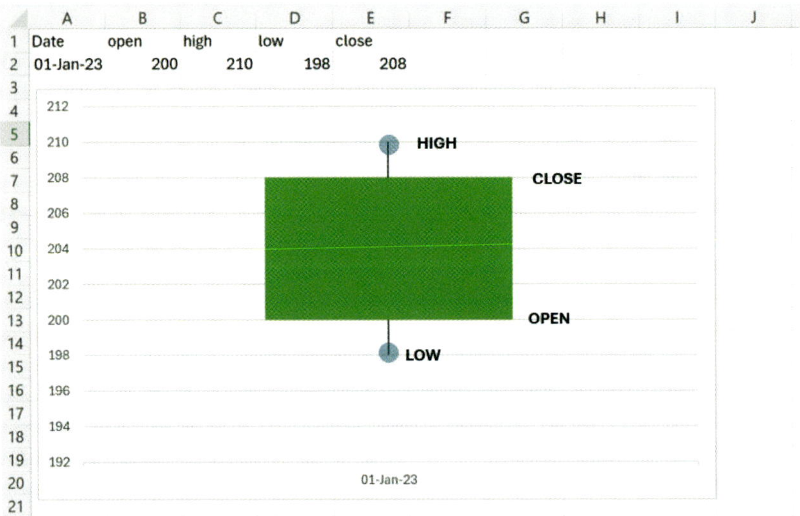

Figure 2.27 Candle formed through input of numbers in Excel

In Figure 2.27, I've added some random numbers as open, high, low, and close and created a candle with the help of the charts in Excel. A simple candle is formed which shows the open, high, low and close. Since this is a green candle, it means that the close is higher than the open. Now let's play with the numbers to see how the story of the candle changes.

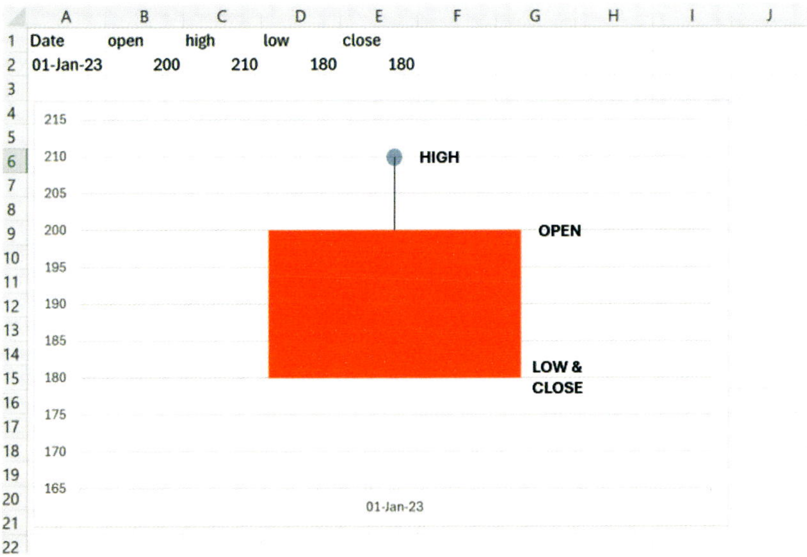

Figure 2.28 Candle formed through input of numbers in Excel

When the closing price is below the opening price, the candle formed is red in colour, as shown in Figure 2.28. To break this complex structure further, let's take the earlier example.

A candlestick, unlike just numbers, tells us a story through its varied formations. In Figure 2.27, the candle opened at 200, made a high of 210, made a low of 198, and then closed at 208. Now the candle could have:

i. either first made a high, then a low and then closed, or
ii. it could have first made a low, then a high and then closed.

In case of situation (i), the story that the candle is trying to tell is that the buyers were stronger when the market opened, then gradually the sellers drove the price down, and then for the later part of the day, the buyers emerged again stronger and drove the price back up again.

In case of situation (ii), the story that the candle is trying to portray is that the sellers were stronger in the first part of the trading session and then the buyers emerged stronger and drove the price up to make a high, with maybe some profit booking in the end to close at 208.

Now in both cases, the buyers emerge stronger for the day, yet the story is different. In the case of (i), there is an intense fight going on between the buyers and sellers, and in case (ii), the intensity of the fight between buyers and sellers is low. To know exactly which, we will have to deep dive into the intraday charts and candles. For now, we will just focus on the end of the day and conclude that the buyers are strong on that trading day.

Suppose the stock closed at 202, the candle would look as shown below:

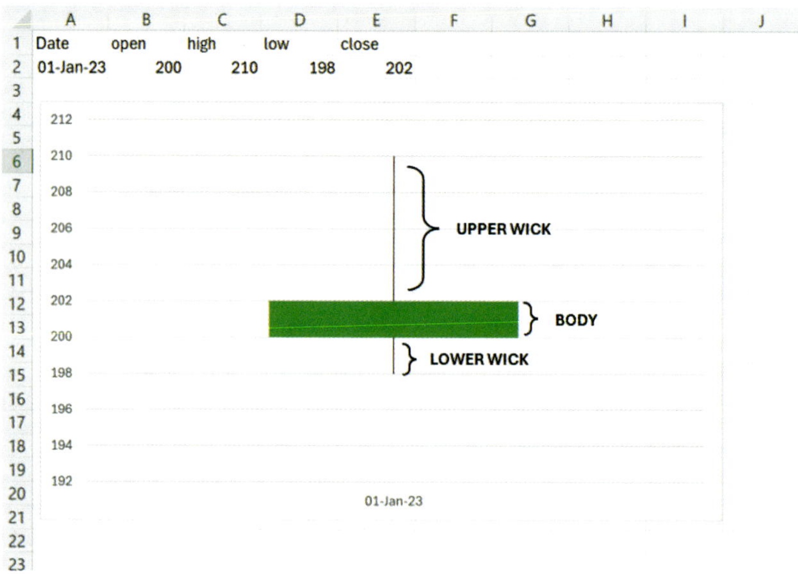

Figure 2.29 Candle formed through input of numbers in Excel

Now if you observe Figure 2.29, it can be understood that the buyers were strong at one point during the day to make a high of 210, but then the sellers took control and dragged the stock down and it closed near its low. There are 3 parts of a candlestick—body, upper wick and lower wick. The size of the body shows desperation of the buyers and the sellers, and a long upper wick indicates that something is wrong as the stock falls from its high. A long lower wick denotes that there is strength as someone has bought at the lower levels.

Every pattern has been given a unique name, and deep studies have been conducted on it. Some traders just rely on candlesticks to trade in the market. There are 2 types of patterns to observe in candlesticks:

- The pattern a combination of multiple candles form
- The pattern a standalone candle depicts

Earlier, when this concept had just started, standalone candles were relied upon but, as complexities increased and this science became popular, a combination of multiple candles were introduced to judge the sentiment of the stock.

Candlestick Chart Analysis

Let us take an example and view the chart of SBI.

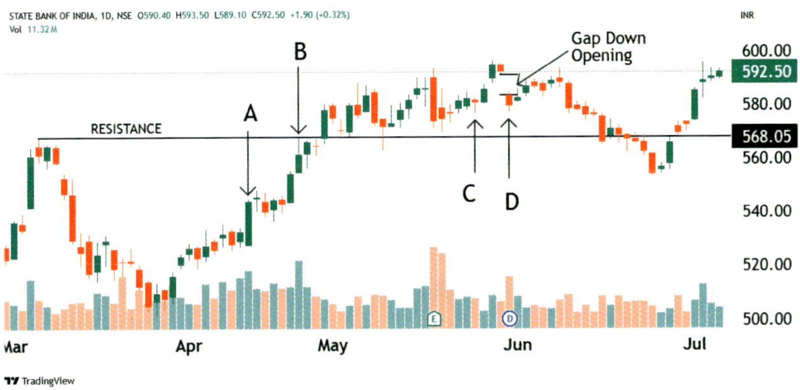

Figure 2.30 Daily candlestick chart of SBI

In Figure 2.30, observe the candle marked as A. The stock moved up by 2% and the candle formed had a long body suggesting a buying pressure at that price point, driving the prices up with intensity. Moreover, there was a very small wick implying that there was not much seller resistance at that price point.

Let's look at the other candle marked as B. Again a green candle, but this time the size of the body and the size of the upper wick are almost the same. The price moved up to a high of 568 and faced resistance driving the price down to 561 level, indicating that there were sellers ready to sell the stock at 568 level. Interestingly enough, the 568 level was also a resistance level or a supply zone as per previous swing high, making the stock pause at this level for some time.

Now let's observe another candle marked as C in Figure 2.30. This red candle depicts a pattern where you can see that the stock hit a low but then it recovered from that low and closed near its high. However, the difference between the open and the close is not much. This means that it is likely that stock will continue its rally as people are not interested to sell; rather, they buy whenever it comes down, and we can see that the stock did move upwards.

Moving on to the candle marked as D, you can see that it is a red candle, which was formed because the close was below the open price. The candle gives a gap down opening—it is when the stock opens at a price much lower than the previous day's low price. This candle is hinting towards the selling pressure and showing weakness in the stock. This does not mean that the stock is weak, it is just showing weakness. There is a difference between being weak and showing weakness.

Probably, the stock has been in a bullish trend for so many days, and so there could be profit booking here. We need to judge how high the intensity of selling or buying is. If the stock has fallen sharply from its high, then the intensity of the sellers is high and if the price has increased sharply from low, then the intensity of the buyers is strong.

The pattern of this red candle tells us that there was not much activity in the stock on that day.

We are designing this system in such a manner that you need to see it holistically. You cannot make a judgement by observing a standalone candle. It's important to understand the basics of what each candle could mean without getting into the theory. If the wick of the candle is long with a single line and without any body, something like in Figure 2.31, what do you think it could denote?

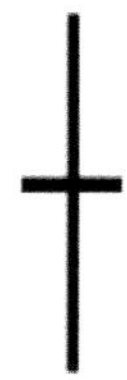

Figure 2.31 Candlestick with no body

This denotes that the open and close are the same. If the lower wick is longer, then it means that there has been buying pressure from the lower levels and if the upper wick is longer, then it means that there has been selling pressure from the higher levels.

The candle shown in Figure 2.31 is a Doji Candle.

Thus, this is what you need to keep in mind and check the length of the wick and the size of the body. A long body gives conviction of entry and exit, and a long wick means more volatility, which indicates uncertainty. Candlestick is a better representation of the market as compared to a line chart and it gives you a deeper understanding of the activities of the market that took place during the day. The more you observe candlesticks, the better you will be able to understand its language and you will be able to form a better judgement.

Volume, Delivery and Open Interest

We've covered the basics of volume, now it's time to dig deeper into the concept and the master combination of volume, delivery and open interest. These 3 components are the guiding light for traders just like the divine Trimurti—Brahma, Vishnu, Mahesh. As a trader, if you master the study of price action, along with volume, delivery, and open interest, the chances of succeeding in your trades become higher.

Volume means the quantity traded at a particular price point. This is a traded quantity which may have been traded intraday, that is, bought and sold on the same day, or bought and sold on different days.

Delivery is the number of positions that is carried forward to the subsequent day or days. Taking a position in a stock implies either buying or selling a stock. When you take a position in a stock and carry the position, that is, do not square off the position the same day, it's called delivery. Thus, a certain percentage of the volume is converted to delivery.

Example: Rakesh bought 400 shares of Reliance and sold 200 shares on the same day. In such a case, the volume will be 600 (400+200) and delivery will be 200 (400–200) for that day.

Open interest is the measure of the 'active contracts' in the derivatives market (futures and options). Unlike volume, which measures how many contracts were traded in a day, and delivery, which shows how many positions were carried forward in the stock market, Open Interest focuses on how many contracts are ongoing.

We will have more clarity on the subject later in the chapter.

What is the significance of tracking these 3 components? The combination of these 3 components is indicative of the operator's intent in a stock.

Judging the Intent of the Market Movers, Operators

Recall that we had talked about operators earlier. Let's understand more deeply who these operators are and why it's important to gauge their intent in a stock.

To put it simply, a group of people with a large investment corpus, who have the capacity to move a stock with their positions, are the operators. Every stock has its own set of operators who control the larger stock movements.

As retail participants we need to gauge the operator's intent as they are the ones who decide the price movement of a stock. If the operator's intent is clear that they are going to drive the prices up further in a stock, then trading in such stocks can be highly profitable.

Volume

The first component that hints towards the operator's intent is the volume. Whenever an operator enters or exits a stock, they participate in large quantities, which is reflected in the volumes traded in the stock. The first thing we do to understand the operator's intent is observe the candle and the volume bar together.

Figure 2.32 Daily chart of HDFC Bank

In Figure 2.32, a few consequent red candles have been highlighted near point A along with big volume bars. In such cases, where the candles are red along with tall volume bars, it is indicative of the selling pressure in the stock. Similarly, green candles supported by tall volume bars denote the buying pressure in the stock. Observe point B where the green candles along with volume bars have been highlighted.

What does a selling pressure or a buying pressure tell us about the operator's intent? In case the price movement breaks an important line of resistance and moves further up with large volumes, in other words gives a breakout with high volumes, then it is indicative that an operator is entering the stock at that level.

Similarly, if the price movement goes beneath a strong support line and if the volume bar is also high, it means that the operator is trying to exit. However, in case of range bound movements, it's difficult to draw conclusions about the operator's intent.

If the large price action is behaving without volume, then the chances of it being a false movement is very high. There could be something fishy going on in the stock. Thus, the price movement needs to be supported by large volumes for conviction in the price move. The aforementioned example gives a very narrow view. Let's look at a broader picture to understand the impact of pricc movements supported by high volumes.

Figure 2.33 Daily chart of CESC Ltd

Observe zone marked as A in Figure 2.33. The price action of the stock was in uptrend supported by high volumes for 2 months. The stock rose from 70 levels to make a high of 90, generating 30% returns in just 2 months. The average volume during this period was roughly 4 times more than usual, reaching almost 30 million on a single day. Do you think people like you and me can trade in such big volumes? Only people with big money can trade with these volumes and drive such an uptrend in a stock.

The next few months saw a range bound price action of the stock with a small correction, and just observe the low volume bars during this period. Does this mean that the operator took an exit from the stock? Well, if the operator had exited the stock, it would have reflected in the volumes and negative price action of the stock.

Moving forward, observe that in the zone marked as B, the stock gave another sharp upmove, giving 70% return in 3 months from 90 level to 150 level, the volume bars were taller than zone A. What does this tell us about the operator? We can presume that there are new operators entering the stock, and/or the existing ones are adding to their position in the stock. The highest volume on a single day reached almost 50 million, almost two-third times more than zone A.

The stock paused post the rally and became range bound with a price correction. This period of low volumes and market correction is indicative of small quantities being sold by the weak people (in terms of capital), or the retail investors. These phases typically do not see any significant price action.

Now let's come to zone C in the chart. The stock gave another rally generating 40% return in 3 months from 150 level to 210 level, and just look at the volumes for this period. We can only presume that the operator became active again during this time, driving the prices further up. The above price action in the stock is a good demonstration of how a typical operator drives the stock.

There are either strong people or weak people in the market, and whenever the stock gives an unexpected move, the weak people get scared, and they run away. That is when the operator sees an opportunity and tries to accumulate the stock as much as he can.

There are 2 components in the volume:

- Intraday volume
- End-of-the-day volume

Intraday volume is when you buy and sell on the same day whereas end-of-the-day volume is if you buy today and keep the position for subsequent day(s) or how I like to say it—take the position back home. Stocks taken home are more important because if you carry the position overnight, then you are carrying a risk, and those who carry risk are stronger. This is reflected in delivery data which an operator is most likely taking.

Delivery

This is a very important topic and is not covered by everyone. If you start tracking this immediately, then it will become your habit. For delivery data we use StockEdge. Let's take an example of NHPC.

Figure 2.34 Delivery data of NHPC

Figure 2.34 is the delivery graph with light blue and a dark blue colour. Dark blue is the delivered quantity and light blue is the total volume. You can choose to track either the data of both exchanges or just NSE. On 6 December 2024, 2.6 crore shares were delivered and 7.4 crores shares were traded. The Volume Weighted Average Price (VWAP) was 85.3. VWAP calculates the average price of a stock, weighted by volume, over a specific period. We will cover this more deeply later in the book.

Pictorially, it is visible that the delivery quantity is higher and on comparing the data of previous few days, you will know that the delivered quantity is more. The price increase on 6 December was

3.3%. To know whether the stock was sold or bought, we would have to track the volume bars on the intraday chart. For an intraday, you can track a 15-minute chart on 6 December.

Figure 2.35 Intraday 15-minute chart of NHPC

Figure 2.35 represents the intraday chart of the stock. An important thing that you might want to take note of: The first 15 minutes candle represents the fight ongoing between the bulls and the bears to take control of the market. We, the retail investors, are like ants in front of these massive elephants, the operators. Hence, it's best to do nothing in the first 15-minutes of the market. Just observe and see what follows through.

If we observe the chart, the price kept increasing on 6 December with long green candles surpassing its previous resistance level of 83.3 in the first one hour of the market, indicating buying pressure in the stock. The price thereon made a high around 86.8 level and then came down to close around 84.8 level. From the above data, we can infer that the operator has bought NHPC at the average buying price of 85.3 (the VWAP level).

We will mark this price point in our chart with a horizontal line as this could be an important good demand or supply zone. In this case, we can assume that this is a demand zone as the operator is interested in buying at this price. If the price falls below this level, then the operator will want to square up his position, driving the prices further down. In the aforementioned figure, observe how the price respected its VWAP level in the upcoming trading sessions.

Similarly, when the operator exits, it is visible in the charts with prices crashing down along with high volumes and high delivery. Hence, tracking volume and delivery data becomes crucial to gauge operator's intent. A price increase with continuous high volumes and high delivered quantity is suggestive of an operator's entry, while a price decrease with high volumes and high delivered quantity hints at an operator's exit from the stock.

Let me show you how a typical chart looks like when the operator is trying to exit the stock. In Figure 2.33, we saw how the stock, CESC, rallied when the operators entered the stock. Let's look at the chart of the same stock at a later date.

Figure 2.36 Daily chart of CESC Ltd

The stock became range bound after making a high of 212 in September 2024. It was oscillating between 205 and 169 levels with fluctuating volumes before it started making a rapid decline. The stock broke its support level of 169, supported by high volume towers. The volume during this decline was also 4 times than the average volume that the stock would have on a normal day. The stock declined 29% since breaking the support level of 169 in a span of only 1 month, and was down by 43% from its high of 212 in a span of 4 and a half months. Such rapid decline, supported by such high volumes, is typically indicative of an operator's exit.

How can we cherry-pick such stocks where the operator is just starting the rally?

One way to do that is filter stocks that had high volume and delivered quantity in the previous trading day. This will help us narrow down the list and track high return probability stocks.

Identifying Stocks That Are at the Initial Stage of an Upward Rally

One way to identify such stocks is through the stock analytics tool. You can find the volume and delivery scans under scans in the StockEdge Homepage and get the list of stocks in which delivery has been high relative to an average delivery quantity.

We can use the scan filter to identify stocks that have been traded in large quantities along with large delivery quantities. You can go for either 1 day or weekly highly traded and delivered quantity (refer to Figure 2.37).

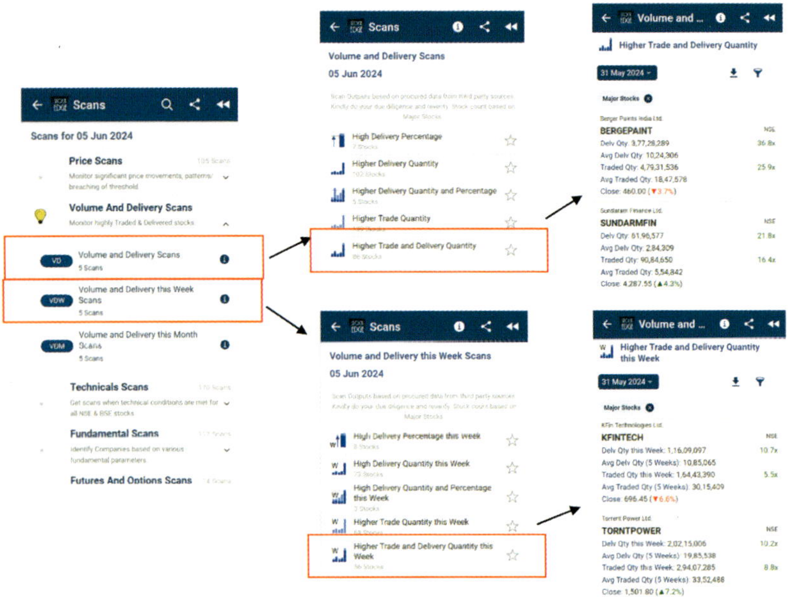

Figure 2.37 Volume and delivery scans in StockEdge

Coming back to the example, the 2 stocks under the scan higher delivered and traded quantity for 1 day are Berger Paints and Sundaram Finance. However, the price of Berger Paints fell along with high delivery, so this is not a good sign, and you might want to omit that, since a high delivery along with a negative price action could indicate that the operator is exiting the stock. We would only want to focus on stocks whose prices had a positive price action along with high volumes and delivery. Let's see the chart of Sundaram Finance.

Let's observe Figure 2.38, the daily chart of Sundaram Finance. The stock seems to be consolidating between 4045 level and 4997 level after an upmove from 3800 level to 4900 level. There was a sharp correction on 28 May and the stock kept falling to 4100 level till there was a huge volume along with a green candle on 31 May, and since then, the price moved up maintaining its range. I would want to keep this stock in my watchlist and find the right time to enter, which we will discuss in the later chapters.

Figure 2.38 Daily chart of Sundaram Finance

Similarly, we will make a list of all the stocks that had high traded and delivered quantity and track their charts to understand the story behind them. Now let's take the example of Torrent Power that had high traded and delivered quantity in the week.

Figure 2.39 Daily chart of Torrent Power

Try to observe Figure 2.39 holistically. In this daily chart of Torrent Power, the trend has been up since 19 March 2024 till 12 April 2024, where the stock gave an upmove from 1233 level to 1631 level, almost a 33% upmove. An interesting thing to note here is that the volume bars beneath the period of upmove were also higher when compared to other dates. Currently the stock is consolidating between 1299 level and 1561 level. However, the high volume and quantity level in the week of 31 May 2024 could be a sign that new buying interest has emerged in the stock, and if this interest sustains for a longer period, the stock could break this consolidation and start a new rally from thereon. The current consolidation zone could just be the accumulation zone for the operators.

I cannot iterate enough the benefits of tracking the delivery data and highest delivered price points of a stock. With regular tracking, you can identify outlier days and levels when the stock gave an unnatural move or had unnatural volumes and delivery. Mark that level in your charts. Eventually you will see several lines being drawn at a price point. This will give you the level where the operator keeps buying and thus, becomes a major demand zone.

When multiple parameters converge at a particular price point, the probability of it becoming a good defence point is high. Each stock is handled by a unique set of operators. You will become familiar with the operator's movement and, next time when the operator gets active, you will immediately be able to identify it.

Open Interest

Open interest is crucial in the derivatives market, but beginners should avoid trading derivatives—as it is a quick way to lose money. Instead, focus on gradual learning and small steps to sustain long-term success in the markets.

Why discuss open interest if you're only trading in the cash market? Many stocks you trade in cash also have derivatives, i.e., futures and options (F&O) segment and to make a holistic view of the stock trend, it's crucial to study the open interest data even if you're just trading in the cash market. While I won't dive into complex details, knowing the basics of open interest is essential.

In the cash market, we track volume and delivery. In the derivatives market, there's no delivery; positions are usually closed before expiry. Operators' positions in derivatives are reflected in the open interest data.

Let us take an example of Godrej Consumer Products. If an operator wants to buy the stock, then he needs to pay the entire amount in the cash market. As of 30 May 2023, Godrej is trading at 1051, and if I buy 500 shares of Godrej Consumer Products Ltd from the cash market, I will have to pay cash of Rs 5,25,500 to take the shares. There is full price engagement on the delivery base and if the operator wants to create a large position in a stock, then he needs to bring in huge money.

There is another option for the operator to take a large position without complete price engagement by leveraging, and this is known as derivatives. It means that you can take a position of Rs 5,25,500 in Godrej Consumer Products by only paying a small amount. This small amount is known as margin. You just need to pay the margin percentage required by the exchange to take full position. Roughly, there is a cumulative margin of around 25–30% in a stock. In the case of Godrej Consumer Products, it is roughly around Rs 1 lakh, and with just 1 lakh, you can take a position worth Rs 5,25,500 in the stock.

Some stocks have a high margin, while some have a lower margin. Stocks with higher risk have a high margin. High risk means stocks having high volatility, and hence, they require high margin, which is decided by the exchange which calculates the volatility-based margin known as *span margin*.

An operator with a large investment can buy more shares in the derivatives market than in the cash market because derivatives require less capital upfront. To understand the operator's position, we need to track *open interest* in derivatives.

Here are some basic terms to know:

Lot of shares: In derivatives, shares are bought and sold in fixed lots. For example, one lot of Reliance Industries might be 100 shares.

Contracts: A contract is an agreement where one party commits to selling a lot of shares to another at a set price on a future date.

Clearing corporation: This institution oversees and confirms contracts between parties, ensuring they're valid until completion.

Open interest (OI): Open interest represents the total number of outstanding contracts in the market at a given time. It helps identify stock trends and gives traders insight into the market by showing how many futures contracts are currently active. OI data changes daily based on the number of open contracts.

Let's take an example to understand the whole picture (Figure 2.40). There are 5 participants in the market: A, B, C, D and E.

On 1 July, A buys 10 contracts from B => OI 10

On 2 July, C buys 20 contracts from D => OI 30

On 3 July, A sells his 10 contracts to D => OI 20

On 4 July, E buys 20 contracts from C => OI 20

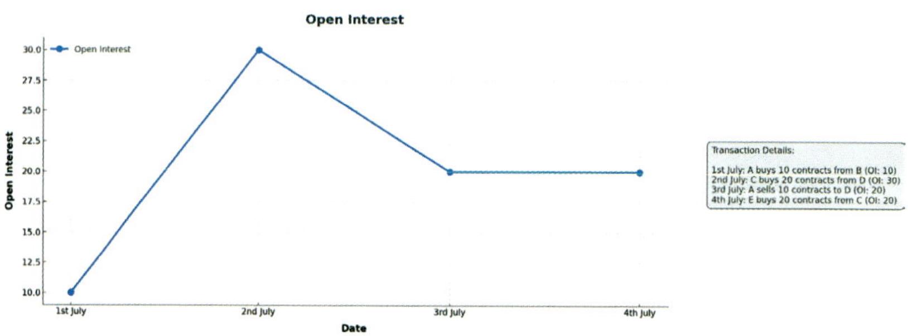

Figure 2.40

So, we can understand how OI changes depending on the change in hand of contracts.

- When a new entrant trades with another new entrant in the F&O market, then the open interest goes up.
- When an existing position holder squares off with entry of a new entrant, open interest remains unchanged.
- When 2 existing position holders square off their positions, we see open interest go down.

Tracking Open Interest

For now, we will only consider the OI data for futures. When the price is going up or down and the future open interest increases alongside the price at a certain level, then we can expect that the price movement is going to sustain.

Taking a longer time period to track the change in OI builds more conviction of the story that OI is trying to show, since the operator could have created a position in previous months. Analysing 3-month data is more than sufficient to get an idea of the operator's position. Let's take an example of SBI. If we observe Figure 2.41, the open interest of 14 March 2023 was 7.36 crores at a price of 525.

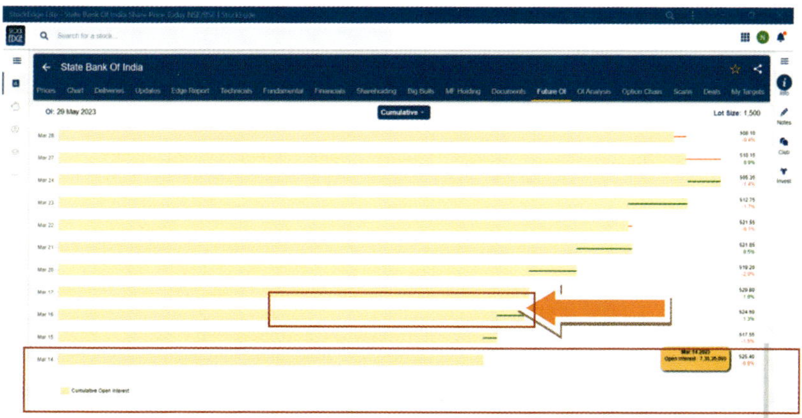

Figure 2.41 OI of SBI for the month of March 2023

The OI as on 29 May 2023 was 6.89 crores at a price of 595, as marked in Figure 2.42.

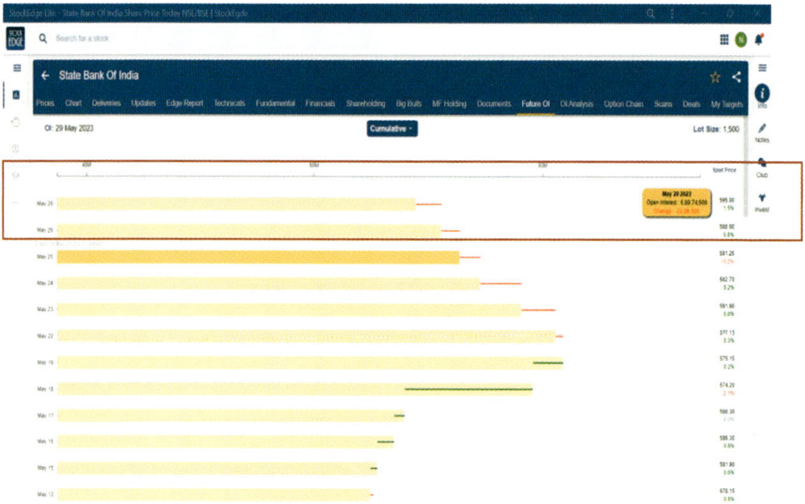

Figure 2.42 OI of State Bank of India for the month of May 2023

In the OI charts, the green line denotes OI build up and the red line indicates decrease in OI. The open interest has decreased, with a slight increase in price. Reading the graph, it seems like the operator has tried to build a position (with the green lines) and the price might have gone up, and has squared up his position in the recent past without adding any new position.

You need to analyse the 3-month trend. There have been times when OI was built up but then OI drastically decreased, indicating a weakish position. There has been a huge OI built up at 575 levels, which indicates that the operator has entered at this price. Tracking the delivery and the price movement simultaneously is equally crucial to draw a fairer conclusion. Combining all 3 elements helps us in determining the operator's intent.

The expiry day of the contract is when all old positions must be closed, hence we do not account that day when analysing. Operators can create both buy (long) and sell (short) positions. Here's what to watch for:

Long Position: If the operator buys in the futures market and prices rise, they are bullish and expect the price to go up.

Short Position: If the operator sells aggressively and prices drop while open interest increases, they are bearish and expect the price to fall.

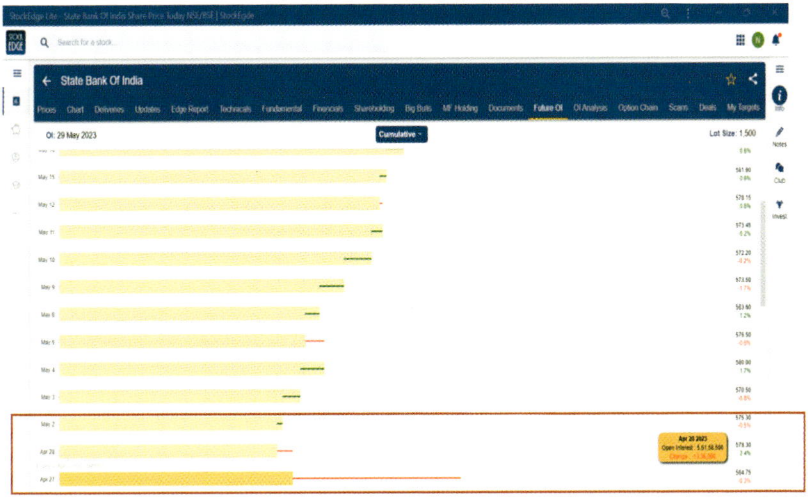

Figure 2.43 OI of State Bank of India for the month of May 2023

If we look at the beginning of May expiry, the OI was 5.61 crores and price was 578 thereafter; initially the OI decreased but then price remained flat and slight OI build up can be seen. Currently, the OI is at 6.89 crores and price is 595. There has been a significant increase in OI with an increase in price. So, we can conclude that the operator seems to be bullish in this stock.

Along with this, we will also look at the delivery data to see the days when the operator has taken delivery in the cash market, and highlight those days. Finally, we check the price chart to see if the stock is in uptrend or downtrend to conclude our analysis.

Your matrix should consist of price, volume, delivery and open interest.

If the price is increasing, along with increase in volume, delivery and open interest, then it is most likely that the operator is taking position in the stock, and if the price is decreasing along with increase in volume, delivery and open interest, then it is most likely that the operator is exiting the stock. There could be more scenarios and Figure 2.44 covers all the possible scenarios and interpretations:

- If the price is increasing and the trend is up, then it is positive.
- If the direction of volume and delivery is a plus, then it is positive.
- If the open interest is increasing with the price, then it is positive.

Check Figure 2.44 for a complete interpretation of the change in price along with OI.

Price	Open Interest	Volume	Delivery	Conclusion
Up	Up	Up	Up	Very Bullish
Up	Down	Up	Down	Short Covering (Bullish)
Down	Up	Up	Up	Very Bearish
Down	Down	Down	Down	Long Covering (Bearish)

Figure 2.44 Interpretation of the change in OI along with price

Let's take an example combining all 3 for better understanding:

Using the scans of StockEdge, I picked up Dr Reddy's laboratories that has had high traded and delivered quantity as on 20 December 2024. Let's look at the chart:

Figure 2.45 Daily chart of Dr Reddy

In Figure 2.45, the stock seems to be in downtrend from September 2024 until December 2024. The stock broke its previous swing high at 1246 level on 6 December, marking a breakout supported by good volumes. Since then, the stock sustained its breakout levels, continuing its upmove and giving another breakout from its historic levels of 1320 on 19 December, supported by a long volume bar. Let's look at the delivery graph on that day:

Figure 2.46 Delivery graph of Dr Reddy

The delivered quantity on 19 December 2024 was roughly 30 lakhs, constituting 41% of the total volume on that day, significantly higher than preceding trading days. Similarly, observe the candle, volume bar and delivery on 20 December 2024 too, all giving bullish signs.

Observe the VWAP levels on both the days of 1313 and 1352. If you see the daily chart of the stock, you'll notice that the VWAP levels were right around historic resistance levels, making these levels very important for us to mark. Theoretically, operators must have entered at these levels and would try to maintain and not let the stock fall below it. Now let's look at the OI data:

Figure 2.47 OI data of Dr Reddy

The OI increased significantly on 18, 19 and 20 December 2024, along with price increase on all the 3 days, giving us more conviction of a start of the bullish trend in the stock. Let's do a quick recap:

- The stock has been breaking its previous swing highs in the past few trading days.
- The support of high volumes and delivery is hinting towards activation of an operator.
- The overall analysis of OI data gives you a picture of aggregate long positions being built up in the stock.
- A significant long build up in OI along with the price increase provides high conviction.

Therefore, this becomes a good stock to add to my tracker to take positions when the risk-reward is favourable.

Observing the OI data on 11 December 2024, there was an increase in OI, with a slight decrease in price by 0.1%. The change in price was so insignificant that we cannot claim that day as short covering. There must be some significant change in both OI and price for us to conclude whether there's long/short build up or long unwinding/ short covering. It's okay to mark these puny changes as neutral.

This requires a lot of practice, and you need to observe this daily in your stocks and track its activity. Our sole objective is to figure out the operator's position and what he is trying to do. If you can study this science properly, you will be able to trade successfully.

Should You Track Open Interest for Trading in the Spot Market?

For stocks with derivatives, monitor open interest, even if you're trading them in the cash market. For those without derivatives, track volume and delivery. Assess price changes, open interest, volume and delivery over the week to spot major movements.

Open interest is good for a short period of time but is not very effective for a longer period as there are frequent entries and exits. People who take delivery generally want to stay in the stock for a long period of time.

My advice is to move slowly and not rush. This concept of open interest is very subjective, and you cannot make judgements easily because you might not be right all the time.

- So, the first weightage should be given to price, trend and the indicators.
- Next, you should focus on volume and delivery. I always use volume and delivery together because without delivery there is no meaning to volume.
- The third weightage should be given to open interest.

Hence, if you follow this, you will be able to create your own trading system.

Analysing open interest can take some time to perfect. If you want to be a full-time trader, I would highly suggest you to take your time and keep practising till you're able to ace analysing the OI. One way to validate your analysis can be done by checking the F&O zone in StockEdge.

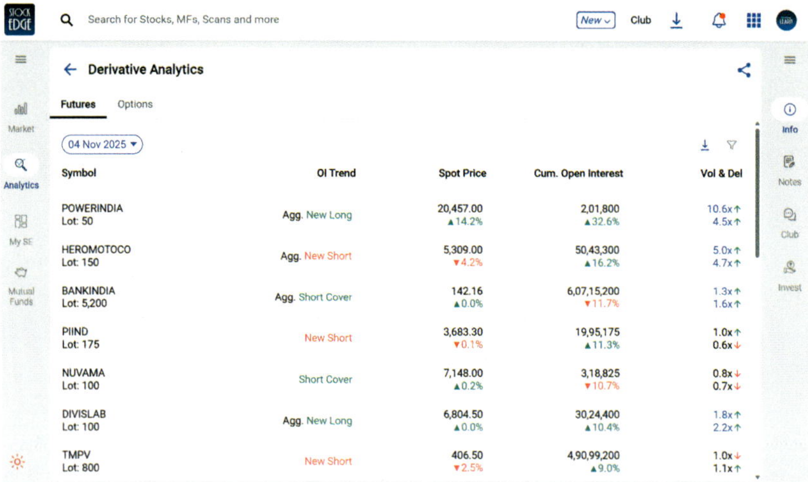

Derivative Analytics

Futures | Options

04 Nov 2025

Symbol	OI Trend	Spot Price	Cum. Open Interest	Vol & Del
POWERINDIA Lot: 50	Agg. New Long	20,457.00 ▲14.2%	2,01,800 ▲32.6%	10.6x↑ 4.5x↑
HEROMOTOCO Lot: 150	Agg. New Short	5,309.00 ▼4.2%	50,43,300 ▲16.2%	5.0x↑ 4.7x↑
BANKINDIA Lot: 5,200	Agg. Short Cover	142.16 ▲0.0%	6,07,15,200 ▼11.7%	1.3x↑ 1.6x↑
PIIND Lot: 175	New Short	3,683.30 ▼0.1%	19,95,175 ▲11.3%	1.0x↑ 0.6x↓
NUVAMA Lot: 100	Short Cover	7,148.00 ▲0.2%	3,18,825 ▼10.7%	0.8x↓ 0.7x↓
DIVISLAB Lot: 100	Agg. New Long	6,804.50 ▲0.0%	30,24,400 ▲10.4%	1.8x↑ 2.2x↑
TMPV Lot: 800	New Short	406.50 ▼2.5%	4,90,99,200 ▲9.0%	1.0x↓ 1.1x↑

Table 2.3 StockEdge screenshot of the F&O zone

Observe in Table 2.3, the OI trend gives you the analysis of the OI itself, whether there was long buildup, short covering, etc.

You may also choose to leverage the above and skip doing the analysis yourself, however I would highly suggest you to do the analysis yourself to make your foundation stronger.

LET'S PRACTICE

Practice tracking operator's position in the following stocks, and fill up the white space beside the bar:

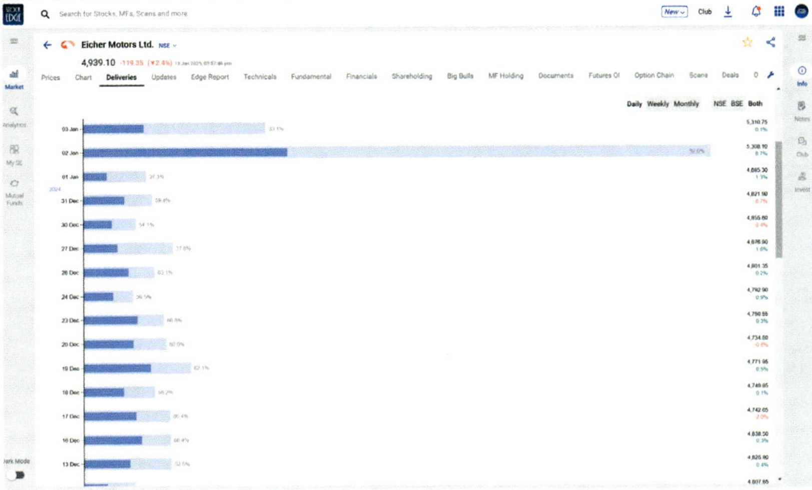

Figure 2.48

Figure 2.49

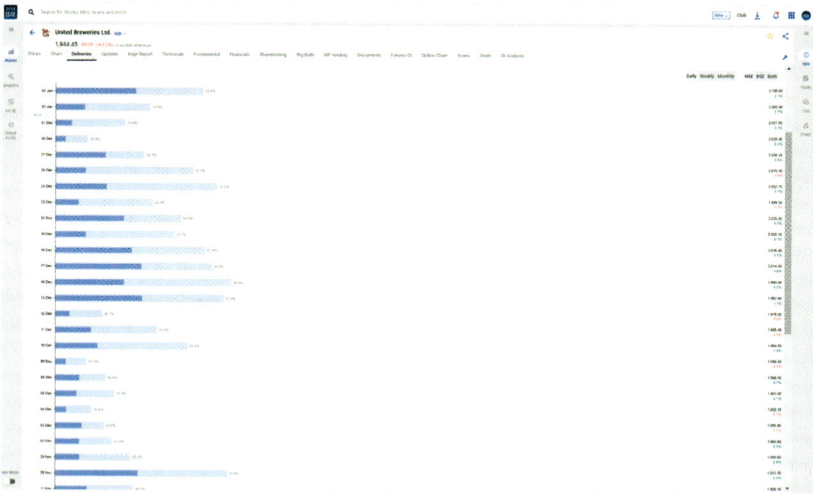

Figure 2.50

Figure 2.51

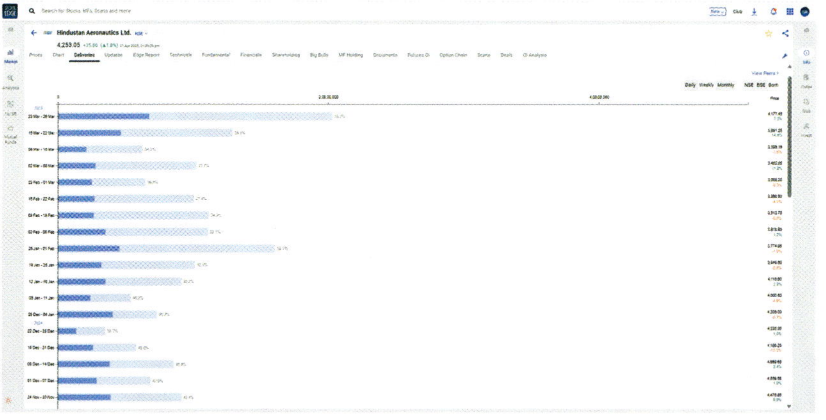

Figure 2.52

Figure 2.53

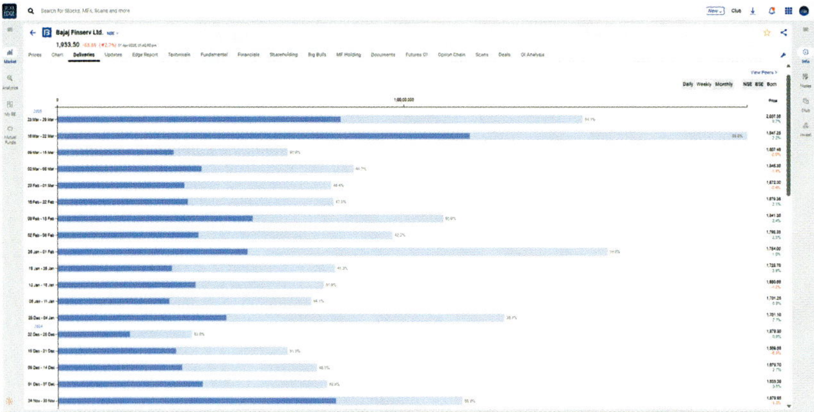

Figure 2.54

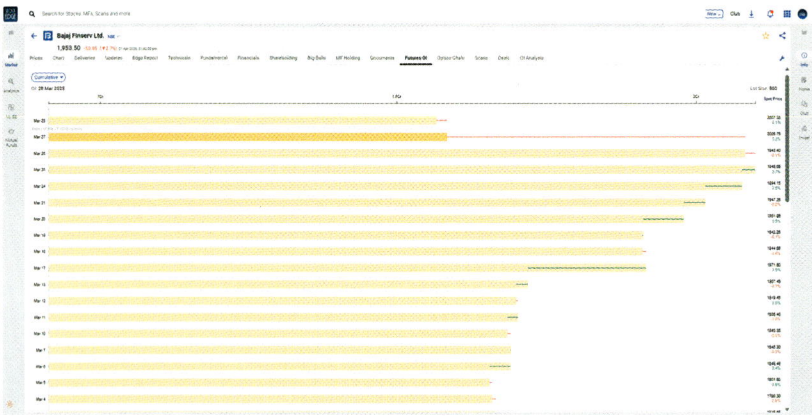

Figure 2.55

Figure 2.56

Figure 2.57

SUMMARY

- Stocks with high liquidity, good market breadth and low impact cost indicate wider market participation in the stock. Always trade in these stocks.
- A knowledgeable trader would always trade with the trend.
- Enter trades where risk:return is 2:1.
- Stop loss is the price point that you fix to sell the stock in case it is not performing well.
- There are 3 different types of charts that you may follow: line chart, bar chart and candlestick chart.
- Candlestick is made of open, high, low and close of price. A longer upper wick indicates selling pressure while a longer lower wick indicates buying pressure, and a long body suggests high volatility.
- Delivery is the portion of traded volume that is carried forward to subsequent days, indicating stronger market participants holding positions overnight.
- Operators are the big guys with a large quantum of capital, and are the ones driving the stock prices.
- Large volumes and price movements supported by delivery data indicate operators' buying or selling actions.
- Open interest (OI) represents the total number of outstanding contracts in the derivatives market, reflecting the level of activity and potential trend direction.
- Increases in OI alongside price movements suggest sustained trends, whereas decreases may indicate position exits.
- Use volume, delivery and open interest data together to validate price moves.

LEARNER'S CORNER

How do I track the liquidity of a stock?

Liquidity of a stock can be tracked by tracking its volume, and the difference between bid and ask. The higher the volume, the higher will be liquidity and lesser the difference between bid and ask, higher will be liquidity. A low difference between bid and ask is indicative of more buyers and sellers in a stock.

Should the risk-reward also be 2:1, or can I change it to something else?

As a trader, you would want to maximize your profits and minimize your losses. When you keep your reward 2 times higher than your risk, then even if you take 10 trades and 5 of them don't work, you still end up making money since your reward in the winning trades was twice that of the losses in your losing trades. For example, you took 10 trades of Rs 10,000 each, deploying 1 lakh capital. Of these, 5 trades incurred 5% loss, making your total loss of Rs 2,500, and the rest 5 trades incurred 10% profits, making your total gain of Rs 5,000. Your net gain adds up to Rs 2,500, even though only 5 of your trades worked. This is just a simple technique of risk management.

Is it important for me to track open interest even if I just intend to trade in the cash market?

Derivative trades are only available in some stocks. You do not have to track OI data for all stocks; track only for the ones that have derivative trading.

Is there something called a time stop loss? What if the stock is consolidating at the same price for more than my trading tenure—should I exit even if it is not hitting my stop loss?

There needs to be a thought-out approach to applying stop losses. It cannot be dependent on just time. We will discuss more about the different approach of putting stop losses later in the book.

Which type of chart should I follow to track the markets?

You can track any type of chart that you're comfortable with.

Can I start trading now by judging the price, volume, delivery and open interest of a stock?

Analysing the price, volume, delivery and open interest are just a stepping stone in a trading journey. These are some crucial elements, and a solid understanding of its functions will help you progress more confidently in your trading journey. Although it's not advisable for a beginner to just start trading based on this analysis, you can start putting in some money now, so that you get in a habit of drawing support, resistance, trendlines and tracking, volumes, delivery and OI on a regular basis. Start by using Scans in StockEdge.

Nice-to-Knows of Technical Analysis

We've covered the must-knows and should-knows of technical analysis. You are now supposed to be knowledgeable enough to understand the story that the charts are trying to communicate to you. The concepts discussed till now are crucial for you to understand, before proceeding further with the book. If it is still not clear, I would highly recommend you give it another read. If you are someone who is serious about pursuing and learning technical analysis, then you would have practised all the exercises mentioned before proceeding. The exercises are there to help you build the muscle memory needed before you move on to the advanced concepts.

Candlestick Patterns

I will not go deep into candlesticks patterns in this book. I suggest you visit my website vivekbajaj.com for more content on this along with the following image and explanation.

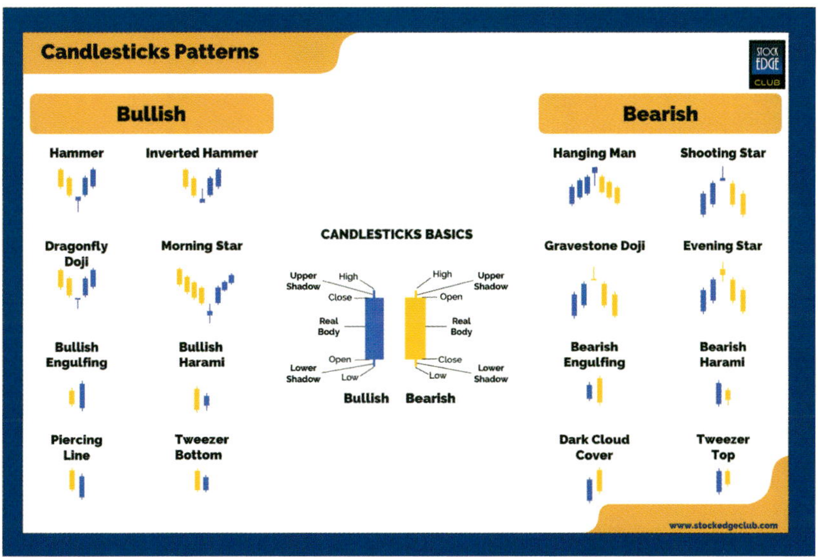

Figure 2.58 Important candlestick patterns

Chart Patterns

Have you ever noticed that we are surrounded by different patterns in our lives?

Every activity around us, our behaviour, our schedules and so on involve a pattern and pattern recognition is one of the biggest strengths of the human mind. This pattern-recognition strength has been lent to us from nature as nature also works in patterns.

Since, we as humans are the creators of science, patterns have become the most important aspect of the scientific definition of everything. This has a very important application in stock markets. The price of a stock also forms patterns, and each pattern signifies or indicates a potential future price movement. Chart patterns is a very widely used study across traders for confirmation of their price action judgement.

In this chapter, we will briefly cover price or chart patterns, which is one of the main reasons behind the evolution of the stock market. There are broadly 3 types of chart patterns:

- Reversal patterns: Reversal patterns signal that there may be a possibility of a reversal in an ongoing trend. There could be 2 types of reversal:
  - Bullish reversal: When the stock may reverse and turn bullish
    - Inverse head and shoulder
    - Double bottom
    - Triple bottom
  - Bearish reversal: When the stock may reverse and turn bearish
    - Head and shoulder
    - Double top
    - Triple top
- Continuation patterns: Continuation patterns hint at the continuation of an ongoing trend. When the price moves in a particular direction and then takes a small pause, it indicates that

the trend might continue. Most commonly used continuation patterns are:

- rectangles
- triangles
- flags
- pennants

- Other patterns: Some patterns form neither indicate reversal or continuation, but are some of the very important price patterns followed by traders:
  - wedges
  - rounding bottom
  - cup and handle

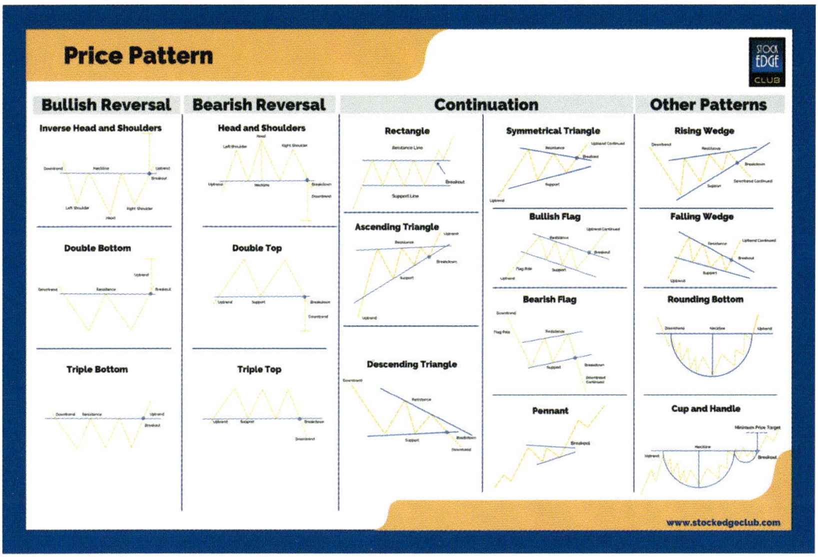

Figure 2.59 Important chart patterns

I will not go deep into each pattern. Figure 2.59 covers all the important chart patterns that you can study about.

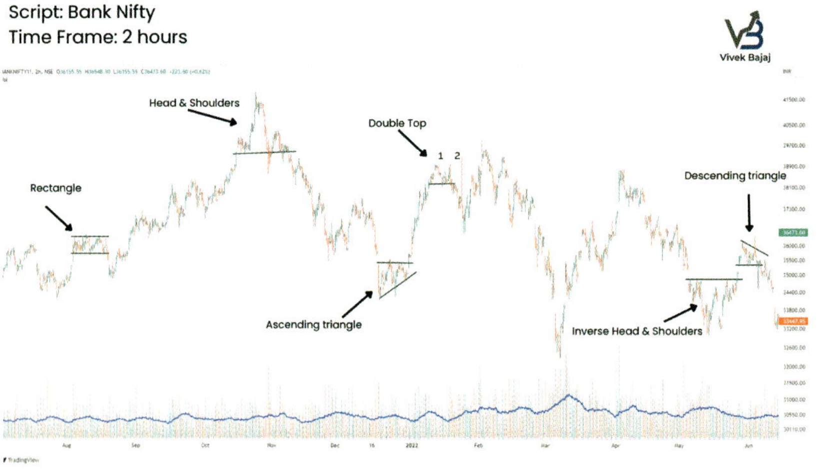

Figure 2.60 All the different chart patterns formed in Nifty50

The chart in Figure 2.60 reveals several trading patterns formed in Nifty50. Initially, a rectangle pattern appeared, and when the price broke below it, it created a chance for a profitable short trade. Following that, a head and shoulders pattern emerged, which provided another profitable opportunity as the price declined post that. Later, amid a falling market, an ascending triangle pattern formed, and once the price broke out of this pattern, it rose, leading to another profit. The chart also featured a double top, an inverse head and shoulders, and a descending triangle.

These examples highlight that multiple patterns can form on a single chart. By mastering pattern recognition and applying it diligently, you can achieve fewer but more effective and profitable trades. To support this, we've integrated an auto chart pattern recognition tool in StockEdge, allowing you to simply check stocks where any chart patterns have been formed. I will cover this in detail later in the book.

Stock Selection: Circle of Competence

This is a concept introduced by Warren Buffet, the father of investing.

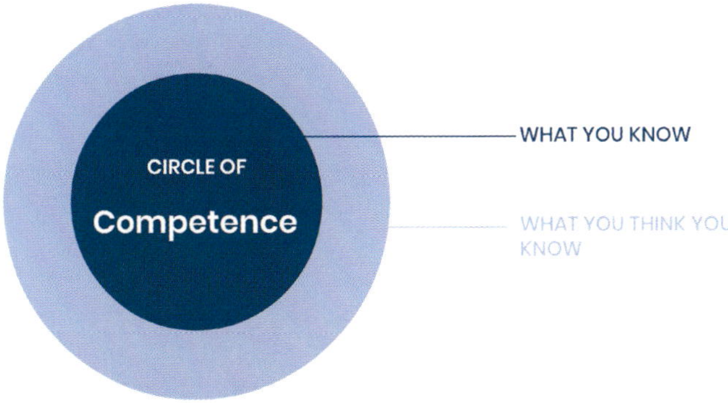

Figure 2.61 Pictorial representation of Circle of Competence

I will try to break down the circle of competence using an analogy about life and your circle of friends.

We all have countless friends, especially if you include those on social media, but only a few close friends. Friendship develops as you get to know and understand each other. Similarly, the stock market works on the basis of familiarity. You need to befriend stocks in a way that mirrors human relationships. Just as a friend can offer support, stocks can provide returns and financial growth. A key aspect of friendship is having compatible wavelengths. If your thoughts don't align with a friend's, the relationship may falter. The same principle applies to stocks—you need to choose those with which you have a higher chance of synergy.

How do you identify stocks that match your wavelength? Your wavelength reflects your thoughts, lifestyle and personal circumstances. When something you read or encounter aligns with your perspective, it falls within your circle of competence—a concept applicable to both trading and investing. Whether you're trading or investing, focus on stocks that resonate with you.

For example, if you lead a simple life and avoid late-night parties, you'll likely bond with friends who share similar traits. If a party-loving friend invites you out at 1.00 a.m., it won't suit your lifestyle. The same scenario applies to stocks. To start with, list stocks that resonate with your life. If you use Colgate to brush your teeth, Dove or Lifebuoy soap, or drive a Maruti car, or have an account with HDFC bank, include the companies these products belong to in your watchlist. (Colgate Palmolive for Colgate, Hindustan Unilever for Dove or Lifebuoy, Maruti for Maruti cars, HDFC Bank.)

Make a list of the products and the brands of the products that you use regularly. Identify the companies the brand/product belongs to and create a watchlist. Experience will introduce you to new stocks, like discovering an FMCG stock when you buy a product or a pharmaceutical stock when you purchase medicine.

Identifying consumption-related stocks is straightforward because they're part of our daily lives. But how do you recognize non-consumption stocks like those in the steel sector? Often, this knowledge comes from personal connections. If a friend is working in the steel industry, then try to understand how the sector is looking and try to get details. Such information also falls within your circle of competence, making the stock a potential addition to your portfolio.

In essence, stay alert and make it a habit to identify stocks. Pay attention to your surroundings, like street hoardings. If you notice any hoardings of any company for a new product launch, for example, if Maruti Suzuki has launched a new car, then do not take it as a casual information. Don't just think of the brand from a consumer's point of view, think of it from a market participant's view. Shift your perspective, be open to new ideas and explore new stocks.

To start with, limit yourself to tracking 30-35 stocks daily and ensure you also keep an eye on the market leaders in each industry. For instance, if you are a customer of ICICI Bank, it naturally falls within your circle of competence, making it a stock you'd want to monitor. However, to make a well-rounded assessment, you should also track the industry leaders. In the banking sector, this means following HDFC Bank and SBI alongside ICICI. By doing so, you gain a broader perspective and better insights into the industry trends.

Identifying the Industry Leaders

You need to take the help of a stock analytics tool to identify the industry leaders.

In the StockEdge web version, go to the Sector section and type or select any sector or industry from the list given. Here we select Banking, for example.

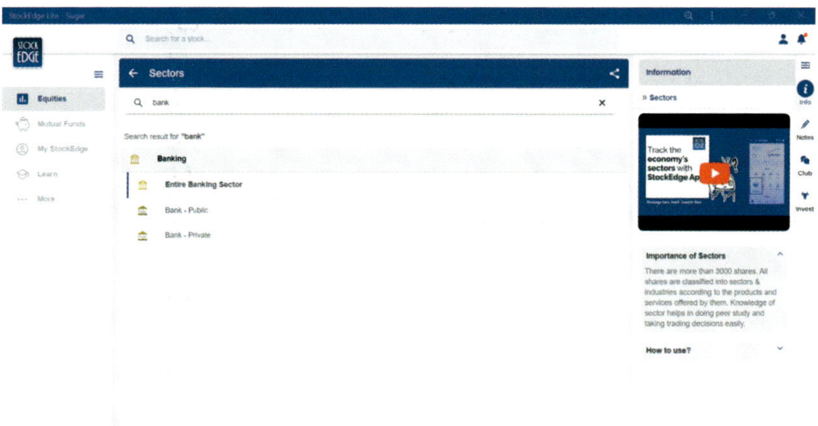

Figure 2.62 Sector page of StockEdge

As we were considering ICICI bank previously as our example, let us go to ICICI Bank under the Entire Banking Sector as illustrated in Figure 2.63. HDFC Bank Ltd is the largest private bank and the leader in the banking industry.

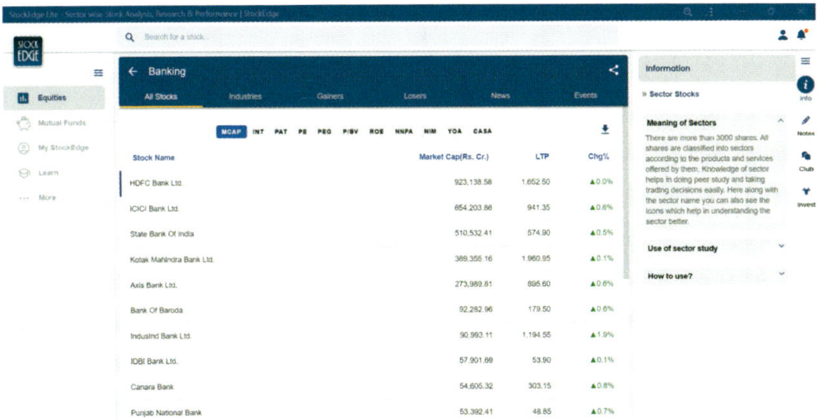

Figure 2.63 Top stocks in Banking Sector

Observing Figure 2.63, the market cap of HDFC Bank is Rs 923,138 crores ranking top in the list, whereas ICICI Bank stands second on the list with a market cap of Rs 654,203 crores. Then comes SBI, which is the largest public bank with a huge market cap of Rs 510,532 crores, followed by Kotak Mahindra Bank with a huge market cap of Rs 388,355 crores.

Along with ICICI Bank, you may track HDFC Bank, SBI, Kotak Bank and even Axis Bank as it also has a significantly large market cap of Rs. 389,355 crores. These are the top 5 banks of the Indian Banking Sector and if you wish to do anything in this sector, then you must track at least these 5 banks. To create your watchlist, add those stocks that are a part of your circle of competence and add the market leaders of the industry to which those stocks belong.

SUMMARY

- Chart patterns are formed by prices that indicate a potential stock movement.
- There are mainly 3 types of chart patterns:
  - Reversal patterns
  - Continuation patterns
  - Other price patterns
- Make note of all the candlestick patterns and the important price patterns.
- Circle of competence is a concept introduced by Warren Buffet, the father of investing. It implies that you stick to companies whose products you use or that you know about or are aware of. Track market leaders of the stocks in your circle of competence before trading.
- Track at least 30 to 35 stocks

LEARNER'S CORNER

Do I need to know all the candlestick chart patterns for technical analysis?

Knowledge of candlestick patterns is definitely an advantage when trading, but it is not necessary. If you are finding it difficult to study them, take it slow. Focus on 4 or 5 important ones to start with.

I know a relative/friend who shares stock tips; can I not trade on those?

Trading on tips is the fastest way of losing your hard-earned money. Unless you know the operator himself who is driving the stocks, do not trade simply based on tips. It's good to get stock ideas from relatives and friends, but do your own analysis before taking the trade. No one else shares responsibility for your money.

3

Seeking Guidance/ Reading Signs: The Priest

Picture a grand temple where the deity represents the heart of the sacred space. The deity's presence is central and extremely pure, adding the most value to the temple. That's the role of price action in the temple of the stock market. Price action holds the highest significance in the field of technical analysis. It's symbolic of the pure movement and value of stock prices.

However, to fully appreciate and connect with this essence, devotees rely on the guidance of the temple's priests. Just as priests offer insights to the spiritual experience, technical indicators provide crucial signals that guide us to understand the underlying trends and potential shifts in stock prices. Each priest has a different perspective and expertise to guide you on how to connect with god. Technical indicators in the financial markets are much like this—each unique in its way of helping market participants navigate the stock price.

As traders, we need to befriend the price, we need to understand its movement. It's the foremost trait of a successful trader. The indicators are much like the language that connects a trader to the price. Whenever a price is about to behave in a certain way, it will communicate its behaviour to you through these indicators. Each indicator signals a certain type of price movement to be anticipated by the traders. Following are the different types of behaviour that the indicators signal to:

- Trend indicators—signal the shifts or the continuation of trends in a stock
- Momentum indicators—measure the speed of the stock movement
- Volatility indicators—help gauge the degree of price fluctuations in a stock
- Volume indicators—help measure the volume support for the price movement of a stock

This book covers the key indicators I think you must track or at least have knowledge of.

Moving Average

The Concept

In cricket, if you want to gauge how well the Indian team is performing, you don't just look at their latest match. Instead, you might consider their average score over the last 10 or 20 matches. This average score helps you understand their general form and performance trend, free from the noise of individual games, where they might have faced exceptionally tough opponents or had an unusually good or bad day.

Similarly, a moving average in technical analysis averages out the stock prices over a specified period, such as 50 or 200 days. This helps investors and traders see the overall direction of a stock's price, filtering out the daily fluctuations.

In the stock market, if the stock price is trending above its moving average, it's like the team consistently scoring above their average—indicating strong performance. Conversely, if the price is below the moving average, it's like the team scoring below their average, signalling a downturn.

Diving Deeper: The Exponential Moving Average

While the simple moving average gives us a balanced view, sometimes recent performances matter more. In cricket, think about how the team's latest matches might be more indicative of their current form than older games. This is where the exponential moving average (EMA) comes into play.

With an exponential moving average, recent match scores are given more importance, or in technical words, more weightage than the older matches. For instance, if the Indian team scored 350 runs in their last match and 200 runs 2 weeks ago, an exponential moving average would emphasize the 350 runs more heavily, reflecting the team's current momentum more accurately. Applying this to the stock market, the EMA assigns greater weight to recent prices, offering a comprehensive view of the stock's trend. It responds more quickly to recent price changes than the simple or weighted moving averages.

This makes it an excellent tool for traders who need to make rapid decisions based on the latest market conditions.

In essence, while the simple moving average (SMA) provides a steady, long-term perspective, the exponential moving average (EMA) delivers a highly responsive and current outlook. Each type of moving average gives traders different insights, just as different ways of analysing cricket scores offer varied perspectives on a team's performance, helping fans and analysts predict future outcomes with greater confidence.

I will discuss only EMA in detail; you can choose to use any other moving averages.

Charting the Indicator

Let's add the EMA indicator to the charts and see what it looks like.

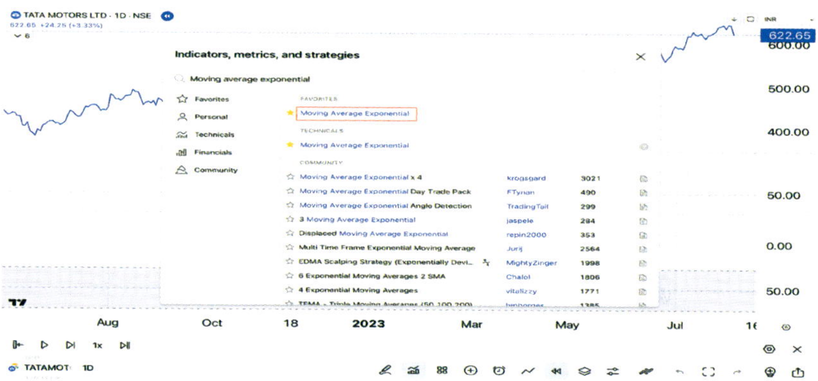

Figure 3.1 Moving average indicators listed in TradingView

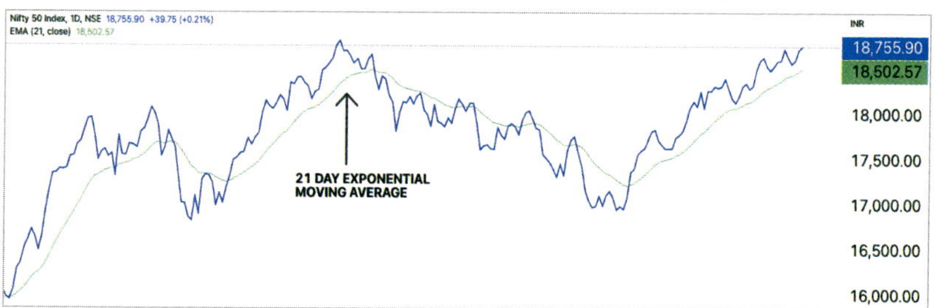

Figure 3.2 EMA 21 added to the daily line chart of Nifty50

As you can see in Figure 3.2, the EMA has been plotted on the graph. By default, it plots this line for 9 periods, but I have changed this to 21 periods from the settings option reflecting the moving average of Nifty50 for the past 21 days. The reason that it's showing for 21 days is because it is a daily line chart. If we change it to 2-hourly or weekly, then it will plot the EMA for 21 periods, each period consisting of 2 hours, or weeks, respectively. Let's add another EMA with 55 time periods.

Figure 3.3 21-day EMA and 55-day EMA plotted on the daily line chart of Nifty50

The red line in Figure 3.3 represents the 55-period EMA. In the short term, prices are more likely to follow the 21-period EMA. Over the long term, the 55-period EMA becomes more relevant. For extended periods, adding a longer-term moving average is beneficial. Let's add 100 and 200 period EMA to judge the longer trend.

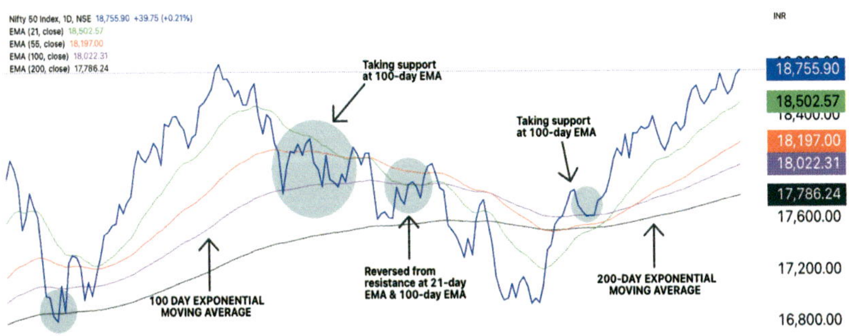

Figure 3.4 21-day EMA, 55-day EMA,100-day EMA and 200-day EMA plotted on the daily line chart of Nifty50

Why 21, 55, 100 and 200?

The number 21 is symbolic of the number of trading days in a month while 55 is symbolic of the number of trading days in a quarter. Similarly, 100 is symbolic of the number of trading days in a half-year and 200 is symbolic of the number of trading days in a year. Moreover, another reason for me to follow 21 and 55 is because they're Fibonacci numbers, the most natural number sequence followed universally. The significance of Fibonacci numbers (0,1,1,2,3,5,8,13,21…) is explained later.

Uses of EMA

Support and Resistance Levels

If you observe in Figure 3.4, whenever Nifty falls, it takes support at/near its moving averages. If it falls below one moving average, then it takes support at/near another moving average. Similarly, if it has been trading below its moving averages, and starts rising, then the EMAs tend to act as resistance points. Typically, moving averages are used as a good support and resistance level in the market. In fact, you can even combine the demand-zone and supply-zone study with the moving average so that you can get more conviction on the key levels of the stock or sector.

Trend Identification

Let us take an example of a stock, ITC Ltd (Figure 3.5).

As you can see in Figure 3.5, the price of the stock is above its 21-day period, 55-day period, 100-day period and 200-day period. This means that this stock has been performing better than its average performance, indicating an uptrend in the short term, medium term, long term, as well as very long term. Moreover, all the short-term tenure EMAs are above the longer-term tenure EMAs indicating that the stock performance in the recent times was better than the longer term. Another sign confirming the uptrend for a long time in the stock. In brief,

- if the stock is trading above all EMAs, and
- all shorter tenure EMAs are above the longer tenure EMAs,

then the stock is in uptrend.

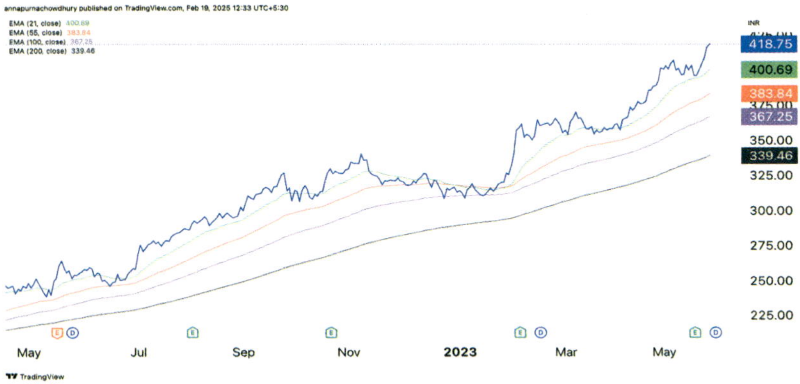

Figure 3.5 21-day EMA, 55-day EMA,100-day EMA and 200-day EMA plotted on the daily line chart of ITC Ltd

One way to identify trends is by using trendline to draw a line where you connect the price points. The other way is to follow the moving averages indicator—if the stock is above its moving averages, then it is in a positive trend.

Stop Loss

You can also use the moving average as a stop loss. It could be 9-day EMA, 21-EMA, or any other as per your trading tenure. If the stock closes below the 9-day EMA, or 21-day EMA, you can trigger the stop loss. The closer the stock price is to its moving average, the more favourable will be the risk-reward as the stop loss will be smaller. In ITC's case, the price is just above the moving average, so you can buy at current levels with a small stop loss.

You can create a model or rule for yourself. It can be

- either you buy the stock if it is above its 100 and 200 moving average and sell if it falls below the 100-day moving average
- or you buy if it is above its 55 moving average and sell once it moves below it.

The closer the stock price is to its moving average, the more favourable will be the risk-reward as the stop loss will be smaller and vice versa.

Which Period of EMA Should You Follow?

There is no magic number for EMA that works with all types of trading styles. Some sets of moving averages work well for some people while it may not work for others. Each trader has their own style of trading and chooses an EMA accordingly. For me, 21, 55, 100 and 200 works well, but you can choose any other number. You can start by using the above-mentioned numbers, and with time, maybe try other numbers too and you will be able to judge what works for you.

Some of the standard practice used by various traders and investors for moving averages:

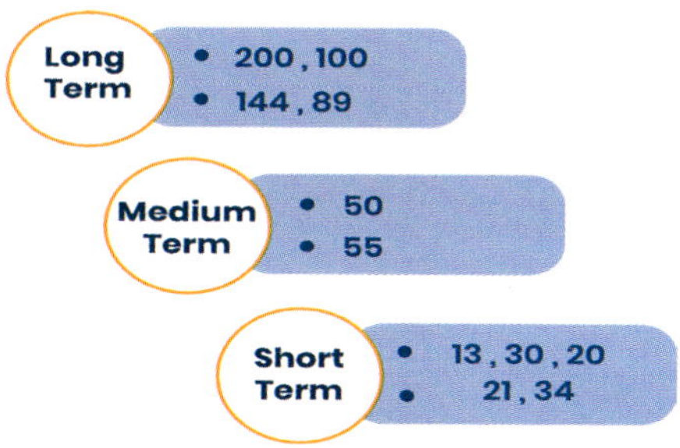

Figure 3.6 Standard EMA durations

Crossovers: Changing Trends

EMA crossovers provide traders with crucial signals about market trends and potential reversals. An EMA crossover occurs when a shorter-term EMA crosses above a longer-term EMA or below a longer-term EMA.

These crossovers are particularly significant because they combine both short-term and long-term market perspectives. They become a very good indicator of changing trends.

- Bullish crossover or golden cross

  This is when a shorter-term EMA crosses the longer-term EMA from below. It signifies a bullish crossover depiction that the average price movement in recent times has been more aggressive than in the longer time frame. For example, in August 2022, after a small phase of downtrend, the Nifty50 Index saw its 21-day EMA and 100-day EMA cross above its 200-day EMA. This golden cross signalled a recovery and subsequent rally, with the index rising from around 16,600 to over 18,800 by December 2022 (refer to Figure 3.7).

- Bearish crossover or dead cross
  This is when a shorter-term EMA crosses the longer-term EMA from above. It signifies a bearish crossover depiction that the average price movement in recent times has declined and is slower than in the longer time frame. For example, in March 2022, the Nifty50 experienced a dead cross when the 21-day EMA and 55-day EMA fell below the 100-day EMA. This indicated a potential bearish trend, and the index did face volatility and downward pressure in the following months, aligning with broader global market uncertainties (refer to Figure 3.7).

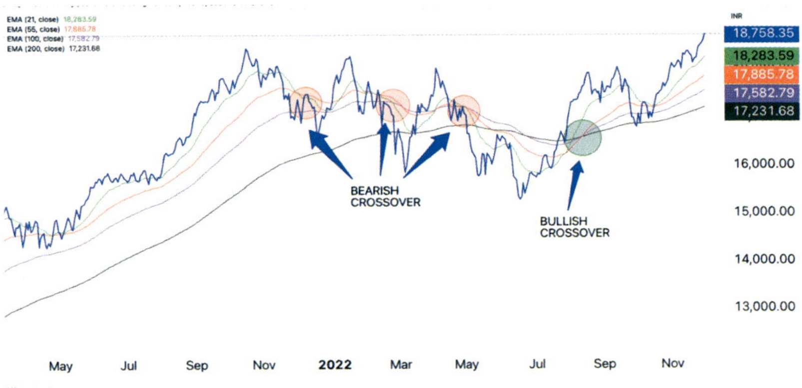

Figure 3.7 21-day EMA, 55-day EMA,100-day EMA and 200-day EMA plotted on the daily line chart of Nifty50

Moving average was probably the first indicator created but now traders consider it outdated. However, in my opinion, at least when you are starting, you should track the moving averages and maybe with time, you move on. It is a very important tool for the understanding of the market.

SUMMARY

- Moving average is a trend identifier indicator.
- Exponential moving average (EMA) gives more weightage to the recent movement of the stock.
- If the shorter tenure moving average is above the longer tenure moving average and the price is above all moving averages, then the stock is in uptrend.
- I use 21-day, 55-day, 100-day and 200-day EMA.
- EMAs are powerful tools that can also help in identifying potential support and resistance levels and stop loss.
- Moving average crossovers indicate the changing trend of the stock.

LET'S PRACTICE

Identifying bullish and bearish crossovers. Use a pen/pencil to mark the bullish and/or bearish crossovers in the following charts:

Figure 3.8

Figure 3.9

Figure 3.10

Figure 3.11

LEARNER'S CORNER

Does the EMA indicator also work on index or sector index charts?

These indicators work wonderfully in any instrument that is traded. You can use it on any sectoral index as well as Gold, USD–INR, etc.

Can I use simple moving average or WMA instead of EMA?

Yes, you can. Find your fit to your style of trading.

How do I decide which time period moving average to follow?

It will depend on the tenure of your trade. The shorter the tenure, the shorter the time frame of EMA you should follow.

If the stock goes below the 21-day EMA, does that mean the trend has changed?

Not necessarily. It could just be a correction rather than a change in the trend. You need to wait for the confirmation of the price action for a longer period of time to conclude whether the trend has changed or not.

Refer to Figure 3.12. The stock was in uptrend from December 2023 to June 2024. Yet there were days when the stock went below 21-day EMA. It was merely retracement before a bounce back.

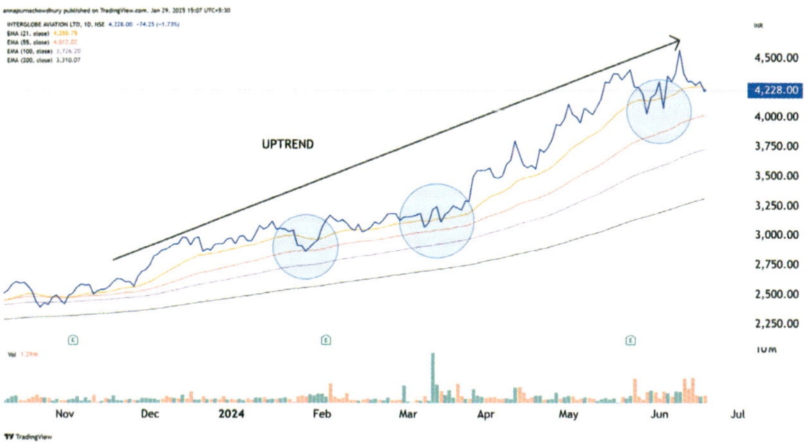

Figure 3.12

Should I consider EMA as support and resistance or the price-based support and resistance as previously discussed in the book?

You can choose both or you could choose either. Like I've mentioned before, you need to look for conviction at price points. If the price-based support and resistance are converging with the EMAs, then it hints towards a strong support or resistance level. Similarly, as we proceed and gather knowledge about more indicators, we need to look for points of convergence to build conviction on the demand or supply zones.

Average True Range and Supertrend

Average true range (ATR) calculates the average range a stock moves over a specified period. It considers highs, lows and gaps between previous closes. It smooths the 'true range' values over a selected period, such as 10 days. You can choose to alter the number of days that you want the ATR of. The supertrend indicator is derived from ATR, where ATR is multiplied by a factor (commonly 3) and applied to a moving average of high and low prices to generate dynamic support and resistance levels.

The ATR in itself is a volatility indicator that signals the degree of volatility in the stock. We will cover volatility more deeply later. A high ATR is indicative of high volatility, whereas a low ATR is indicative of low volatility.

Supertrend–The Concept

The technical indicators keep evolving, and there is rapid introduction of new theories that lead to formation of new indicators. Supertrend is one such new trend identifying indicator.

Imagine you're driving on a scenic but unpredictable mountain road. The road signs you encounter—sharp curve ahead, steep descent or caution—guide you to adjust your speed and steering to stay safe. Similarly, the supertrend indicator overlays on a stock's price chart, acting as a visual guide that indicates when to enter or exit a trade. It is a trend identifying indicator which tells you when the stock is in a trend and when there has been a change in the trend.

The core of the supertrend indicator is volatility as ATR is the base of this indicator.

Charting the Indicator

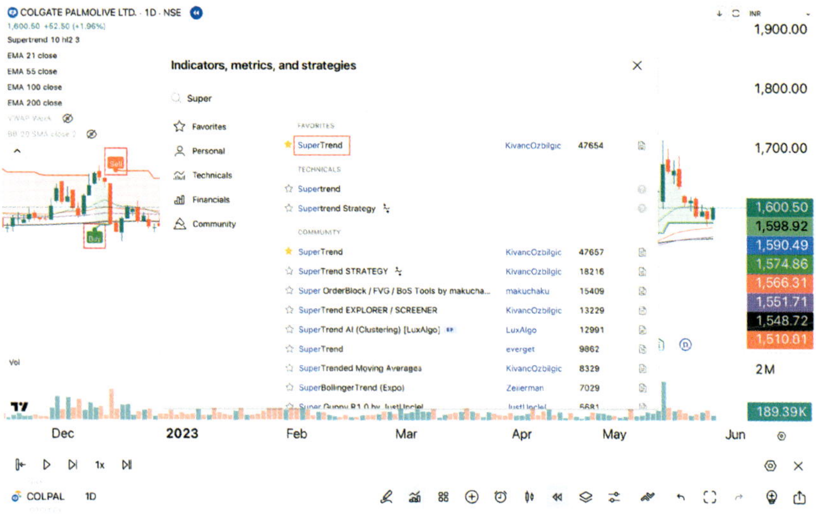

Figure 3.13 Adding the supertrend indicator to the chart

Figure 3.14 Daily chart of Colgate Palmolive with supertrend indicator and EMAs

In Figure 3.14, there are new signals added to the chart that highlight 'buy' and 'sell'. Observe that when the indicator changed to 'sell', a significant downtrend was witnessed in the stock, and when the indicator changed to 'buy' the second time, the stock changed its direction and moved towards uptrend. Even though there has been some correction in the last 12 trading sessions, the long-term trend is still up which implies that as a trend-following trader I would still be positive on the stock, till it signals 'sell' to me.

Use of Supertrend

It navigates the trader for the following:

- Identifying trends
- Entry/exit levels

As discussed in the above example, supertrend is a trend-identifying indicator that confirms an uptrend/downtrend in the stock. You can use the shift in the signals as entry/exit levels too. In the case of the above example, the stock gave a buy signal roughly around 1450 levels, so that could be the entry point for traders. Similarly, when the stock signals 'sell', that could be the exit level for traders. In the above case, if the stock closes below 1575, it will show 'sell' indicating a potential downtrend.

Another important point that I want to highlight is the misleading signals that these indicators can give. Let's use the above example to understand this. Observed in Figure 3.14, the stock had given a 'buy' signal around December too near 1650 level; however, there was no uptrend witnessed later and the stock crashed to give a 'sell' signal on the 4th trading session at the 1575 level, witnessing a massive downtrend later. As traders, if we entered seeing the 'buy' level around 1650 and exited at the 1575 level, we would have to book a loss of Rs 75 or 4.5%.

Imagine you are looking to get married. Do you rely only on one aspect such as age or hobbies? No, you have multiple areas on your mind and you consider all of them. Similarly, *we cannot rely on only 1 indicator to take a trade*. We need to have a setup that includes at least 2 or more indicators as well as price action that are all indicating the same thing to build conviction in the trade.

Moving Average and Supertrend

Now that you've learnt 2 trend-identifying indicators, we will combine both and confirm whether both are signalling towards the same thing. Let's take the example of Coal India.

Figure 3.15 Daily chart of Coal India with EMA and Supertrend

Observed in Figure 3.15, Coal India is trading at 486.95, and trading above all the 21-day EMA, 55-day EMA, 100-day EMA, and 200-day EMA, so the stock seems to be in an uptrend, as per EMA. However, the supertrend is still a 'sell'. In such a case, if we follow both the indicators, then you will wait for the supertrend to signal 'buy' before you enter the trade. Let's look at a different example now.

In Figure 3.16, the stock is currently trading at the 192 level, right near the resistance level of 199. The stock was in downtrend since December 2023, but it seems that new buying interest has emerged in May 2024, which is reflected well in price action, tall volume bars, and the supertrend changing to buy. However, the 21-day EMA is still below the 100-day and 200-day EMA. Moreover, the stock keeps reversing from its resistance level, indicating that the stock has transitioned into the consolidation zone.

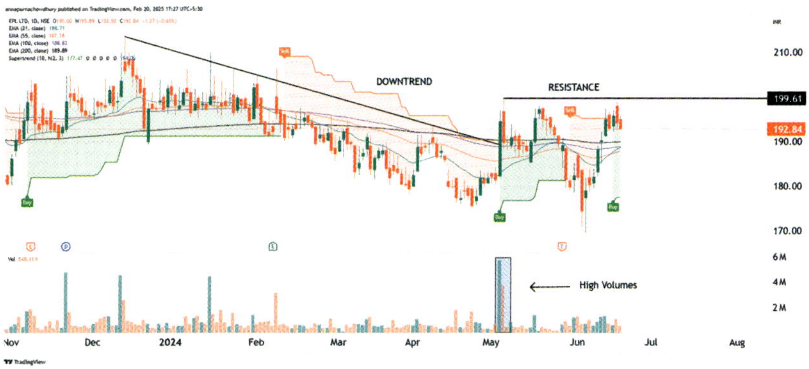

Figure 3.16 Daily chart of EPL Ltd with EMA and Supertrend

In such a case, till the shorter-term EMA goes above the longer-term, price trades above all EMAs, the stock is in uptrend and the supertrend indicator is also a buy, we will not be positive on the stock.

This was the introduction of the basic concept of supertrend and moving average crossover. You can now add this to your template and use it to track your stocks from your watchlist.

SUMMARY

- Supertrend is a trend-identifying indicator derived from ATR and gives 'buy' and 'sell' signals.
- Supertrend can be used for identifying trends and defining entry and exit levels.
- You can go long on a stock when the supertrend has turned 'buy' and square off or sell the stock when it has given a 'sell' signal.
- A combination of moving average and supertrend adds conviction to the trades.

LET'S PRACTICE

Some charts have been provided below with the EMAs and supertrend drawn. Analysing the graphs, write whether you would have a bullish, a bearish or a neutral sentiment towards the stock.

Figure 3.17

Figure 3.18

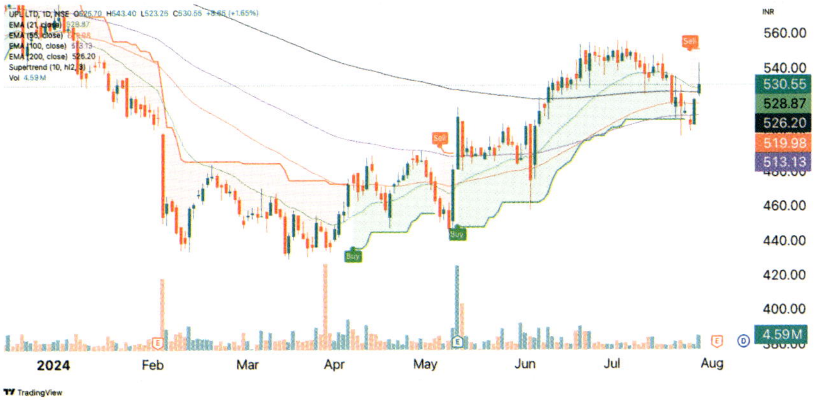

Figure 3.19

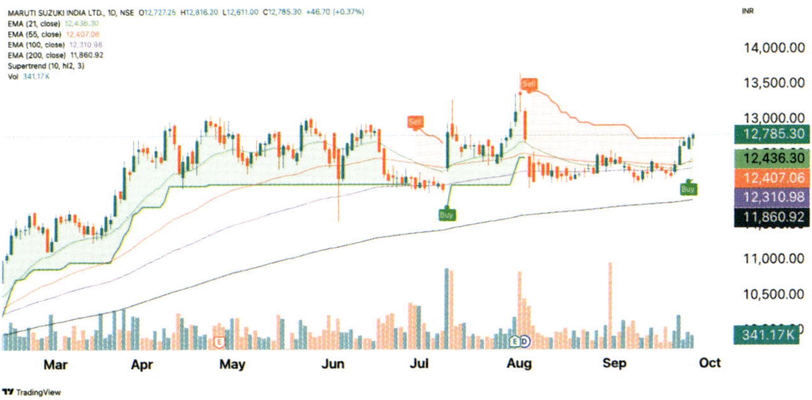

Figure 3.20

LEARNER'S CORNER

Can I trade solely based on supertrend?

It will depend on your trading style and your chart duration. The stock market is all about probabilities. When trading, you need to assess the probability of the stock movement. The probability becomes much clearer when multiple parameters are assessed together than just one. Hence, it's best to combine other indicators before taking a trade.

Can I use supertrend as a stop loss?

Yes, you can. We will discuss more on stop loss later in the book.

Fibonacci and Fibonacci Retracement

The Concept

Fibonacci retracement is an interesting and natural concept that helps us to judge the price retracement.

What Are Fibonacci Numbers?

Named after the Italian mathematician Leonardo Fibonacci, the Fibonacci number sequence consists of the most natural numbers, and everything in this world works in this format, from the arrangement of leaves on a stem to the pattern of a seashell.

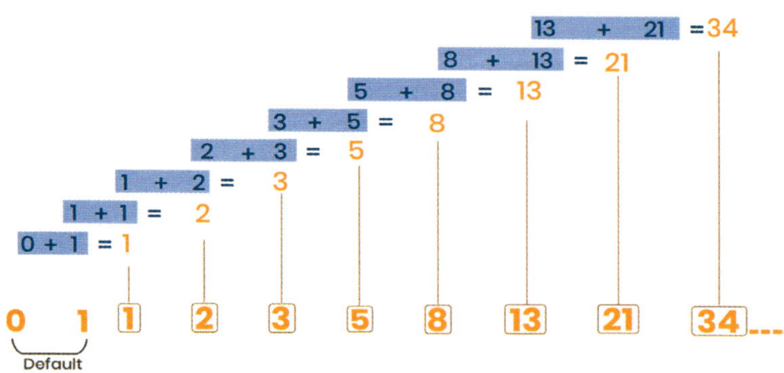

Figure 3.21 Fibonacci sequence

The Fibonacci number sequence can be seen in Figure 3.21. Fibonacci numbers form a sequence starting with 0 and 1, where each subsequent number is the sum of the 2 preceding ones. This series looks like this: 0, 1, 1, 2, 3, 5, 8, 13, 21, and so on. It is widely believed that the natural shapes in the world are as per the Fibonacci pattern. Decisions based on this number pattern increase the accuracy.

Figure 3.22 Fibonacci numbers as observed in nature.

Let's see why these numbers are known to be the most natural numbers. They work in sync to create ratios (Table 3.1) that are observed in all things around us, including our bodies.

	A	B	C	D	E
	Fibonacci Series	A_i / A_{i+1}	A_i / A_{i+2}	A_i / A_{i+3}	A_i / A_{i+4}
2	0				
3	1	**A3/A4 = 1/1 = 1**	1/2 = 0.5	1/3 = 0.333	1/5 = 0.2
4	1	**A4/A5 = 1/2 = 0.5**	1/3 = 0.333	1/5 = 0.2	1/8 = 0.125
5	2	2/3 = 0.667	2/5 = 0.4	2/8 = 0.25	2/13 = 0.154
6	3	3/5 = 0.6	3/8 = 0.375	3/13 = 0.231	3/21 = 0.143
7	5	5/8 = 0.625	5/13 = 0.385	5/21 = 0.238	5/34 = 0.147
8	8	8/13 = 0.615	8/21 = 0.381	8/34 = 0.235	8/55 = 0.145
9	13	13/21 = 0.619	13/34 = 0.382	**13/55 = 0.236**	13/89 = 0.146
10	21	21/34 = 0.618	**21/55 = 0.382**	21/89 = 0.236	21/144 = 0.146
11	34	**34/55 = 0.618**	34/89 = 0.382	34/144 = 0.236	
12	55	55/89 = 0.618	55/144 = 0.382		
13	89	89/144 = 0.618			
14	144				

Table 3.1 Fibonacci ratios

These ratios, especially 61.8%, known as the 'golden ratio', are fundamental in the study of patterns and play a very important role in your life too. In the human body, ratios between different body parts (e.g., length of the forearm to the hand) often approximate the golden ratio (61.8%). Studies even suggest that people are more likely to pause and evaluate their progress at key milestones, often aligning with Fibonacci proportions (e.g., 38.2% or 61.8% through a task). Fibonacci has the biggest application in nature and even gravity has Fibonacci patterns. The stock market is not alien to the concept either, and they are used to predict how far a price might move in a given direction after a significant change.

Understanding Fibonacci Retracement

Recall the concept of retracement and correction: whenever a stock bounces after creating a high or a low, without the change in the trend of the stock, while a small pullback is known as retracement, a deeper decline is known as correction. Fibonacci retracement levels help traders pinpoint these intervals—where prices might pause, pull back, or reverse before continuing their journey.

When applied to financial markets, Fibonacci retracement uses the key ratios derived from the Fibonacci sequence to identify potential points where the price might find support (if it's falling) or resistance (if it's rising) during its trend. Here's how it works in practice:

- Identify a significant price movement: Suppose a stock rises from 100 to 200.
- Apply Fibonacci ratios: You then apply the Fibonacci ratios (23.6, 38.2, 61.8 and 100%) to this price range. These levels will help you determine that the stock might pull back to 161.8, 150, 138.2, or 123.6 before possibly resuming its upward trend.

Uses of Fibonacci

Fibonacci levels can be used to identify the following:

- Support and resistance
- Stop loss
- Right price for entry/exit

Fibonacci retracement levels are often used as part of trend-trading strategies. The stock should be in a strong uptrend or a downtrend. Traders identify a retracement taking place within the trend using Fibonacci levels. Traders using this strategy anticipate that a price has a high probability of bouncing from the Fibonacci levels back in the direction of the initial trend.

Fibonacci levels can be useful if a trader wants to buy a particular stock but has missed out on a recent uptrend. In this situation, you could wait for a pullback. By plotting Fibonacci ratios—23.6, 38.2 and 61.8%—on a chart, traders identify possible retracement levels and enter potential trading positions at a better risk-reward level.

The same concept also holds true for a downtrend. Traders can also choose to use these levels as stop loss since these levels act as a strong support zone. So in case the price goes below these levels, it could be indicative of a selling pressure in the stock.

The best way to use this indicator is along with moving averages and supertrend. When combining all 3 indicators, we could get points of convergence, i.e., all 3 indicators direct to a similar price level, building more conviction on those price levels for a trader to initiate a trade.

Drawing the Levels

Learning how to correctly draw the indicator is the key in getting the right retracement levels in this case. For that, you need to know what a swing is.

Figure 3.23 Chart depicting swings

The highs and lows of these swings are very important for us to mark the Fibonacci levels.

Figure 3.24 Daily chart of Tata Motors

In Figure 3.24, the stock is in uptrend and the supertrend, and moving averages are also positive. This is a good stock for you to add. Now let's try to see what the retracement levels of the stock are. As depicted through the candlestick chart in Figure 3.25, the uptrend in the stock started from 400 levels and continued till 537 making these 2 important levels for us, the high and the low of the large swing. When we draw Fibonacci levels on this distance, we get the retracement points.

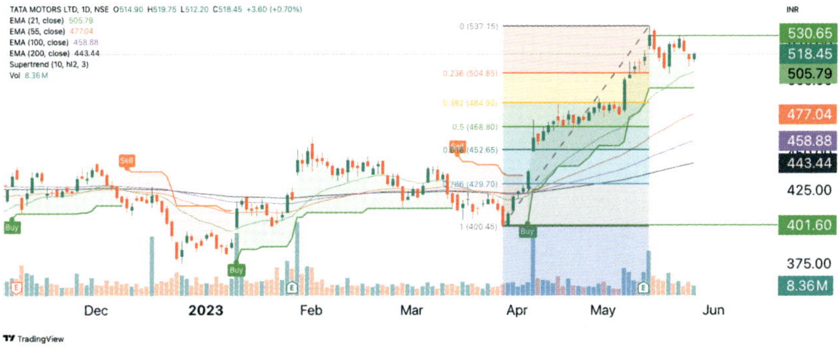

Figure 3.25 Daily chart of Tata Motors along with the Fibonacci retracement

To draw the Fibonacci retracement, select it from the left panel in TradingView and then select the low point (400) and the high point (537). As per Figure 3.25, the Fibonacci retracement levels of the stock are:

- 505 at 23%
- 485 at 38%
- 469 at 50% (this is not a Fibonacci level, but generally people feel that price can reverse from that point)
- 453 at 61.8%
- 430 at 78.6%

This entails that the stock is most likely to give a bounce back from the above-mentioned levels, making it good price points to enter the stock. In the case of Tata Motors example, the ideal price to enter the stock would be around the 505 level, as the stock is most likely to reverse from this level in case it is able to sustain its uptrend. On close observation, you will be able to see that the stock has already reversed and found a good support at 505 levels.

While Fibonacci retracement helps identify potential pullback levels within an ongoing trend, there's another concept—Fibonacci extensions—that goes a step further. It predicts where the price might move beyond its current range, providing targets for future movements.

Fibonacci Extensions

The Concept

Fibonacci extension levels are used by traders to forecast the potential continuation of a trend beyond its previous high or low.

	A	B	C	D	E
3	Fibonacci Series	$^{A_i}/_{A_{i-1}}$	$^{A_i}/_{A_{i-2}}$	$^{A_i}/_{A_{i-3}}$	$^{A_i}/_{A_{i-4}}$
4	0				
5	1				
6	1	A6/A5 = 1/1 = 1			
7	2	A7/A6 = 2/1 = 2	2/1 = 2		
8	3	3/2 = 1.5	3/1 = 3	3/1 = 3	
9	5	5/3 = 1.667	5/2 = 2.5	5/1 = 5	5/1 = 5
10	8	8/5 = 1.6	8/3 = 2.667	8/2 = 4	8/1 = 8
11	13	13/8 = 1.625	13/5 = 2.6	13/3 = 4.333	13/2 = 6.5
12	21	21/13 = 1.615	21/8 = 2.625	21/5 = 4.2	21/3 = 7
13	34	34/21 = 1.619	34/13 = 2.615	34/8 = 4.25	34/5 = 6.8
14	55	55/34 = 1.618	55/21 = 2.619	55/13 = 4.231	55/8 = 6.875
15	89	**89/55 = 1.618**	89/34 = 2.618	89/21 = 4.238	89/13 = 6.846
16	144	144/89 = 1.618	**144/55 = 2.618**	144/34 = 4.235	144/21 = 6.857
17	233	233/144 = 1.618	233/89 = 2.618	**233/55 = 4.236**	233/34 = 6.853

Table 3.2

Derived from the Fibonacci sequence, these levels (161.8, 261.8, and 423.6%) are applied to the price movements to project possible targets where the price might extend after breaking out of a known range.

Uses of Fibonacci Extensions

It is majorly used to set target levels by traders to book the profits. Suppose a stock rises from 100 to 150 and then pulls back to 125. Using Fibonacci extension, traders can project potential future resistance levels at 175, 200 or 225, based on the stock's prior move. These levels help traders set profit targets and make strategic decisions about where to exit their positions.

Drawing the Levels

Figure 3.26 Daily chart of Anant Raj Ltd

To draw the Fibonacci extension, you need to select Trend Based Fib Extension from the left panel in TradingView. You need to select the following points to map it:

a) Swing low—the point from which the actual trend started—650 in the above case.
b) Swing high—the point at which price started to retrace—948 in the above case.
c) Low of the last swing correction—807 in the above case.

In Figure 3.27:

- The stock has been in uptrend for a while, transitioning into consolidation from end October 2024 to mid-December 2024, before giving another upmove.
- The price is trading above all EMAs and all the shorter-tenure EMAs are trading above longer-tenure EMAs.
- Supertrend is buy.
- Uptrend is supported by high volumes.

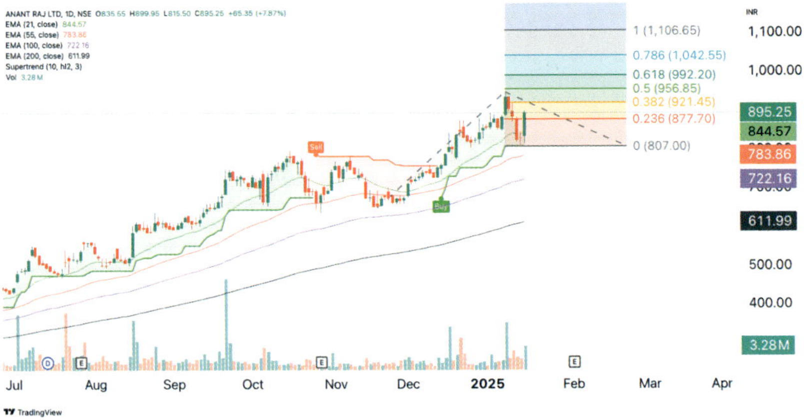

Figure 3.27 Fibonacci extension drawn on the daily chart of Anant Raj

This helps us build conviction in the stock. To estimate the potential target and the next resistance, we draw the Fibonacci extension as per the levels mentioned above. The new potential levels are estimated at 992/1042/1106. Now that we have a potential target, we can easily evaluate risk-reward before deciding whether to initiate the trade.

So far, we've covered the basics of trading with simple charts and price action. Moving averages and supertrend are straightforward, but Fibonacci analysis is more complex. From here, things will get a little more advanced but remember, over time, as you spend more hours in the market, you'll develop a 'trader's gut'—an instinctive ability to read charts and make judgements. This gut feeling is invaluable and cannot be taught directly; it's earned through experience. As we explore more complex topics, remember that practice is key. The more you engage with the market, the sharper your skills will become. Ultimately, this practice is what will perfect your approach and give you your own 'Brahmastra' in trading.

SUMMARY

- Fibonacci numbers are the most natural numbers that can be seen followed by nature.
- Ratios derived from Fibonacci numbers are used as potential retracement and target levels by traders.
- Traders use Fibonacci retracement tools to project the retracement level in a stock for favourable trading opportunities.
- Fibonacci extension tool is used to project the future potential targets or resistance levels.
- Fibonacci retracement is drawn by identifying the swing high and swing low.
- Fibonacci extension is drawn by identifying swing high, swing low, and low of the recent swing correction.

LET'S PRACTICE

Use a pen/pencil to mark the points from where you will draw the fibonacci retracement and extension in the following charts:

Figure 3.28

Figure 3.29

Figure 3.30

Figure 3.31

Figure 3.32

Figure 3.33

LEARNER'S CORNER

Can Fibonacci tools be used in all the different time-frame charts?

Yes, they can be. It depends on your trading tenure. If you're trading for a short tenure, then you can use Fibonacci tools in the shorter time-frame charts.

Can we use Fibonacci on index charts?

Yes, you can.

Does Fibonacci work in all market conditions?

Fibonacci retracements and extensions are most effective in strong trending markets where price moves in clear waves than when the stock or the broader market is range bound.

Volatility

Just as our emotions can fluctuate wildly in response to different events, the prices of stocks and other financial instruments can swing dramatically due to market news, economic indicators and investor sentiment.

Volatility measures the extent and speed of price changes in the market. High volatility means prices can rise or fall sharply in a short time, while low volatility suggests more stable, gradual price movements, similar to a calm, steady emotional state.

Think about how you feel during a typical week. Some days, you might be ecstatic at one moment and highly irritable at the next triggered by internal or external reasons. On other days, you might feel calmer and more relaxed, without getting affected much by the day's events. Such mood fluctuations are akin to the volatility in the markets. There will be days when the market fluctuations are higher than other days, indicating high volatility in the markets, while there will be other days when the price changes are minimal, and the trading environment is calmer and more stable, indicating low volatility.

Each market has its own index to measure volatility. In India, it is captured through the index INDIAVIX. Let's look at a chart of Nifty50 at the time of the Covid-19 scare as an example.

In Figure 3.34, note the sharp market drop from 12,000 to 7,600 in a month. This period of high volatility in the Indian markets, driven by uncertainty, is mirrored in the INDIAVIX chart. Observe how the VIX spikes when the market crashes and remains mostly flat during stable periods.

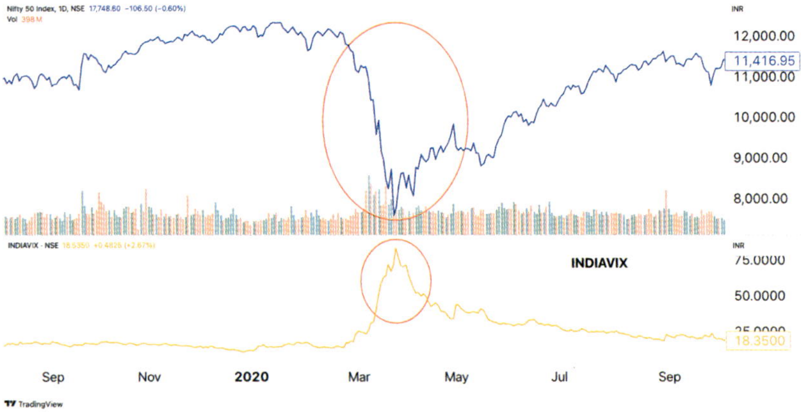

Figure 3.34 Daily chart of Nifty50, along with the chart of INDIAVIX

Also, notice the VIX's decline as the market begins to recover, eventually trending downward. This illustrates the correlation between market crashes and volatility. During corrections or crashes, volatility spikes due to panic-driven exits. Although volatility is higher during rallies compared to sideways markets, it is still lower than during crashes. Thus, a high VIX typically indicates a corrective phase in the market.

Market Movement	Volatility Level
Crash/correction	Very high
Uptrend	Moderate to high
Downtrend	Moderate to high (spikes in panic-selling)
Sideways	Low

Table 3.3

Why Is It Important to Judge Volatility in Stocks?

Just like how 2 people can never be the same, even 2 stocks can never be the same. Each stock has its own character, which is mostly driven by the character of the operator of the stock. Some stocks are highly volatile in nature, while some stocks move in a slow and steady form. Each stock will give you different opportunities to enter and exit the stock, hence making it important for us to have different strategies for stocks that are less volatile from that of stocks that are highly volatile in nature.

Figure 3.35 Daily chart of DCM Shriram

In Figure 3.35, we see that the stock is volatile since it has been making frequent high lows.

Figure 3.36 Daily chart of Firstsource Solutions (FSL)

If we see Figures 3.35 and 3.36, FSL is less volatile as compared to DCM Shriram. If a stock is volatile, then there are 2 aspects to it.

On one hand, the take profit will come faster, and on the other hand, the stop loss will get frequently hit. You need to adjust your take profit and stop loss accordingly for every stock.

I would suggest staying away from highly volatile stocks with the help of indicators that help measure a stock's volatility.

Bollinger Bands

The Concept

Bollinger bands are a versatile tool that help traders understand the volatility and potential price movements of a stock. Created by John Bollinger in the 1980s, these bands provided a visual representation of a stock's price range, indicating whether it is high or low compared to its recent past.

Figure 3.37 Bollinger Bands

Observe the indicator in Figure 3.37: Bollinger Bands consist of 3 lines plotted on a stock chart:

- The middle band—a simple moving average (SMA) of the stock price, typically set over 20 periods.
- The upper and lower bands—standard deviations away from the middle band, usually set at 2 standard deviations.

- The bands expand and contract based on the stock's volatility—widening during high volatility and tightening during low volatility.

Let us try to understand how the upper and lower bands are formed more deeply. Standard means a benchmark, and deviation measures how much it is deviating or fluctuating from its benchmark or mean. Imagine the Cricket World Cup T20 was going on, and for the first few matches Shubman Gill was not playing. The average score per match was 140, but as soon as Gill joined the squad, the average went up to 210. This was a deviation from the mean (the average) or the benchmark, meaning that the data set changed significantly. Similarly, when market conditions shift, prices can fluctuate considerably. The upper and lower bands of the bollinger band take into consideration these fluctuations and suggest that even if the prices fluctuate in either direction, there is a 95% probability (as per the normal distribution curve, or the bell curve)[1] that the prices would still move within this range.

The second concept we need to understand is the gap between the bollinger bands, also known as the BB gap. This gap, which is the distance between the upper and lower bands, changes over time.

Bollinger Bands Analysis

Let us now try to understand its application. Prices tend to move between the upper and lower bands. When the bands are close together, or the BB Gap is narrow, it indicates low volatility, and when they are far apart, or the BB Gap is wide, it signifies high volatility. Additionally:

- When price touches the upper band, or crosses the upper band, it could mean
  - either an overbought condition, if the volume is low, and the price is more likely to reverse and come back down to the middle band
  - or an onset of uptrend, or continuation of uptrend, as per the chart setup, if the volume is high.

- When price touches the lower band, or crosses the lower band, it could mean
  - either an oversold condition, if the volume is low, and the price is more likely to reverse and bounce back up to the middle band
  - or an onset of downtrend, or continuation of downtrend, as per the chart setup, if the volume is high.

Charting the Indicator

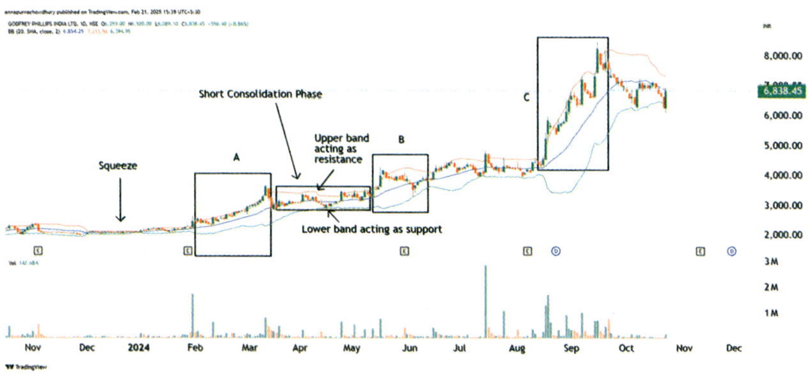

Figure 3.38 Bollinger Bands indicator added to daily chart of Godfrey Phillips India

Observe in Figure 3.38 how the stock moved within the range of the bollinger bands. Whenever the stock moved beyond its upper band supported by strong volumes, as observed in point C, the BB gap widened, and the strong price action stretched the upper band along with it, shifting the complete range of the stock, and making an uptrend. This move can also be noted at point A.

Additionally observe at point B that whenever the stock went above its upper band without much volume support, it came back to trade near its middle band. This is typically how the bollinger bands work.

Uses of Bollinger Bands

Indicative of Overbought/Oversold Conditions of Stocks

Figure 3.39 Bollinger Bands indicator added to the daily chart of DCM Shriram Ltd

In Figure 3.39, observe how the price moves within the Bollinger Bands. At Point A, the price sharply increased and moved outside the band in December 2023. The bands widen, showing an increase in volatility. However, the price eventually reverses inside the bands to trade near the middle band, confirming a temporary overbought condition.

Similarly, at Point B, the price pierces the lower band indicating high volatility due to panic selling. The bands widen, showing market stress. However, the price eventually reverts back inside, suggesting a temporary oversold condition and a mean reversion.

Although a price move outside the bollinger bands suggests overbought or oversold conditions, it does not guarantee an immediate price reversal.

Identifying Support and Resistance Levels

As the probability of a stock moving between the upper and the lower bands of bollinger band is 95%, the upper band is considered to be a good resistance level, while the lower band is considered to be a good support level. These levels typically work very well when the stock is in consolidation.

As observed in Figure 3.38, when the stock was moving in a sideways range, the upper band acted as resistance, while the lower band acted as support. Please note, bollinger bands as support and resistance levels only work when the stock is moving sideways.

Trading Strategies

When a stock consolidates around a particular price level, the gap narrows. This means that the volatility of the stock has decreased. After a period of low volatility (squeeze), price typically experiences a strong move in either direction.

Bollinger bands are widely used as trading strategies, where the traders try to analyse the gap of the bollinger band. Keeping stocks, whose price action is in a squeeze, under radar, can be very beneficial. A breakout post the squeeze, supported by high volumes is a good buy level for traders. In Figure 3.40, Nifty50 gave a breakout, after a period of squeeze. A high volume on a breakout is a sign that the stock is no more in consolidation, and it could go on to form an uptrend. A similar pattern can also be identified in Figure 3.37, when a BB squeeze was noted in the stock, and post that the stock went on to make higher highs and higher lows, starting a fresh rally.

Figure 3.40 Bollinger Bands indicator added to the Nifty50 daily chart

Integrating the Indicators

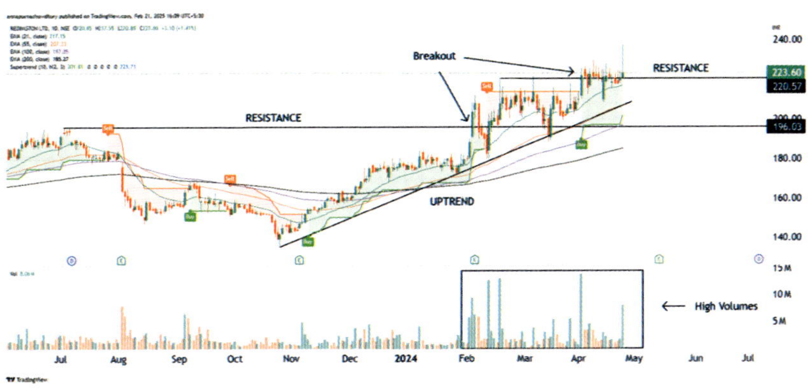

Figure 3.41 Supertrend and EMAs added to the daily chart of Redington

Figure 3.42 Bollinger Bands added to the daily chart of Redington

When we try to integrate all the indicators together, we get a very cluttered view, unable to make any sense of the chart. Hence, I've added 2 charts, one with bollinger bands, and the other with EMAs and supertrend for a clearer view. In Figure 3.40 and Figure 3.41,

- the stock is in uptrend and trading at 223 level dragging the Bollinger Bands along with it;
- price is above all EMAs, and all shorter tenure EMAs are above longer tenure EMAs;
- supertrend is buy;
- high volumes on breakout.

The stock has had medium to high volatility due to the ongoing uptrend in the stock and there have been occasional strong breakouts. Moreover, the stock recently gave another breakout and is respecting this new breakout level. Hence, I will have a bullish sentiment on the stock.

I hope you are now able to identify the relationship between price, Bollinger bands, moving averages, and supertrend.

Note to self: Trading is not tough. It is a matter of time and practice.

SUMMARY

- Volatility measures the degree of the price fluctuation in a stock.
- INDIAVIX is the volatility index that measures the volatility of the broader markets.
- A high volatility is indicative of intense price fluctuation, which is typically observed when the market is correcting.
- Volatility is completely flat during consolidation phase and on a slight rise during bull run or uptrend.
- Bollinger bands is a volatility indicator consisting of 3 bands, with the middle band being the 20-day moving average, and the upper and lower bands being 2 standard deviations away from the middle band.
- Any stock or index is typically supposed to move in this bollinger band range.
- The gap between the upper band and the lower band is known as BB gap, and if the gap is very narrow, it is known as bollinger bands squeeze with an anticipation of a large movement either up or down.
- If the price crosses the upper band taking the band along, it signifies strength of the price movement, whereas if the price crosses the lower band taking the band along, it signifies further breakdown in the stock.
- If price moves beyond the upper band, without any volume support, it is indicative of an overbought market, whereas if the price moves beyond the lower band, it is indicative of an oversold market.
- Bollinger bands is also used as a trading strategy where the breakout levels, supported by high volumes, are used as buying levels.

LET'S PRACTICE

Some charts have been provided below with the EMAs supertrend in 1 chart and bollinger bands in the other chart. Each stock has 2 charts to avoid overcrowding in 1 chart. Analysing the graphs, write whether you would have a bullish, a bearish or a neutral sentiment towards the stock. Additionally, if you identify any squeeze, please mark that too.

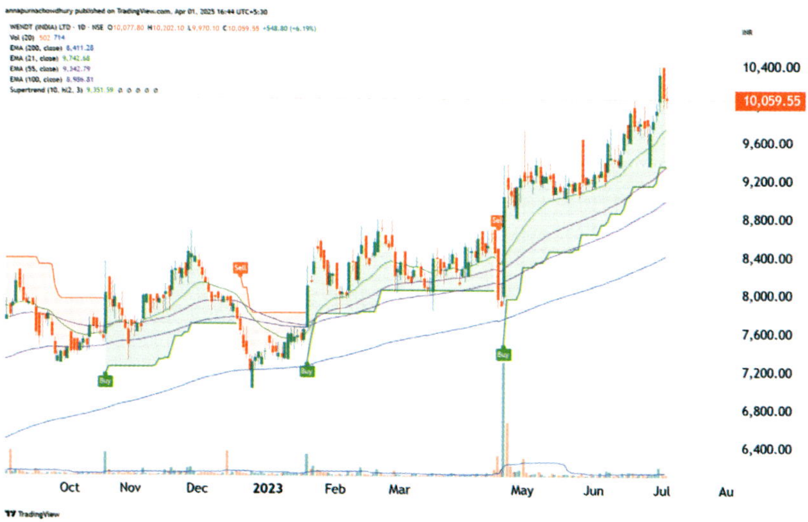

Figure 3.43

Figure 3.44

Figure 3.45

Figure 3.46

Figure 3.47

Figure 3.48

Figure 3.49

Figure 3.50

Figure 3.51

Figure 3.52

LEARNER'S CORNER

Should I choose to trade in highly volatile stocks or low volatile stocks?

This is not a yes or no question as it depends on your trading style. When trading in highly volatile stocks, the chances of hitting stop losses also becomes high. If you have an aggressive trading style and can be calm and patient when stocks give high fluctuations, only then opt to trade in highly volatile stocks.

If the volatility is high, should I stay away from the markets?

If the market volatility is high, it is indicative of falling markets. Typically, markets are highly volatile on specific event days (like election-result day, budget day), amid geopolitical tensions, or during the onset of economic turmoil. It is advisable to stay calm and patient when the market is in a panic mode, but it is equally important to cut your losses if your stop loss was triggered even on such volatile days.

What is the normal volatility range?

On a daily basis, a VIX reading between 15 and 20 indicates moderate volatility, while a reading above 20–25 indicates increasing uncertainty in the market. During periods of market stress (like global financial crises, major political events or economic downturns), Nifty50's volatility can spike to 30% or higher. For example, during the Covid-19 pandemic, volatility soared to unprecedented levels as markets reacted to the uncertainty.

Momentum Indicators

Picture the stock market as a horse race. Here, the stocks are the horses, and we, the traders, place our bets on these horses. Would you want to bet on a losing horse? No, we would always want to bet our money on the winning horse.

How do you judge which horse could be a winning horse? You would want to judge the strength, the fitness and the past performance of the horse to evaluate whether the horse is in form or not. This is the concept of momentum.

Momentum measures motion. Momentum indicators are tools used to determine the strength or weakness of a stock's price. Although their main use is to indicate the strength of a trend, momentum indicators also indicate when a trend has slowed and possibly ready for a change.

One way to judge the horse's potential would be to see how it is performing vis-à-vis the average speed of all the horses in the race, or the benchmark. In the case of the stock market, the major index, Nifty50 or Sensex, is a good benchmark to compare the performance of a stock. If a stock performs better than these indices, it is worthy of being bet on. This concept is known as relative strength (RS).

Another way is to compare its own performance with its historical performance. Consider this analogy: if Horse 1 has been winning the past 10 races at an average speed of 55 km/hr while Horse 2 has an average speed of 50 km/hr, but on race 11, Horse 1 runs at a speed of 45 km/hr, while Horse 2 runs at 52 km/hr. Who will win? Of course Horse 2, as Horse 1 is not using its full potential, while Horse 2 is outperforming its previous performances.

Similarly, a stock might have great potential, but if it's underperforming its own potential, then as traders it's not worth your bet. This concept is known as relative strength index (RSI). We always want to invest in horses or stocks that are the fastest runners and are using their full potential.

The above-mentioned indicators are known as momentum indicators. To summarize:

- When a stock is outperforming the benchmark index, Nifty50 or Sensex, it's exhibiting a higher relative strength (RS).
- When a stock is performing at its full potential or outperforming its own historical performance, it's exhibiting a good relative strength index (RSI).

Relative Strength (RS)

The Concept

Relative strength measures the strength of the stock by comparing its performance to that of the benchmark index, as discussed previously. How do we compute the relative performance of a stock? There are different ways we can do this. The simplest way of computation is to check the stock analytics platform and compare the return of a stock for a specified period of time with Nifty50's return over the same period of time.

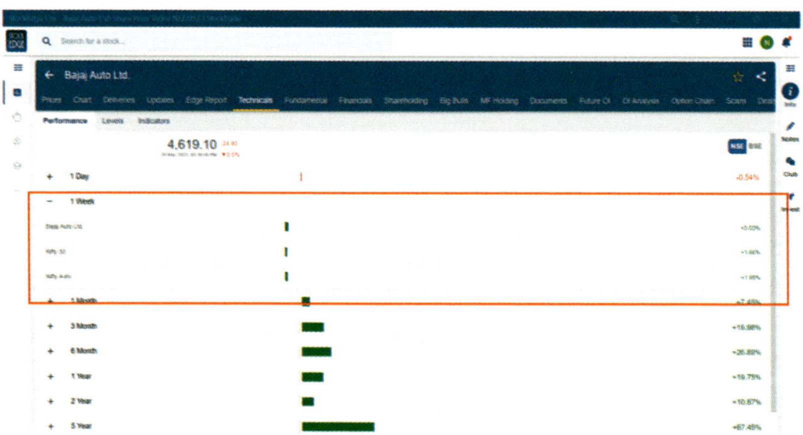

Figure 3.53 Bajaj Auto's return vis-à-vis Nifty50 and Nifty Auto for 1 week in StockEdge

As observed in Figure 3.53, the return of Bajaj Auto has been 3.03%, while Nifty50 has increased by 1.66% giving a clear indication that Bajaj Auto has been outperforming Nifty50 in the past 1 week.

Similarly, Bajaj Auto has also been outperforming its own sectoral index, Nifty Auto as the latter recorded a return of only 1.99% in the same period. Please note that a sectoral index can be an additional benchmark to compare the performance of the stock.

The outperformance of the stock is called alpha. It is the extra returns generated by a stock than its benchmark index. Let's take a look at a longer time frame.

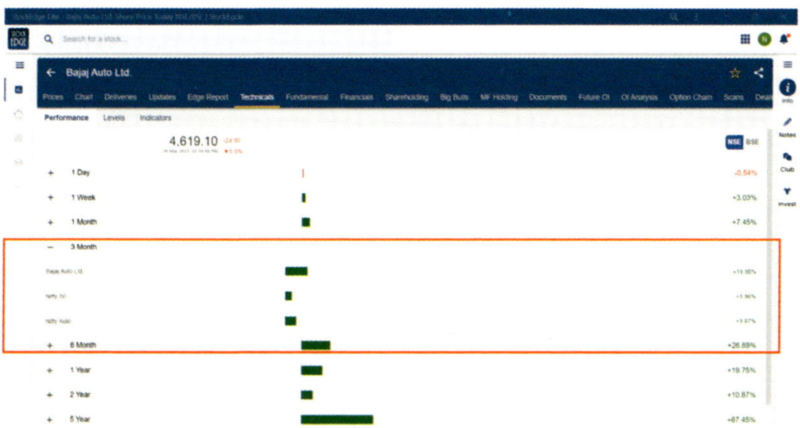

Figure 3.54 Bajaj Auto's return vis-à-vis Nifty50 and Nifty Auto for 3 months in StockEdge

Observe in Figure 3.54 that Nifty Auto has outperformed Nifty50 in the past 3 months, a longer time frame, while the stock has increased by 19%, outperforming both Nifty and Nifty Auto. Moreover, the sector is also outperforming the benchmark index for the same period. A crucial learning from the above is that:

If a stock belongs to a sector that is outperforming the market and that stock also outperforms both the indices, then it is a strong stock.

To compute the relative strength of a stock compared to the Nifty50, follow these steps:

- Choose the time frame: Decide the period over which you want to compare the performance, such as one week, one month, or one year.
- Calculate increase in stock: Determine how many times has the stock increased in your chosen time frame. For example, if a stock's price increased from ₹100 to ₹120 over a month, the stock increased 1.2 times.
- Calculate increase in index: Similarly, find how many times has the Nifty50 increased over the same period. If the Nifty50 went from 15,000 to 16,000, the return increased 1.07 times.
- Compare the returns: Divide the stock's return by the Nifty50's return to get the Relative Strength ratio.
  Relative Strength (RS) = (Stock Return/Nifty50 Return) – 1

Example Calculation

Let's say you're analysing the relative strength of ITC Ltd compared to the Nifty50 over 55 days. I have decided to compare the past 55 days of rolling return data because I believe that if a stock is outperforming the market for the past 3 months on an average, then it is a strong stock. 55 is approximately 3 months and it is also a Fibonacci number and hence, I use RS55. Some people use 123 or 21 and you can choose your own period. I use the 55-day period.

ITC Return: Suppose ITC's stock went up from 269 to 300 in a period of 55 days giving a return of: 300/269 = 1.12

Nifty50 Return: Nifty went up from 16661 to 17494 for the same time period, giving a return of: 17494/16661 = 1.05

Relative Strength = (1.12/1.05) – 1 = 0.06

RS Analysis

This indicates that ITC has outperformed the Nifty50 by a factor of 0.06 during this period. It's like saying ITC is running 0.06 times faster than the average performance of the stocks in the Nifty50, indicating that ITC is strong vis-à-vis Nifty50. Similarly, in the case of RS55, RS is calculated for every 55 days on a rolling basis showing the strength/ weakness of that stock.

As long as the RS>0, the stock is considered to be strong. RS<0 indicates a weak stock.

Charting the Indicator

Now I will show you how to do the same thing in TradingView. You need to search for Relative Strength of a stock under the indicators tab in TradingView and you will find one indicator by Bharat Trader. He is one of my friends and has been very generous to make this and share it with us.

Figure 3.55 RS indicator in TradingView

As you select this as shown in Figure 3.55, you will see RS at the bottom of the chart in red and green. We will change the period from

123 to 55 in the settings. 123 is by default since it is used by a lot of people, you can use your own time frame. I use 55 days.

Figure 3.56 RS indicator added to the daily chart of ITC Ltd

If you see in Figure 3.56, the green and the red line added below the price chart is the RS55 indicator. Whenever RS is above 0, it's green and demonstrates strength or momentum in the stock, and whenever RS is below 0, it's red and demonstrates weakness. In the above example, observe how the stock was in strong uptrend when RS55 was above 0, and now look at the period when RS55 went below 0, the stock lost its upward momentum and came down by 10% from November 2022 to January 2023. As soon as the RS55 went back up above 0, the stock gave yet another breakout supported by high volumes, demonstrating strength in the stock movement, making us very bullish in the stock.

Uses of RS

The beauty about RS is that it can show that the stock is weak, even if the price action is consolidating or in slight uptrend. You need to understand that when there's a bull run in the markets, most of the stock will be in uptrend. However, selective stocks will outperform Nifty50. As traders, you need to identify such stocks that can help generate alpha returns, and RS is a way to do that. Let's see some examples for clarity.

Figure 3.57 RS indicator added to daily chart of Balkrishna Industries

In Figure 3.57, observe the period between mid-April and May; the stock gave a breakout above the 2100 level from its previous swing high and was making a higher high and higher low; moreover, even the supertrend was indicating a buy. However, the RS was still below 0 signalling that even if the stock has changed the trend, it's still not able to outperform Nifty50 in 55 days, and not a strong stock still.

This right here is the magic of RS, it can show the real picture or the strength of the stock, even when the price action and the other indicators are implying otherwise. In the above case, the stock became strong during mid-May when it went above 0. As traders, we would wait for the confirmation of the indicators and price both to be positive on a stock.

A common question that comes to the mind of a beginner is that RS eventually follows suit of the price action and becomes positive. Is it not delaying the entry into a stock? Had we not waited for the RS to go above 0, we would have been able to enter at a lower price level with a more favourable risk-reward ratio reaping higher profits. Let's look at another example.

In Figure 3.58, observe that from 27 March 2024 to 3 May 2024, the price gave a good upmove, and gave a breakout from its previous swing high at the 2951 level; the supertrend was also buy, and seemed like it could reverse the ongoing downtrend. But observe that RS during that period was still below 0, and the stock soon went back down continuing its downtrend. This is the power of RS; it clearly indicated the underperformance of the stock vis-à-vis Nifty.

Figure 3.58 RS added to the daily chart of Angel One

There will always be cases like that of Balkrishna Industries where the RS did follow the suit of the price action, and there will also be cases like that of Angel One where the RS did not follow the suit of the price action and soon the price reversed back to the original downtrend, leading to a failed breakout.

As mentioned earlier, *always look for conviction and wait for confirmation*. An important trait of a successful trader is to have patience, and not rush into taking trades; wait for all the indicators and the price movement to point to the same thing. Doing so builds conviction in the trades that you take.

Another very important point to note is that you may still go wrong with the trade, but that's okay. We as humans cannot be right all the time. Even expert traders go wrong with their trades. We need to plan for such situations, and that's the power of risk management and stop loss. I will cover this in more detail later in the book.

SUMMARY

- Momentum measures the strength or weakness of a stock's price trend and indicates when a trend might change.
- Relative strength (RS) compares a stock's performance against a benchmark index (e.g., Nifty50 or Sensex), showing if it's outperforming.
- Relative strength index (RSI) compares a stock's current performance to its own historical performance, indicating if it's maximizing its potential.
- I use the 55-day period duration of RS to judge the strength of the stock.
- If RS55>0, then stock is strong; if RS55<0, the stock is weak.
- Stock could be in uptrend, yet the RS could be below 0, indicating that the stock is not strong vis-à-vis Nifty in the 55-day period
- To have a positive outlook on a stock, we will wait for the RS55 to go above 0 supported by an uptrend in the stock.

LET'S PRACTICE

Some charts have been provided below with the supertrend and RS55 drawn. Analysing the graphs, write whether you would have a bullish, a bearish or a neutral sentiment towards the stock.

Figure 3.59

Figure 3.60

Figure 3.61

Figure 3.62

Figure 3.63

LEARNER'S CORNER

Can I compare the strength of the stock with its sector?

Yes, you can. In fact, if a stock is outperforming its benchmark index and sectoral index, then it could be claimed as a strong stock. All you need to do is change the setting of the RS in TradingView.

Can I compare the strength of 2 stocks together?

Yes, you can. All you need to do is change the setting of the RS in TradingView, and you will be able to compare the strength of the 2 stocks together.

Can I use RS in weekly or 2-hourly time-frame charts?

Yes. In fact, later in the book, we've used different time-frame templates that have RS in it.

Will the RS go up even if the market and stock are falling? What to do in that case?

If the RS is going up even if both the stock and market are falling, it implies that the rate of the fall of the stock is relatively lower than the rate of the fall of the market. Only following RS will not help us in determining anything. We have to consider multiple factors to determine what to do in that case.

Relative Strength Index (RSI)

The Concept

RS is the relative strength of a stock vis-a-vis the benchmark index, while RSI measures the stock's own speed. RSI is developed by James Welles Wilder, who is also known to have developed ATR, used to derive supertrend. Wilder has made great contributions towards technical analysis.

RSI is a vast subject, so I will cover only the relevant aspects. Let's begin by understanding its computation.

Calculation of RSI

Every stock has its own speed, be it bullish or bearish. If the stock is running faster than its average speed, then it simply means that it's in momentum. Wilder suggests that we should consider the past 14-day performance of a stock as a base to judge whether a stock is in momentum or not.

To compute the RSI, follow these steps:

- Calculate the average gains and losses: Over a specific period (commonly 14 days), calculate the average of the gains and the average of the losses.

  Gain: If today's closing price is higher than yesterday's closing price, it's considered a gain.

  Loss: If today's closing price is lower than yesterday's closing price, it's considered a loss.

  For example, if over the past 14 days, a stock had gains on 10 days and losses on 4 days, sum up all the gains and losses separately to find the average.

  Average Gain = Sum of Gains over 14 days/14

  Average Loss = Sum of Losses over 14 days/14

- Calculate the relative strength (RS): The RS is the ratio of the average gain to the average loss.
  RS = Average Gain/Average Loss
- Calculate the RSI: Finally, use the RS value to calculate the RSI using the formula:
  RSI = 100 – {100/(1+RS)}

Example calculation:

Date	close	Difference	Gains	Losses
08-May-23	2,471.90			
09-May-23	2,479.55	7.65	7.65	
10-May-23	2,496.60	17.05	17.05	
11-May-23	2,480.30	-16.30		-16.30
12-May-23	2,484.35	4.05	4.05	
15-May-23	2,489.25	4.90	4.90	
16-May-23	2,453.80	-35.45		-35.45
17-May-23	2,439.30	-14.50		-14.50
18-May-23	2,434.05	-5.25		-5.25
19-May-23	2,441.95	7.90	7.90	
22-May-23	2,455.00	13.05	13.05	
23-May-23	2,454.55	-0.45		-0.45
24-May-23	2,440.25	-14.30		-14.30
25-May-23	2,439.95	-0.30		-0.30
26-May-23	2,506.50	66.55	66.55	
			121.15	**86.55**
			Total Gains	Total Losses

Table 3.4 Gains and losses of Reliance Industries

In Table 3.4, we've computed the gains and the losses of Reliance between 8 May 2023 to 26 May 2023. We've segregated the gains in the fourth column and the losses in the fifth column.

- Calculate the average gains and losses:
  Total gains in 14 days was 121.15.
  Total loss in 14 days was 86.55.
  Average gain = 121.15/14 = 8.65
  Average loss = 86.55/14 = 6.18
- Calculate the relative strength (RS):
  RS = 8.65/6.18 = 1.4
- Calculate the RSI:
  RSI = 100 – {100/(1+1.4)} = 58.33

RSI Analysis

As long as the RSI>50, the momentum in the stock is strong, and if the RSI<50, the momentum is low. Reliance has an RSI of 58.33 as on 26 May 2023, indicating that the momentum is strong. Another very common practice with RSI is to identify the overbought and oversold levels of the stock. When RSI>70, it denotes an unreasonable buying in the stock, it is said to be in the overbought zone, and a correction is anticipated. On the other hand, when the RSI<30, it denotes an unreasonable selling in the stock, it is said to be in the oversold zone, and a bounce back is anticipated.

Another interesting thing to note is the underlying logic behind using 14 periods. For the daily chart RSI 14 implies 14 days which is also the lunar phase. Just like Fibonacci levels, this is the most natural number that is very commonly followed across the world for various applications.

Charting the Indicator

Let's add the indicator to our charts.

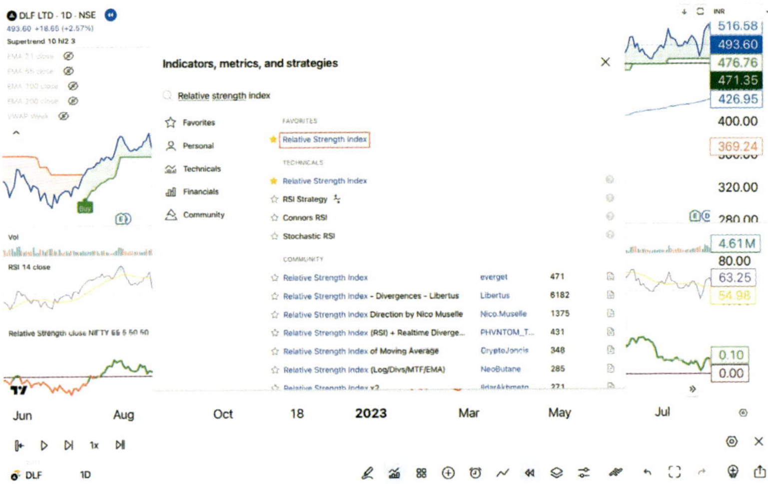

Figure 3.64 RSI indicator in TradingView

While adding the RSI indicator, I change the settings and remove the upper and lower band of the RSI that indicates the overbought and oversold zone. If you want, you can keep it. Let's look at the ITC's daily chart.

Figure 3.65 RSI added to the daily chart of ITC Ltd

In Figure 3.65, the purple line added between the price chart and RS indicator is the RSI indicator. Observe the correlation between the RSI and price action of the stock, it is almost synchronized. Whenever the RSI is above 50, the stock is outperforming its own strength indicating momentum. I'm not taking any more examples, as in most cases you will observe that the price of the stock movement will be synchronous with the movement of RSI.

Uses of RSI

We will use RSI to judge the strength of the stock movement and decide whether we want to stay invested in the stock or not, or before initiating a trade. I will cover this in detail while explaining the trading strategies later in the book.

Divergence between Price Action and RSI

Till now we've observed that the price action of a stock and its RSI's movement is mostly synchronous. However, in some cases, they're not, and that's the concept of divergence in technical analysis. Divergence occurs when the price of the stock and indicator are moving in opposite directions. They do not match with each other. Divergence occurs because momentum indicators like RSI track the strength of price movements. If price continues to rise but RSI fails to confirm, it suggests momentum is weakening, which can lead to a reversal. In case of divergences, it's typically observed that the signals of indicators is more promising than the price action. There are 2 types of divergence:

- Negative divergence—It occurs when the price is in an uptrend and RSI moves downward. It is a condition where price makes higher highs and higher lows whereas indicators fail to do so. They make lower highs and lower lows.

- Positive divergence—It occurs when the price is in a downtrend, but RSI starts to rise. It is a condition where price makes lower tops and lower bottoms whereas indicators fail to do so. They make higher highs and higher lows.

Divergences often act as early warning signals for potential reversals, but traders should use confirmation signals (trendlines, support/resistance, volume or candlestick patterns) before taking action. Serious technical analysts often focus on divergence across various indicators, such as RS, RSI or MACD. It's crucial to check if the price and the indicator align. When there's a discrepancy, the indicator usually prevails, and the price tends to reverse. This is because the operators can try to fool retail investors by manipulating the price movements but they can't manipulate the underlying indicators.

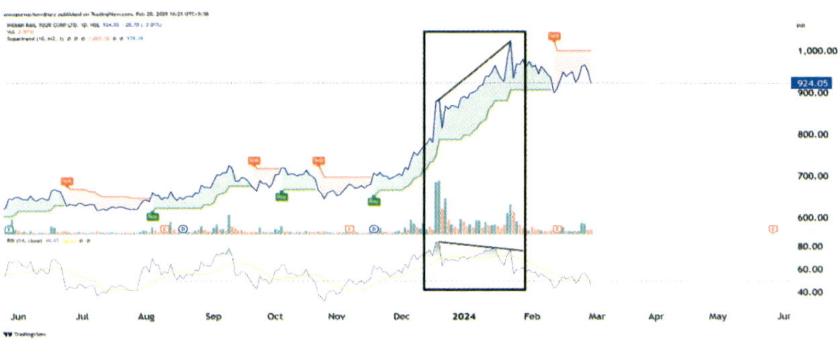

Figure 3.66 RSI added to the daily chart of IRCTC

In Figure 3.66, observe the marked area, where we can see a clear divergence between the price action and RSI. The price was in uptrend, however RSI reversed its trend after making a top and showcased downtrend from thereon. The price corrected and was in consolidation period for 2 months before giving a breakout again. RSI was signalling a weakness in momentum.

However, this might not always be the case. In strong trends, prices can still rise despite divergence, so traders should confirm signals using trendlines, volume and moving averages.

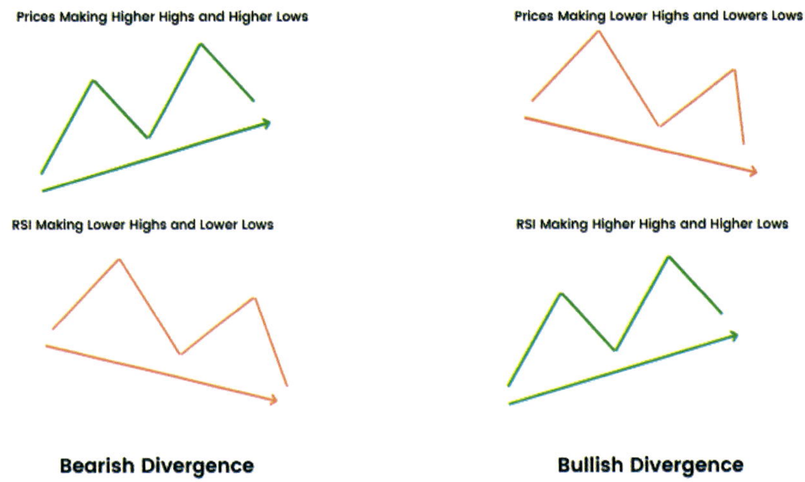

Figure 3.67 Difference between bearish divergence and bullish divergence

I'll not go deep into details about trading in divergence. Figure 3.67 is sufficient as a beginner to understand the basic concept of divergences.

LET'S PRACTICE

Identifying divergence and its type: Use a pen/pencil to identify and draw the divergence in the following charts:

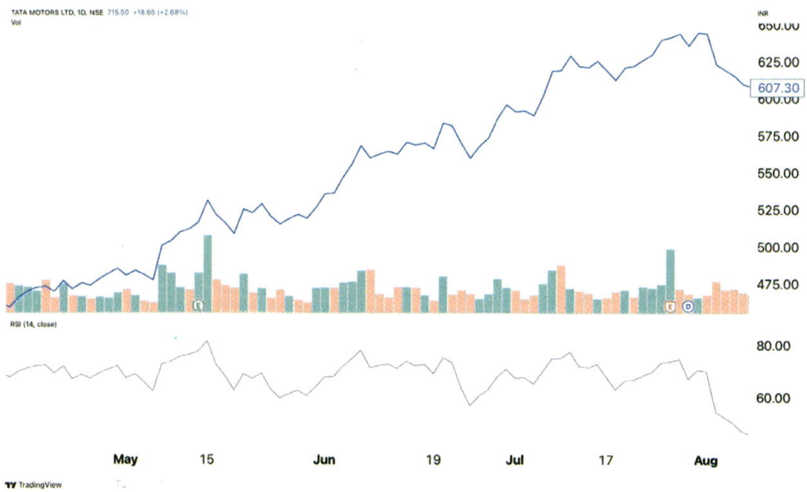

Figure 3.68

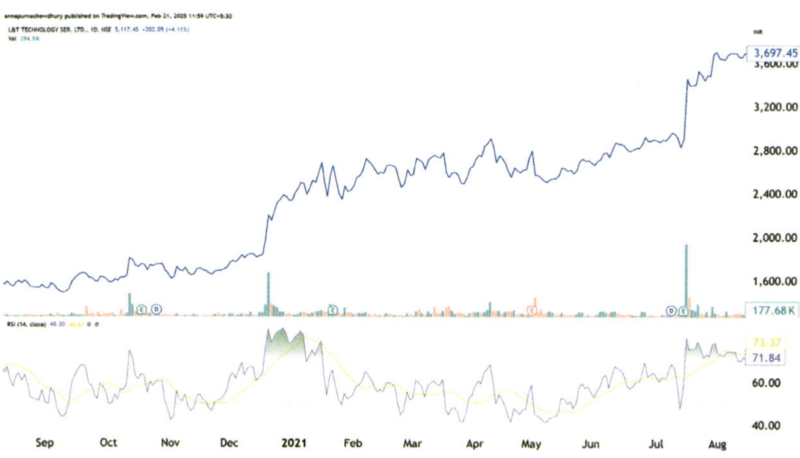

Figure 3.69

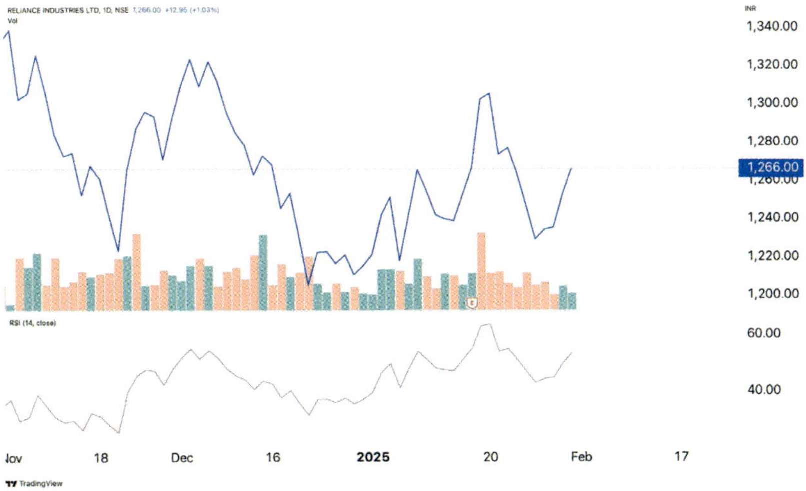

Figure 3.70

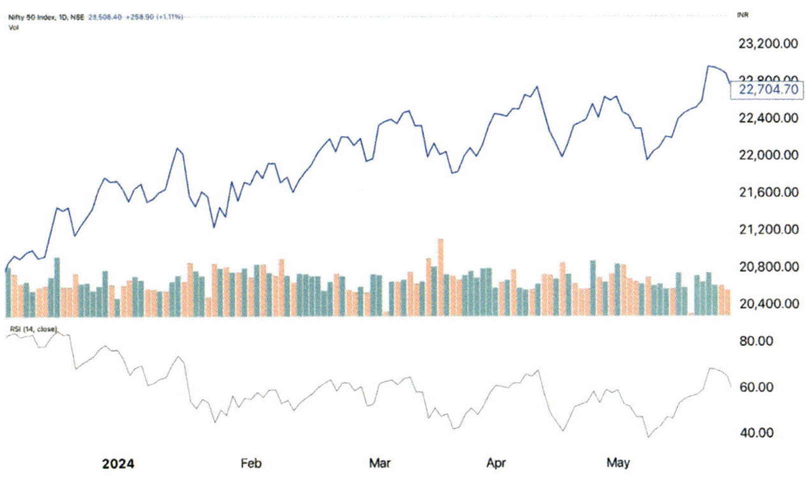

Figure 3.71

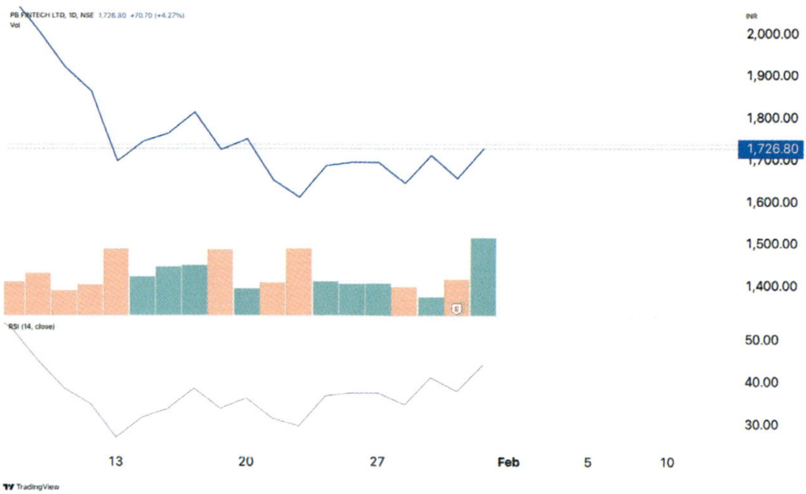

Figure 3.72

Try finding some divergences in the stocks added to your watchlist.

SUMMARY

- RSI measures the strength of the stock relative to its past 14-day performance.
- If RSI 14>50, it is indicative of momentum or strength in the movement of the stock.
- If RSI 14<50, then there is no momentum in the movement of the stock.
- RSI 14 is used to judge momentum of the stock movement.
- There could be divergence between the price movement and RSI 14, indicative of a reversal in the price.
- There are typically 2 types of divergences—bullish divergence and bearish divergence.

Volume Weighted Average Price (VWAP)

The Concept

VWAP is a volume indicator and the only volume indicator that we will cover in this book. Recall that price and volume are the 2 most important components of chart analysis that help in building the foundation of technical analysis.

In the world of technical analysis, volume-weighted average price (VWAP) is a powerful tool that helps traders understand the average price at which a stock was traded throughout the day, considering both its price and volume, volumes being used as weights. The higher the volume, the higher the weightage given to a price point. VWAP is a short-term indicator used mainly in intraday trading. It resets at the beginning of each trading session and helps traders identify whether a stock is trading at a fair value on that day.

The day that the operator is entering into a stock, the VWAP level of that day becomes important for us to understand the average price at which the operator could have potentially entered. Recall that operators are the big guys with a large investment corpus.

Charting the Indicator

Figure 3.73 VWAP added to the daily chart of Hindustan Unilever

In Figure 3.73 VWAP is the light blue line drawn along with the price line. Normally, it is calculated as per the duration of the chart, but I have changed the settings to weekly. Hence, the VWAP line in the above graph is weekly VWAP. Observe how VWAP's movement is synchronous with the price action.

VWAP Analysis

Let's understand its interpretations. Stocks trading below the VWAP line are considered 'cheap' or 'of value'. On the other hand, stock prices above the VWAP line are labelled 'expensive'. But when a stock is above VWAP and rising with strong volume, it indicates buying pressure. However, if price deviates too far from VWAP, it could indicate overbuying and price reversal could be likely.

Anchored VWAP (AVWAP)

The Concept

The anchored VWAP (volume weighted average price) provides insight into the average price of a stock, adjusted for volume, from a specific starting point. Unlike the traditional VWAP, which resets daily, the anchored VWAP allows you to 'anchor' or start the calculation from any significant date or event, such as a market top, bottom, earnings report or news release. AVWAP then calculates the average price from that point forward, factoring in the volume traded.

Charting the Indicator

As observed in Figure 3.74, the VWAP has been anchored on the day the stock made a very big candle and bottomed out (reversed) in the near short term.

Figure 3.74 AVWAP added by anchoring VWAP at the end of December 2022 on the daily chart of DLF Ltd.

It reflects the market's average trading price from a significant point, which can indicate whether a security is overbought or oversold relative to its anchored average.

Uses of AVWAP

One of the biggest applications of AVWAP is to identify support and resistance. Anchored VWAP lines often act as dynamic support or resistance levels. Traders watch how prices interact with these lines to make trading decisions. Observe Figure 3.74: when the price went below the AVWAP, a further downtrend was seen in the stock, indicating the breakdown of a major support zone, and as soon as the stock gave a breakout above the AVWAP with high volume bars, it marked the beginning of an uptrend, indicating that it broke a major resistance level. To conclude, we can say that *if the price is above the anchored VWAP, it is suggestive of a bullish sentiment*. Conversely, if below, it may suggest bearish sentiment.

Selecting the anchor point: Choose a date or event significant to your trading strategy. Common choices include recent highs/lows, earnings releases, or significant news.

Like VWAP, AVWAP is a tool to identify the levels at which the operator has entered/exited, and operators tend to defend their positions near AVWAP, making it a key level for support and resistance. By anchoring the VWAP to significant events, traders can gauge the level at which operators might have entered or exited the market. A breakout above AVWAP with strong volume suggests operators are buying, while a breakdown below AVWAP with high volume signals distribution by large players.

Example:

Suppose you're analysing a stock after its quarterly earnings report, which was released on 1 June 2023. You can anchor the VWAP on that day to track how the average price, adjusted for volume, has evolved since the earnings release. If the stock's price consistently stays above the anchored VWAP, it indicates that most trading has occurred at higher prices since the report, suggesting a positive market reaction.

Conversely, if the stock price remains below the anchored VWAP set on 1 June, it indicates that the market has not responded favourably to the earnings report or subsequent events. The volume-weighted average price since the report is higher than the current price, suggesting that the recent trading activity has been dominated by sellers, reflecting a bearish sentiment.

AVWAP is a very powerful tool for traders to

- decide entry price points/exit price points;
- judge the sentiment of the stock; and
- identify operator's price points to enter/exit.

I felt this is an important concept that you should be aware of if you're trading in the markets, hence I've covered it in brief for you. Although AVWAP is a powerful tool, I have chosen not to include it in my model because my strategy prioritizes other indicators. However, you can experiment with it and see if it adds value to your trading approach.

SUMMARY

- VWAP is a volume indicator that shows the average price a stock has traded at during the day, weighted by volume.
- Stocks below the VWAP are considered 'cheap', signalling potential for short trades, while stocks above it are considered 'expensive', signalling potential for selling.
- Useful for intraday trading to determine entry/exit points based on stock price relative to VWAP.
- AVWAP anchors the VWAP from a specific event or date to track price trends from that point.
- Helps identify dynamic support and resistance levels and can indicate bullish or bearish sentiment.
- Useful for traders to judge sentiment, identify entry/exit points, and track operator activity from key events.

Conclusion

By following indicators, we are enabled to make data-driven decisions. Adopting this in our everyday practice brings us a step closer to the turtle mindset. Turtles, especially sea turtles, are known to use the Earth's magnetic fields, ocean currents, angle of sunlight and various smells to navigate across oceans. In trading, these indicators are those navigational tools that help you make data-driven decisions.

A trader should always optimize the number of indicators that they're adding to the template. We cannot add all the indicators. As the saying goes, 'Too many cooks spoil a broth.' Similarly, too many indicators can confuse a trader and have the opposite effect of building conviction.

Each indicator has its own way of directing, some might indicate a bullish sentiment, some a bearish sentiment. Too many indicators will all indicate different sentiments, adding to the confusion of traders.

I would advise you to keep only 3-4 indicators in your template that will make up for your trade setup. However, you must be well equipped for any situation. *Remember the most important parameter amongst all is the price action.*

I have taught you 7 indicators till now, and I would urge you to make a template that consists of only 3-4. The template should be according to your trading style. If you're someone who likes to play in volatility, then maybe ATR, bollinger is a must for your template, and if you're someone who is more of a momentum investor, then RS and RSI is essential for your template. Feel free to choose your style and make your own template.

What if I don't know my trading style?

Trading style can be identified by knowing your own nature, characteristics and traits. Don't worry if you're not sure of your trading style; I will share a standard template with you. This template should be good enough to get you started and eventually with more time and experience you can mould it as per your trading style.

Figure 3.75 Trading template

In the above template, I've added

- 21-day EMA, 55-day day EMA, 100-day EMA and 200-day EMA;
- supertrend;
- RSI 14;
- RS55.

The EMAs and supertrend will help in identifying trends, while the RS and RSI will help in confirming momentum in the stock trend and identify strong stocks for us. A stock needs to fit into our template for us to be positive on it and selecting it for trading. By fitting into our template, I mean

- price is in uptrend;
- there is high volume and delivery in the stock in the last couple of days;
- price is trading above all the EMAs, and the shorter tenure EMAs are trading above the longer tenure EMAs;
- supertrend is buy;
- RSI 14>50;
- RS55>0.

There are 5,000+ stocks in the market, do I have to track all to identify the stocks that fit into my template?

Of course not. The next chapter will now cover all the different methods that we can use to filter the stocks that most likely will fit into our trading template.

LET'S PRACTICE

Some charts have been provided below in our mentioned template. Analysing the graphs, write whether you would have a bullish, a bearish or a neutral sentiment towards the stock.

Figure 3.76

Figure 3.77

Figure 3.78

Figure 3.79

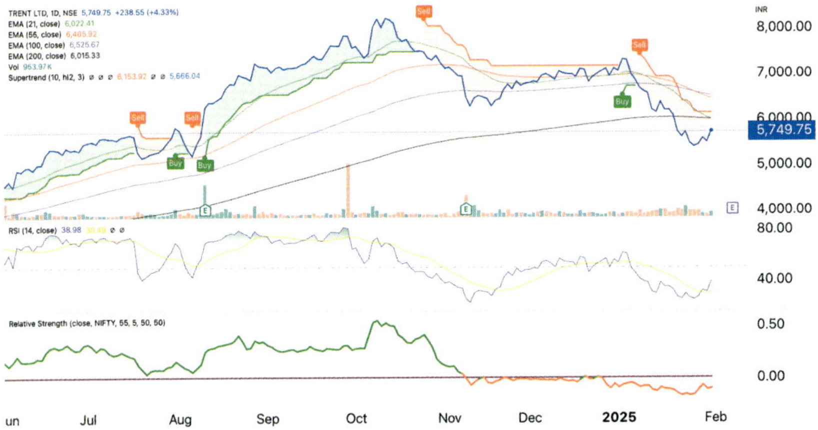

Figure 3.80

I would highly suggest that you start entering some stocks with a small capital of, say, Rs 5,000. Now that you have a template, you can start by putting in some money where you see a bullish sentiment in the stock.

The more you practice, the more you will understand how the indicators work in your template. Anytime you feel stuck, I will be happy to help you.

4

The Art of Picking Stocks

Before we proceed, remember:

We will only trade in stocks that are in uptrend.

We will only trade in stocks that fit our trading template.

Stock market trading is a game of probability and not a linear path. Each stock has a unique probability, so the focus should be on 'high probability setups'. With over 5,000 listed stocks, trading them all isn't feasible.

There are different methods of picking stocks, I will cover all the approaches that I take and work best for me. You can try them all and see what works for you.

In the stock market, the final goal is to make money, and we have different stocks available to achieve that objective. To identify which stock is good for you is dependent on your approach in identifying the stocks. I have penned down a few approaches here:

Sector Rotation

The Concept

> 'If you are in the right sector at the right time, you can make a lot of money real fast.'
>
> —Peter Lynch, author, investor, mutual fund manager

Let's understand why some sectors perform better than others. Every sector/business/economy moves in a cycle. They may be in different stages of the cycle at the same time, but they all typically move in a cycle.

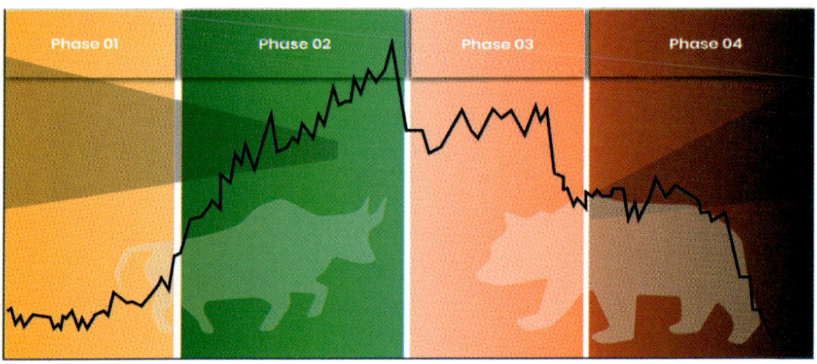

Figure 4.1 Market cycle

What Drives the Cyclical Movement in a Stock/Sector?

A part of the strategy of the ace investors or fund managers is to rebalance their portfolio and divert their funds from one sector to the other in anticipation of the change in economic cycle and for optimized returns. This concept is known as sector rotation.

A sector that attracts such funds by the investors typically starts gaining momentum. As traders we need to identify these sectors and the top-performing stocks in these sectors to get an early entry.

The cycle typically has 4 phases:

Phase 1	Phase 2	Phase 3	Phase 4
Accumulation	**Markup or Bull Run**	**Distribution**	**Decline or Bear Run**
The initiation phase where the institutions gradually accumulate shares without triggering major price increases. Price moves in a range with an increase in volumes and delivered quantity with long positions.	An uptrend driven by the operators with the price in upward momentum.	A trend conclusion triggered by institutional exit. The price becomes range-bound again with sellers gaining control of the price. This phase may include sharp spikes and false breakouts before sellers fully take control.	A downtrend driven by the seller with the price crashing significantly and erasing most of the gains made during the bull run.

Table 4.1

A stock or a sector can go through this cycle many times. Some sectors such as metals, oil and gas, cement, real estate, capital goods, etc. are highly cyclical in nature where they go through the entire cycle as their performance is directly related to the broader economic cycle. These sectors thrive in economic expansions and decline during downturns.

On the other hand, there are defensive sectors, such as utilities, consumer non-durables, pharma and IT, that are unbothered by any economic downturn. For instance, even if there is a recession, people do not stop or cut down expenses on utility services like electricity, healthcare services, consumer goods and other basic necessities. Hence, these sectors are non-cyclical in nature. Consider the 2020 Covid-19 crash and recovery:

- 2020 Market Crash (decline phase: phase 4): IT and pharma outperformed while metals, real estate and banking collapsed.
- 2021 Recovery (accumulation to markup: phase 1 to phase 2): Banking, auto and capital goods saw institutional buying, leading to a rally.

- 2022-23 Distribution and Rotation (phase 3 to 4 for some, phase 2 for others): IT and pharma corrected, while commodities and energy peaked before slowing down.

This demonstrates why sector rotation is crucial—smart investors allocate funds to sectors that are just entering an uptrend (phase 1-2), not the ones already near their peak (phase 3). Let's look at the chart of metal index, and chart of IT index.

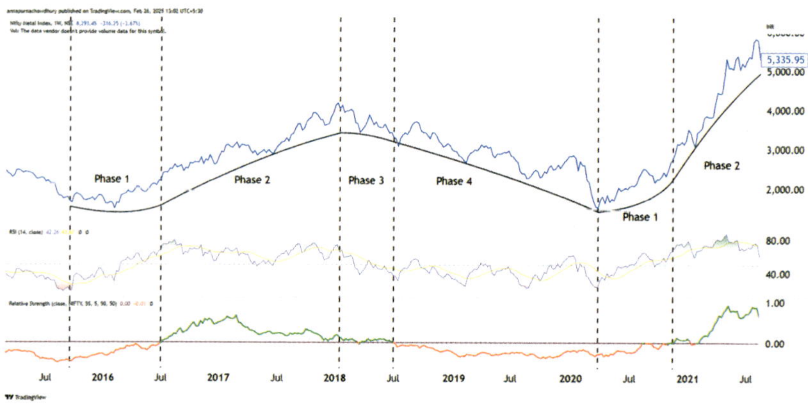

Figure 4.2 Weekly chart of metal index

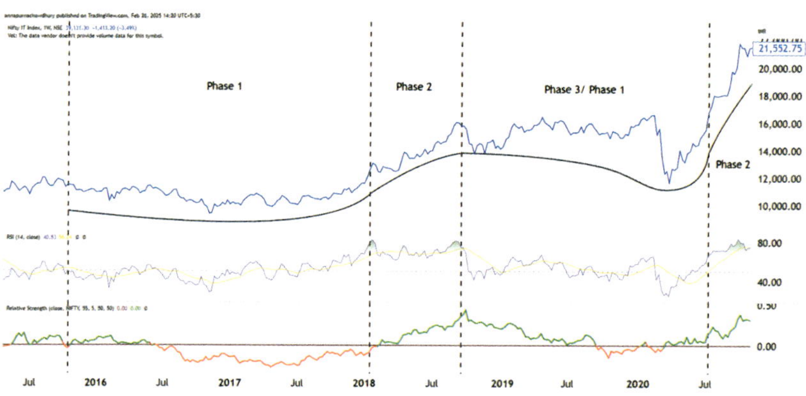

Figure 4.3 Weekly chart of IT index

The metal index, as a cyclical sector, follows the complete 4-phase cycle. In contrast, the IT index, being more defensive, transitioned from distribution (phase 3) back to markup (phase 2), bypassing a major decline (phase 4). Although a small correction can be witnessed during the Covid-19 crash, when uncertainty creeped in the economy, yet there was no major decline in the sector to claim that the sector entered phase 4. Another interesting thing to note here is the movement of RS55 in the 4 phases of the sector. Observe how RS55 was above 0 during the bull run (phase 2) and below 0 during accumulation (phase 1) and decline (phase 4). That's a classic case of RS, where strong sectors in momentum would typically have a positive RS.

The bottom line is that there will always be some sector/some company that will give you good returns, even when the economy has gone for a toss. Being able to read and analyse the data will help you in identifying these sectors/stocks that are going to benefit due to the ongoing economic/geopolitical event, and are going to enter phase 2—giving you a good rally.

As traders, in which phase should you enter the stock? The answer is pretty simple, you'll enter when chances of making money are highest, i.e., at the end of phase 1 or at an early stage of phase 2, when the stock is in upward momentum. When do you think we should exit the stock? In technical terms, when the stock loses its momentum, i.e., early stage of phase 3. Rather than going into details for each phase, let's try to understand how, as traders, we can leverage this knowledge and identify and select stocks that are trading at the end of phase 1/accumulation phase or the beginning of phase 2/bull run.

Indices and Sector Indices

Exchanges create indices to represent the overall market or specific sectors by grouping select company stocks. The Indian market uses the Sensex and Nifty indices. Sensex includes thirty companies, and Nifty includes fifty. These indices mostly cover the same stocks but differ in how much weight each stock has in the index. NSE has fewer indices than BSE. For sector analysis, following NSE indices is the norm as NSE stocks are more liquid.

Each sectoral index has its own composition of a different number of stocks. There are more than 5,000 stocks in NSE, out of which there are a huge number of companies in this sector, and it is not possible to include all of them. Hence, top companies are taken and represented through the index. Nifty Metal consists of the top metal companies while Nifty Auto represents the top automobile companies and Nifty Bank represents the top banking companies. To conclude, we can say that if a sectoral index is doing well, that's because most of the stocks in that sector are doing well and vice versa.

Method 1: Simple Method

The first thing that we do is identify the trend of a sector by analysing the movement of the sectoral index. For analysis, we need to use a Stock Analytics tool.

Daily Updates

Updates | Forthcoming | Indices | Trending Stocks | FII/DII | Future OI | Options OI | Deals | Results

Major | Gainers | Losers

Tue, 16 May 2023 — NSE BSE — 1D 1W 1M 3M 6M 1Y 2Y 5Y

Index Name	LTP	Chg	Chg%	Last Update
Nifty50 Dividend Points	44.33	+42.39	▲2,185.1%	17 May 2023
Nifty Realty	469.30	+39.90	▲9.3%	17 May 2023
Nifty Midcap Select	7,548.60	+533.80	▲7.6%	17 May 2023
Nifty Microcap 250	11,722.50	+812.00	▲7.4%	17 May 2023
Nifty Auto	13,911.20	+915.05	▲7.0%	17 May 2023
India VIX	13.12	+0.85	▲6.9%	17 May 2023
Nifty Smallcap 250	9,731.80	+615.00	▲6.7%	17 May 2023
Nifty Midcap 50	9,274.15	+574.95	▲6.6%	17 May 2023

Table 4.2 List of indices as per their 1-month performance

In Table 4.2, we have the list of indices given as per their 1-month performance. We can see that Nifty Realty and Nifty Auto are the top 2 sectoral indices that have given a good upmove in the past 1 month. We overlook the Nifty50 Dividend Points, Nifty Midcap Select, and Nifty Microcap 250 that's at the top 5 of the list as these are not sectoral indices. Now let's look at the stocks in Nifty Realty.

Nifty Realty

Prices | Chart | Stocks | Aggregated Deliveries | Updates | Technicals | Scans | My Targets

All | Gainers | Losers

Wed, 17 May 2023

Company Name	Market Cap Rs. Cr	Close Price	Price Change	Percentage
DLF Ltd.	116,748	468.45	-3.30	▼0.7%
Macrotech Developers Ltd.	48,048	981.70	-16.60	▼1.7%
Godrej Properties Ltd.	38,624	1,387.60	-2.10	▼0.2%
Oberoi Realty Ltd.	35,469	930.90	-44.25	▼4.5%
The Phoenix Mills Ltd.	26,453	1,490.30	+7.95	▲0.5%
Prestige Estates Projects Ltd.	20,195	494.85	-8.90	▼1.8%
Brigade Enterprises Ltd.	12,398	541.00	+2.35	▲0.4%
Mahindra Lifespace Developers Ltd.	6,174	396.65	-2.25	▼0.6%

Table 4.3 Stocks that make up the Nifty Realty index

DLF Ltd is a part of this index with a market cap of 116,748 crores followed by Macrotech Developers, Godrej Properties, Oberoi Realty, etc., as observed in Table 4.3. Just because a sector is showing strength does not mean that all the stocks in that sector will show the same strength. Typically, there are a few stocks that demonstrate most strength dragging the index higher along with them. All we need to do is identify these strong stocks in the sector. Let's look at the list of gainers in the Nifty Realty Index.

Stocks	LTP	Chg	Chg %	17 May 2023
Nifty Realty	467.70	+38.30	▲8.9%	10:21:59 AM
Sobha Ltd.	537.95	+103.20	▲23.7%	10:21:57 AM
DLF Ltd.	468.45	+53.10	▲12.8%	10:21:57 AM
The Phoenix Mills Ltd.	1,490.30	+155.55	▲11.7%	10:21:57 AM
Prestige Estates Projects Ltd.	494.85	+46.70	▲10.4%	10:21:57 AM
Mahindra Lifespace Developers Ltd.	396.65	+31.85	▲8.7%	10:21:59 AM
Brigade Enterprises Ltd.	541.00	+42.35	▲8.5%	10:21:53 AM
Godrej Properties Ltd.	1,387.60	+108.30	▲8.5%	10:21:58 AM

Table 4.4 List of gainers of Nifty Realty

Nifty Realty was up by 8.9% in the last one month while Sobha Ltd was up by 23.7%, DLF Ltd by 12.8% and Phoenix Mills by 11.7% (refer to Table 4.4). This is a clear indication that these stocks have been the strongest in the realty sector outperforming the sectoral index too. The look of it indicates an uptrend in these stocks and a potential to enter at the early stage of phase 2; the confirmation can only be done by tracking the charts. First, let's confirm the trend of the sectoral index.

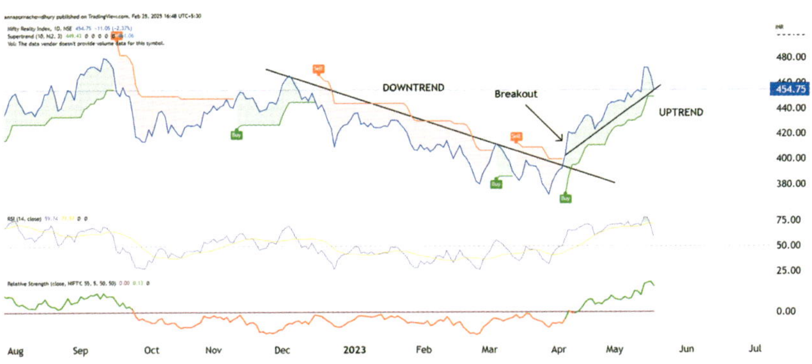

Figure 4.4 Daily line chart of Nifty Realty index

In Figure 4.4, Nifty Realty has been making higher highs and higher lows, confirming an uptrend. Coming to stocks, let's track the charts of the strongest stocks in the sector, starting with Sobha Ltd.

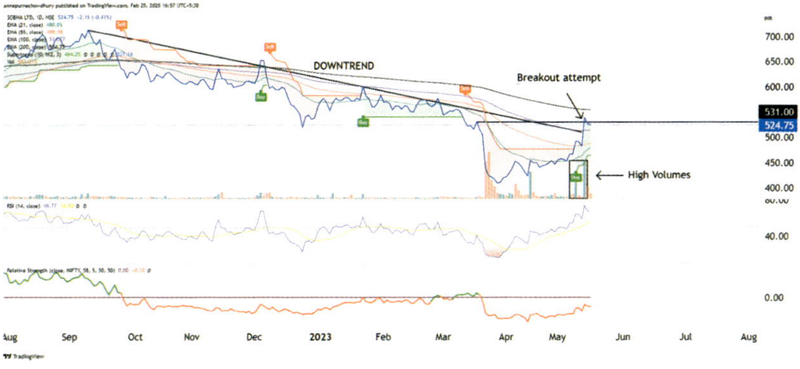

Figure 4.5 Daily line chart of Sobha Ltd

Let's see if the stock fits into our template. As observed in Figure 4.5, the stock has been in downtrend, although it appears that it has been attempting to break out of it with the recent price upmove from April 2023 onwards supported by high volumes. Coming to the template, the stock is trading at 524, and

- has had high volumes with the recent price movement;
- the stock is still below 200 EMA;
- the shorter tenure EMAs are below the longer tenure EMAs;
- the supertrend has recently changed to buy;
- RSI 14>50; but
- RS55<0.

We can safely conclude that the stock does not fit into our trading template now. It appears that the stock is still in Phase 4 or bear run, or maybe in the early stage of phase 1 or accumulation phase.

Hence, we will wait and observe the stock, till it is able to sustain the upmove and fit into our trading template, i.e, we will wait till the stock enters phase 2.

Let us pick DLF Ltd from this sector and track its chart.

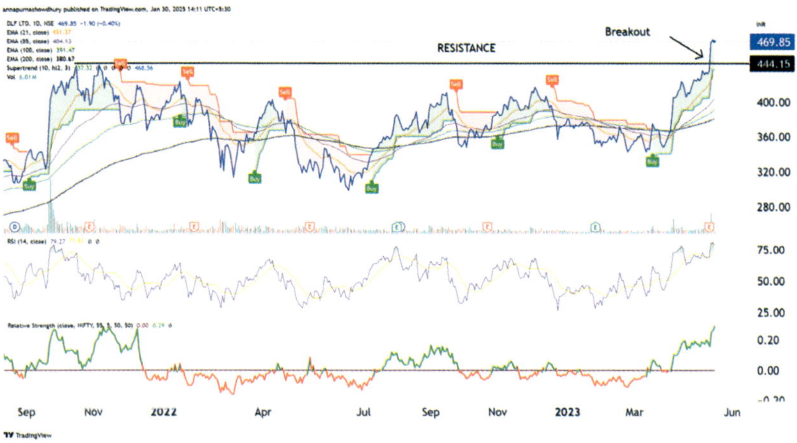

Figure 4.6 Daily line chart of DLF Ltd

In Figure 4.6, the stock was range-bound from 300 level to 444 level since November 2021. The stock recently gave a breakout above its resistance of 444 and trading at 469, and

- has had high volumes with the recent price movement;
- the stock is trading above all EMAs;
- all the shorter tenure EMAs are trading above the longer tenure EMAs;
- supertrend is 'buy';
- RSI 14>50; and
- RS55>0.

The stock fits perfectly into our template, making me positive on the stock. It appears that the stock was in the accumulation phase or phase 1, and is now breaking out of it to enter phase 2. This could be a potential early entry to phase 2 or the bull run of a stock. We will wait for the stock to retrace and be available at a favourable risk-reward ratio to accumulate the stock. To get back to our example, we need to track the charts of at least the first 5 stocks as per the last 1-month gainer list of the sectoral index, and track stocks that are in uptrend.

To conclude:

- Identify the trend of a sector by analysing the movement of the sectoral index by checking the top gainer list for the past 1 month.
- Pick up the top 5 stocks as per the gainer list and add it to the watchlist.
- Check the charts of the sector and of these 5 stocks, check if it's in uptrend and fits into our template.
- Assess the risk and reward and wait for the right price to enter the stock and initiate the buy trade.

Method 2: Advance Method

The second and a far more efficient way to identify strong sectors would be through a combined analysis of the following:

1. Breadth
2. Delivery
3. VWAP

Breadth Analysis

When we say that a sectoral index is in momentum, we need to check whether it's being dragged by a select few stocks that have a higher weightage in the index, or most of the stocks in the index are doing well. If the latter is true, that's when we can conclude that the sector momentum is in play. This analysis is known as breadth analysis.

Imagine you're attending a party along with a lot of other guests (stocks). Just like how the party's energy is affected by the number of guests dancing (advancing stocks), the music volume (trading volume), and the overall mood (market sentiment), market breadth measures the overall health of the market by considering the number of stocks participating in the uptrend or downtrend, rather than just focusing on the index's overall value. Think of it like this:

- A strong market is like a packed dance floor, where most guests are dancing (many stocks are advancing).
- A weak market is like a weak party with an empty dance floor, where only a few guests are dancing (few stocks are advancing).

The index might go up in both cases. However, an experienced trader would always know to participate in a strong market rather than a weak market through breadth analysis.

Advancing stocks imply that the stocks are trading higher than previous day's close; conversely declining stocks imply that stocks are trading lower than previous day's close. By considering market breadth, traders can get a better sense of the market's underlying strength and potential future direction, rather than just relying on the index's value alone.

There are different ways to do such analysis. The most popular ways are through:

- Advance decline ratio: This ratio compares the number of advancing stocks to the number of declining stocks. A ratio above 1 means more stocks are rising then falling, while a ratio below 1 indicates the opposite.
- Percentage of stocks above key technical indicators: This method looks at the percentage of stocks of an index trading above key technical indicators, such as the 50-day or 200-day moving average, or its relative strength, or any other momentum or trend identifying indicators. If a high percentage of stocks in a sectoral index are above their moving averages, it signals broad market strength.
- Percentage of stocks making new highs: In this method we check the number of stocks in an index making new highs. The higher the number of stocks making new highs the stronger the market.

There are more ways to measure market/sectoral breadth, but let's stick to the popular ones as beginners in the market.

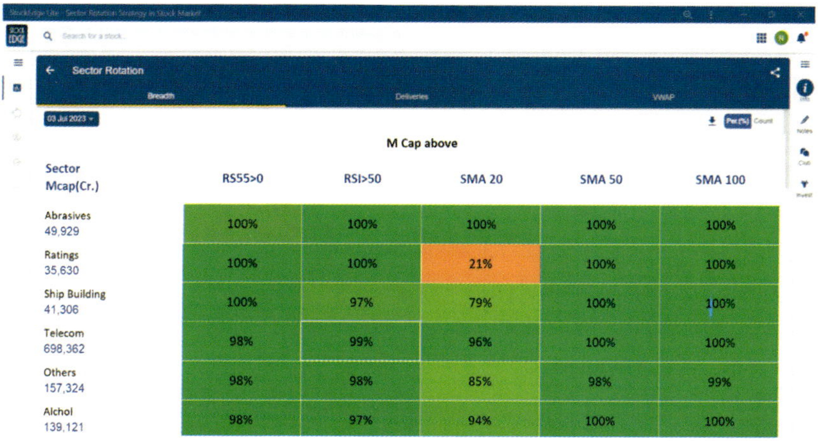

Sector Mcap(Cr.)	RS55>0	RSI>50	SMA 20	SMA 50	SMA 100
Abrasives 49,929	100%	100%	100%	100%	100%
Ratings 35,630	100%	100%	21%	100%	100%
Ship Building 41,306	100%	97%	79%	100%	100%
Telecom 698,362	98%	99%	96%	100%	100%
Others 157,324	98%	98%	85%	98%	99%
Alchol 139,121	98%	97%	94%	100%	100%

Table 4.5 Sectoral breadth analysis in StockEdge

If we look at Table 4.5, in the first column are sectors based on the market cap. Please note that the different shades of green represent varying levels of strength within sectors. The deeper shades of green at the top indicate maximum strength, suggesting strong bullish momentum that may continue. It's a good idea to consider strong stocks in these sectors for potential investment. As you scroll down, the shades become lighter (refer to Figure 4.7), indicating sectors that have just begun to show bullish strength. Entering stocks in these sectors could be advantageous in the future.

Figure 4.7 The colour scale of sector rotation

Green signifies that most stocks in that sector are in momentum. However, you avoid a sector if it has been the deepest shade of green for the past 2 to 3 weeks, as that could mean it is an overheated/ overbought sector. Yellow signifies the neutral zone for a sector with no significant movements. As the shades turn orange and deep red, it indicates weakening strength in the sector. It's advisable to avoid bullish trades in these sectors. The changing colours within sectors reflect the strength observed on a particular day.

In StockEdge, we've identified a few technical indicators, already covered in the book, which are important to measure the breadth and momentum of a sector. The indicators include:

- relative strength: RS55>0
- relative strength index: RSI>50
- price > simple moving average: SMA 20
- price > simple moving average: SMA 50
- price > simple moving average: SMA 100

If all the stocks in a sector fulfil the above-mentioned criteria, then the box will be dark green. If most of the stocks in the sector fulfil the above criteria, then the box will have a lighter shade of green or a shade of yellow and if most of the stocks in the sector do not fulfil the above criteria, then the box will be orange or red in colour.

Observe Table 4.6: as per the market cap 100% of the abrasives sector are fulfilling the criteria indicating a strong momentum in the sector, and 98% of the telecom sector's RS55>0, 99% of the market cap's RSI is above 50, 96% are trading above SMA 20 and 100% are trading above SMA 50 and SMA 100. Let's check the count of the stocks that are fulfilling the criteria, although it is slightly overheated, i.e., it has rallied quite a bit.

Stocks above

Sector / Stocks	RS55>0	RSI>50	SMA 20	SMA 50	SMA 100
Abrasives 3	3	3	3	3	3
Ratings 3	3	3	2	3	3
Ship Building 5	5	4	3	5	5
Telecom 32	17	21	17	23	23
Others 27	10	8	8	7	11
Alcohol 15	9	12	9	13	12
Aviation	3	4	4	4	3

Table 4.6 Count of stocks in sectoral breadth analysis in StockEdge

Observe in Table 4.6; as per the count there are 32 stocks in total in the telecom sector and only 17 stocks' RS55>0, which has a market cap of 98% of the entire sector. Thus, combining the market cap and the count data, we can conclude that these 17 stocks have the highest market cap and RS55 for only these stocks are above 0.

Similarly, RSI is above 50 for 21 out of 32 stocks with the market cap of 99% of the entire sector, inferring that these 21 stocks have the highest market cap and only these stocks have a higher buying propensity in this sector. Likewise, most of the stocks that cover a major part of the market cap of the sector are above SMA 20, SMA 50, and SMA 100. With most of the stocks fulfilling the criteria, we can say that the sector momentum is in play and keep a close watch on all the top stocks in the sector.

Let's look at the stocks in the telecom sector.

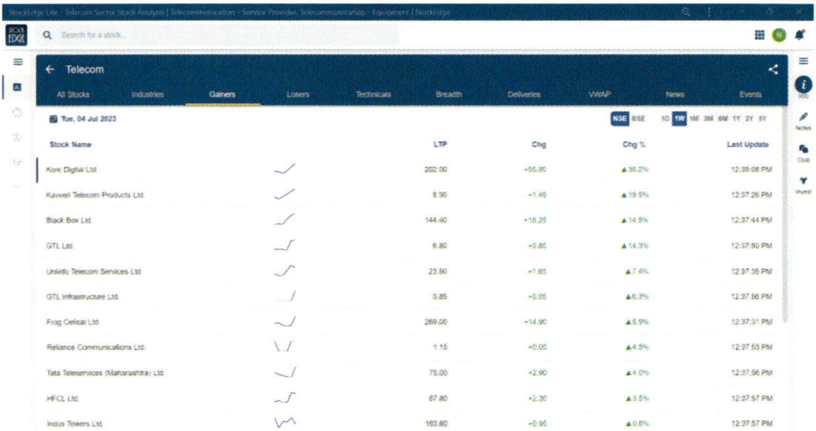

Stock Name	LTP	Chg	Chg %	Last Update
Kore Digital Ltd	202.00	+55.80	▲38.2%	12:38:08 PM
Kavveri Telecom Products Ltd	8.90	+1.45	▲19.5%	12:37:28 PM
Black Box Ltd	144.40	+18.25	▲14.5%	12:37:44 PM
GTL Ltd	6.80	+0.85	▲14.3%	12:37:50 PM
Unlnfo Telecom Services Ltd	23.90	+1.65	▲7.4%	12:37:35 PM
GTL Infrastructure Ltd	0.85	+0.05	▲6.3%	12:37:56 PM
Frog Cellsat Ltd	269.00	+14.90	▲5.9%	12:37:31 PM
Reliance Communications Ltd	1.15	+0.05	▲4.5%	12:37:53 PM
Tata Teleservices (Maharashtra) Ltd	75.00	+2.90	▲4.0%	12:37:56 PM
HFCL Ltd	67.80	+2.30	▲3.5%	12:37:57 PM
Indus Towers Ltd	163.60	+0.95	▲0.6%	12:37:57 PM

Table 4.7 Stocks in the telecom sector sorted as per the highest gainer in a week

Observed in Table 4.7, the stocks in the telecom sector have generated good returns in the past 1 week as on 4 July 2023. Let's check the charts of the third stock, Black Box Ltd.

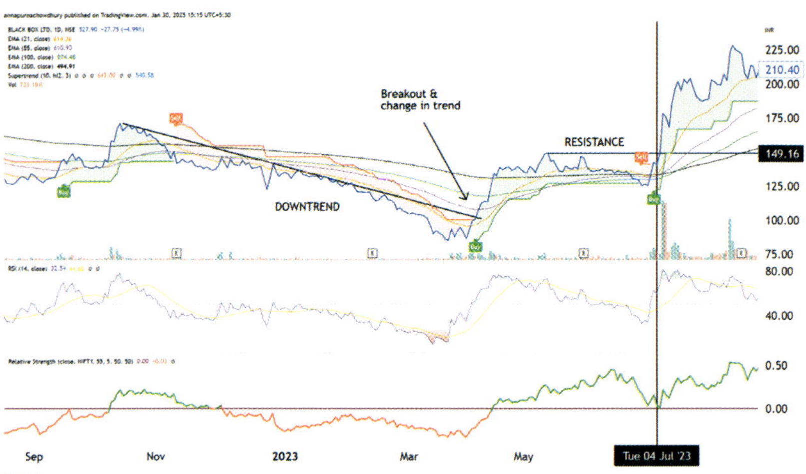

Figure 4.8 Daily chart of Black Box Ltd

In Figure 4.8, observe the stock trading at 140 on 4 Jul 2023 and

- the stock has been in an uptrend since April 2023;
- has had high volumes in the past week;
- the price is above all EMAs;
- the shorter tenure EMAs are above longer-tenure EMAs;
- the supertrend indicator gave a buy signal on 3 July 2023;
- RSI>50; and
- RS55>0.

This stock fits perfectly into the template, but should you enter at the 140 level? For that we need to assess the risk-reward.

Considering that there is resistance at the 149 level, from which there is a probability for the stock to reverse, it's best to wait and let the stock cross 149 supported by high volumes and delivery to enter, or if it reverses then accumulate near the demand zone for a favourable risk and reward.

One thing that you want to be cautious about is participating in an overbought sector that has already given a rally. To avoid such sectors, pick sectors that are in the middle section, i.e., those sectors that are between rows 2 and 5.

Sector Stocks	RS55>0	RSI>50	SMA 20	SMA 50	SMA 100
Abrasives 3	3	3	3	3	3
Ratings 3	3	3	2	3	3
Ship Building 5	5	4	3	5	5
Telecom 32	17	21	17	23	23
Others 27	10	8	8	7	11
Alcohol 15	9	12	9	13	12
Aviation 6	3	4	4	4	3

Table 4.8 Sectoral breadth analysis in StockEdge

Extreme green and extreme red indicate high greed and fear zones. For example, it was better to enter the abrasives sector when it was a lighter shade of green and book when it is in extreme green shade or zone.

Now let's move to delivery analysis.

Delivery Analysis

We know the importance of delivery in the stock market, be it stocks or sectors. High delivery along with a significant upmove in the price is suggestive of the operator's new position in the stock. Delivery data for a particular sector is of higher importance because sectors that have higher delivery along with an increase in price is indicative of buyer's demands in that sector. It usually suggests confidence in that sector's potential for near-term growth or stability.

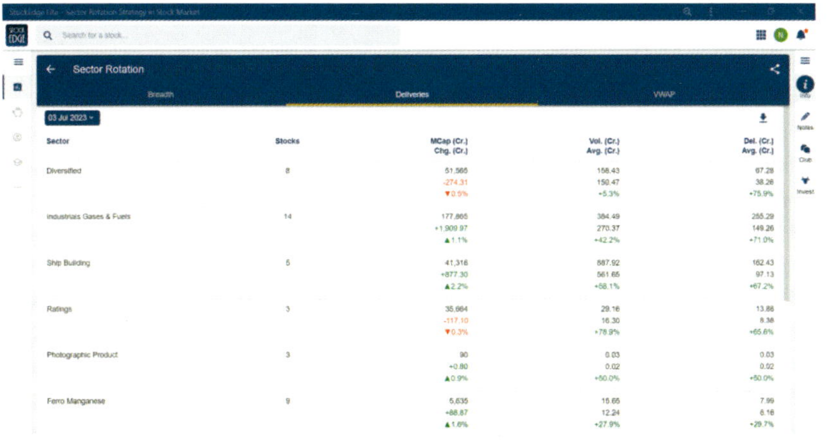

Sector Rotation

Breadth | Deliveries | VWAP

03 Jul 2023

Sector	Stocks	MCap (Cr.) Chg. (Cr.)	Vol. (Cr.) Avg. (Cr.)	Del. (Cr.) Avg. (Cr.)
Diversified	8	51,565 -274.31 ▼0.5%	158.43 150.47 +5.3%	67.28 38.26 +75.9%
Industrials Gases & Fuels	14	177,865 +1,909.97 ▲1.1%	384.49 270.37 +42.2%	255.29 149.26 +71.0%
Ship Building	5	41,318 +877.30 ▲2.2%	887.92 561.65 +58.1%	162.43 97.13 +67.2%
Ratings	3	35,664 -117.10 ▼0.3%	29.16 16.30 +78.9%	13.88 8.38 +65.6%
Photographic Product	3	90 +0.80 ▲0.9%	0.03 0.02 +50.0%	0.03 0.02 +50.0%
Ferro Manganese	9	5,635 +88.87 ▲1.6%	15.66 12.24 +27.9%	7.99 6.16 +29.7%

Table 4.9 Delivery analysis of sectors in StockEdge

Table 4.9 highlights sectors with high daily delivery volume. On 3 July 2023, the Diversified Sector had the highest delivery activity despite a slight decrease in market cap. With 8 stocks in this sector showing significantly increased volume and delivery, it's a prime candidate for closer examination. We should monitor this sector closely and identify potential stocks for trading. Let's look at the stocks that belong to this sector (Table 4.10).

Diversified

All Stocks | Gainers | Losers | Technicals | Breadth | Deliveries | VWAP | News | Events

Date Wise | Stock Wise

Mon, 03 Jul 2023

Stock Name	Delivery Value (Rs. in Lacs)	5 Days Avg. (Rs. in Lacs)	LTP	Chg%
3M India Ltd	374.84 +22.1%	306.94	27,122.35	▼0.4%
DCM Shriram Ltd	244.47 -57.0%	566.71	885.60	▼0.9%
Surya Roshni Ltd	5,526.71 2.3x	2,443.11	802.20	▲1.2%
Balmer Lawrie & Company Ltd	233.43 +19.1%	196.06	134.40	▼1.0%
Gillanders Arbuthnot & Company Ltd	22.91 3.9x	5.82	70.10	▲1.4%
TCI Industries Ltd	0.01 -88.2%	0.66	1,250.00	-
Binani Industries Ltd	2.84 +2.7%	2.77	18.55	▲1.4%

Table 4.10 Delivery analysis of stocks in diversified sector in StockEdge

We have the list of all the stocks in the diversified sector in Table 4.10. Let's check the chart of the top stock in the sector, 3M India.

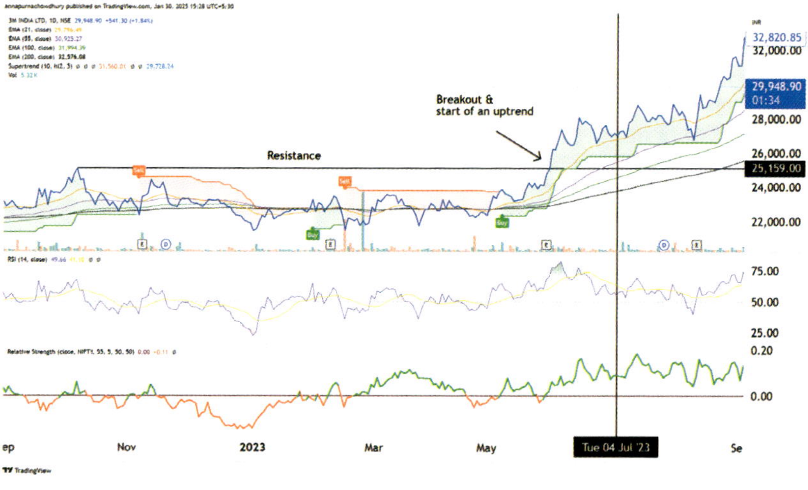

Figure 4.9 Daily chart of 3M India Ltd

In Figure 4.9, observe the stock trading at 27,077 on 4 July 2023. The stock was moving in a range for a while before giving a breakout above the 25,159 level in May 2023, and since then it was making a higher high and higher low indicating a change in trend. As of 4 July 2023,

- the stock is in uptrend;
- the stock is trading above all moving averages;
- all shorter-tenure EMAs are above longer-tenure EMAs;
- supertrend indicator is buy;
- RSI is above 50; and
- RS55 is greater than 0.

This is again a good stock for traders to trade. Moreover, the stock is currently retracing and taking support at EMA21, making it a good and favourable price point to enter at with respect to risk and reward. Observe how the stock rallied and went up till 33,000 as of 11 September 2023. It looks like the stock was at the end of phase 1 in July 2023, making it the perfect stock to trade in. This is the power of trading in the right stocks that belong to the sectors in momentum.

As mentioned earlier, delivery data is one of those rare data that is often missed by traders to track, as the accessibility of the data is not very easy. Tracking delivery has been rewarding in my trading journey, and hence I'm stressing on it again and again for you to track.

VWAP Analysis

We've already covered the meaning and implications of VWAP. We will now simply apply that to the sectors to form a judgement on its momentum. When stock price trades above its VWAP, it is generally considered bullish and vice versa. Hence, when more stocks in a sector are trading above their VWAP, it reflects the overall strength in that sector or industry.

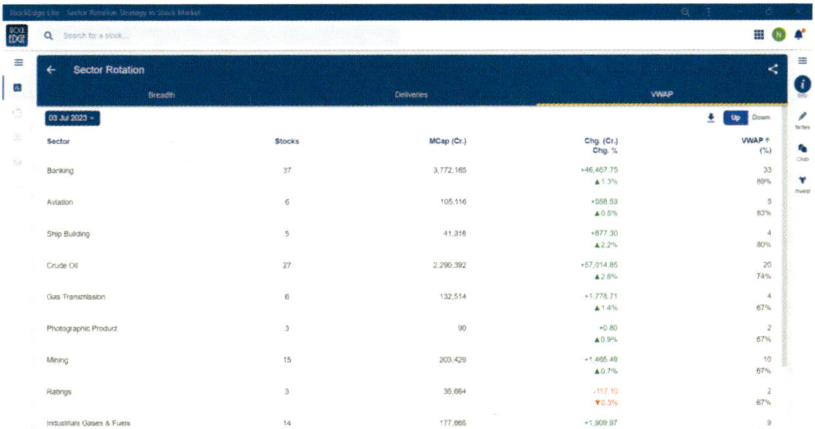

Sector	Stocks	MCap (Cr.)	Chg. (Cr.) Chg. %	VWAP ↑ (%)
Banking	37	3,772,165	+46,467.75 ▲1.3%	33 89%
Aviation	6	105,116	+558.53 ▲0.5%	5 83%
Ship Building	5	41,316	+877.30 ▲2.2%	4 80%
Crude Oil	27	2,290,392	+57,014.85 ▲2.6%	20 74%
Gas Transmission	6	132,514	+1,778.71 ▲1.4%	4 67%
Photographic Product	3	90	+0.80 ▲0.9%	2 67%
Mining	15	203,429	+1,465.48 ▲0.7%	10 67%
Ratings	3	35,664	-117.10 ▼0.3%	2 67%
Industrials Gases & Fuels	14	177,865	+1,909.97	9

Table 4.11 VWAP analysis of sectors in StockEdge

In Table 4.11, the top sector that has been above VWAP is banking with 33 out of 37 stocks having a close above its VWAP and a gain of over 1.3% in the overall sector. Another is the ship building sector with 4 out of 5 stocks closing above its VWAP and a gain of 2% in the sector.

Recall that ship building was also listed in the third row while analysing the sectoral breadth as shown in Table 4.5 and was also listed in the third row while doing delivery analysis as seen in Table 4.6. Since this sector has been demonstrating strength across all parameters—breadth analysis, delivery analysis and VWAP analysis—let's pick stocks in this sector.

Stock Identification

In Table 4.12, we can see the price of all the stocks as compared to its EMAs in the sector. Mazagon Dock Shipbuilders is trading above all 5-day EMA, 20-day EMA, 50-day EMA, 100-day EMA and a 200-day EMA indicating an uptrend. Cochin Shipyard is also trading close to 20-day EMA, and above all the other longer-term EMAs. Both stocks look good to add to the radar. Let's look at the chart of Mazagon Dock.

Table 4.12 Technical levels of ship building stocks

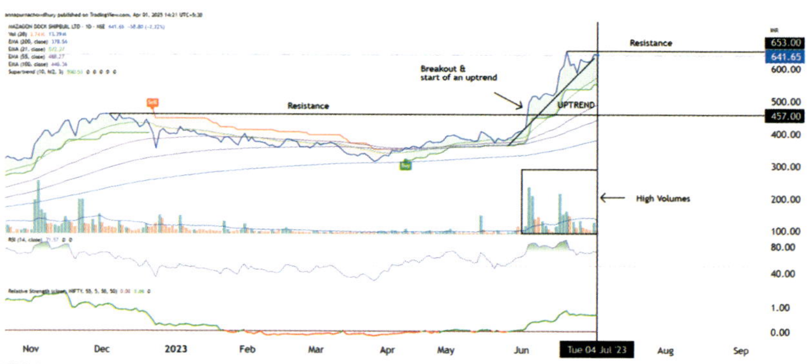

Figure 4.10 Daily chart of Mazagon Dock

Please note: When we were adding these examples using StockEdge screenshots, Mazdock was trading at the 1300 level. However, to increase the visibility of the charts, we worked on the charts much later, during which Mazdock underwent a split and hence the trading level mentioned in Table 4.12 is not matching Figure 4.10. However, the idea is to understand the concept and not match the levels.

In Figure 4.10, Mazagon was trading at 641 as on 4 July 2023, close to its resistance level of 653.

- The stock had already given a breakout above 457 level and started an uptrend.
- It has tall volume bars at the breakout level.
- The stock was trading above all EMAs.
- The shorter-tenure EMAs were all above longer-tenure EMAs.
- Supertrend was buy.
- RSI 14>50.
- RS55>0.

These make it a good pick for the traders.

By the look of it, the stock seems to have been trading in phase 1 of its cycle till June 2023. If you open the chart of Mazdock in your phone/ipad/laptop now and see the period from June 2023 to September 2023, you will see how the stock rallied up in its phase 2, generating massive returns for traders who entered at an early stage of the phase.

This is the power of sector rotation: by identifying the strongest stocks within a strong sector, you can generate alpha returns. However, it's crucial to remember: if you bought a stock based on the strength or momentum of a sector, and that sector starts losing strength, then the basis for your trade no longer holds. In such cases, it's wise to exit the stock immediately even if your stop loss hasn't been hit. If a sector is losing strength, then it is indicative of the operators pulling out funds, hinting to loss of confidence in the sector. Hence, it's best to exit the stock.

SUMMARY

- Every sector/business/economy moves cyclically.
- Each cycle has 4 phases—accumulation, markup or bull run, distribution, decline or bear run.
- The best way to make money is to enter at an early stage of phase 2, and exit around phase 3.
- Sector rotation is when the ace investors rebalance their portfolio by divesting from one sector to another in anticipation of the change in economic cycle and optimized returns
- Method 1:
  - Identify the strong sectors by highest gain in the past 1 month.
  - Pick the top 5 stocks as per the gainer list.
  - Check the chart of these stocks to confirm if it fits in our trading template.
  - Assess risk-reward and enter when it is most favourable.
- Method 2:
  - Identify strong sectors through breadth analysis, delivery analysis, and VWAP analysis.
  - Identify strongest stocks by checking the technical levels.
  - Add it to your watchlist.
  - Check the chart of these stocks to confirm if it fits in our trading template.
  - Assess risk-reward and enter when it is most favourable.
- Avoid overheated or overbought sectors.
- Only stay invested in a stock in case it was identified through sector rotation, till the sector is strong. As soon as the sector becomes weak, exit the stock.

LET'S PRACTICE

Some charts have been provided as follows. Analysing the graphs, identify the different phases of the stock cycle in each chart. Please use a pen/pencil to distinctly mark the different phases. Please note that it's not mandatory that stocks go through all the 4 stages consecutively in the ascending order.

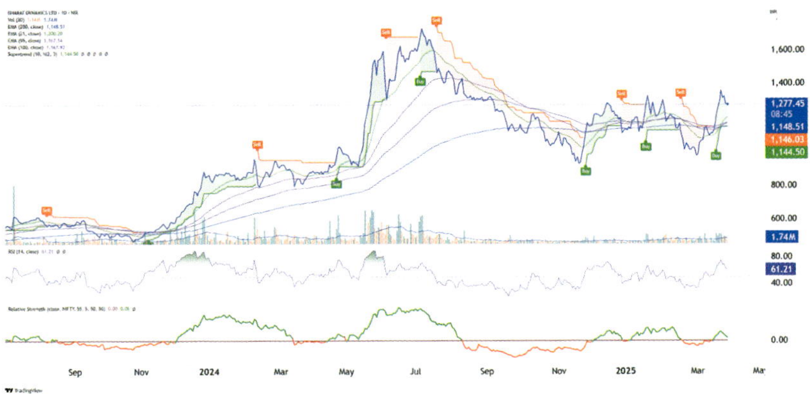

Figure 4.11

Figure 4.12

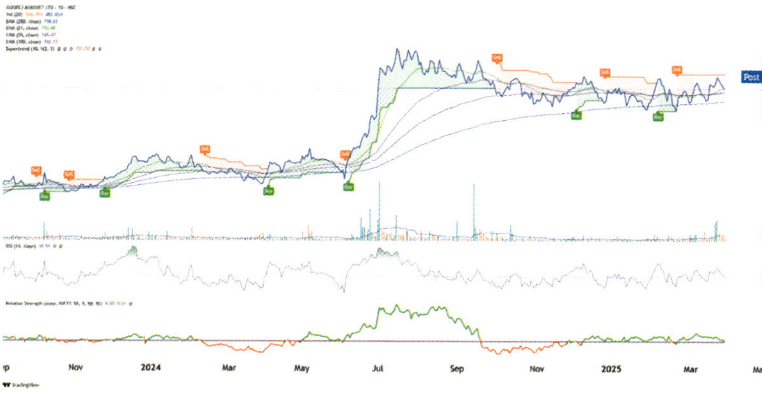

Figure 4.13

Figure 4.14

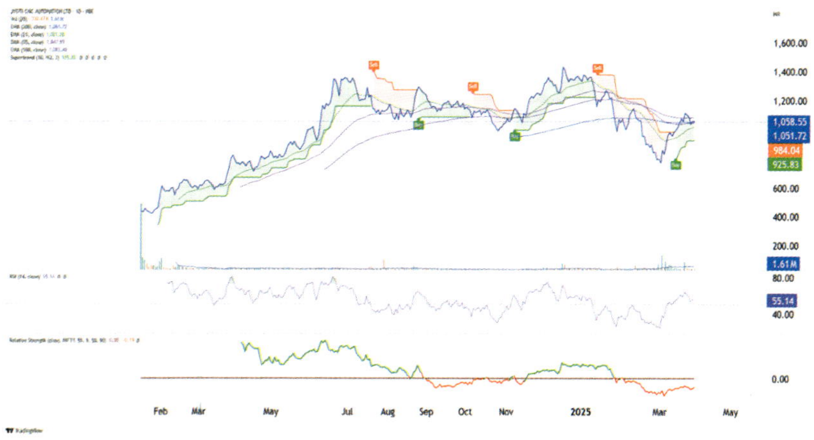

Figure 4.15

LEARNER'S CORNER

Should I only look for sectors that appear in all 3—breadth, delivery and VWAP analysis?

Any sector that appears under all 3 sections clearly has something going in it that is being reflected through the data, and would naturally have higher conviction than any other sector that appears under either 1 or 2 sections. However, if no common sector emerges across all 3, it doesn't mean there are no opportunities. In such cases, track the different sectors across all 3 sections, and find sectors that are demonstrating momentum.

What if I entered a stock based on sector rotation, but now the sector is turning down while the stock is still in an uptrend?

If your entry was based on sector strength, and the sector has now started to weaken, ideally that weakness should reflect in the stock as well. If it hasn't yet, it could be because the stock has a lower weightage within the sector index. When the basis of your entry—the sector's strength—no longer holds true, it's best to exit the stock, regardless of whether the stop loss is hit. Alternatively, if the stock continues to trend upward, evaluate it independently using your stock-specific parameters. If it continues to meet all your criteria on its own merit, you may choose to hold it—but your conviction should now come from the stock's individual setup, not the sector trend.

Just because a sector is in the overheated zone, does it mean that all the stocks in that sector will also be in the overheated zones?

A sector is made up of the stocks that operate that sector. Any movement in a sector is mostly reflective of the movements of the stocks that have a high weightage in the sector. Hence, if the sector is in the overheated zone, then the underlying reason behind it is the overheated zones of the sector. However, if a stock does not have a lot of weightage in the sectoral index, then might or might not be in the overheated zone.

If sector rotation is driven by ace investors shifting their money, can't I just track news to find out where they're investing?

Whenever an operator invests in a stock, they do not add in one go. They start accumulating in small quantities, which is reflected in the volume and delivery data, and then buy a big chunk driving the rally in the stock. By the time it's reflected in the news media, it would already be stale and the stock would have already given a rally. People who add/exit on the basis of news more often than not get trapped by narratives and false hopes.

Combo Scans (Combining Parameters)

Another great way to identify stocks to trade is by combining multiple different parameters, a combination that will filter out stocks as per our defined criteria and should be perfect as per our trading setup. We will first define a concept and then list and combine different parameters that fit the concept.

52-Week Zone–Strong Zone

If the stock trades in a 15% window of its 52-week high price, it is considered a strong stock. The 52-week high is the highest price the stock reached in the past year. For mid-caps the window is 20% while for small caps it is 25%. For ease, let us consider only 15% as of now. If a stock is near its 52-week high it means the operators are not letting the stock price fall signifying strength in the stock.

Let's take 2 examples for better clarity:

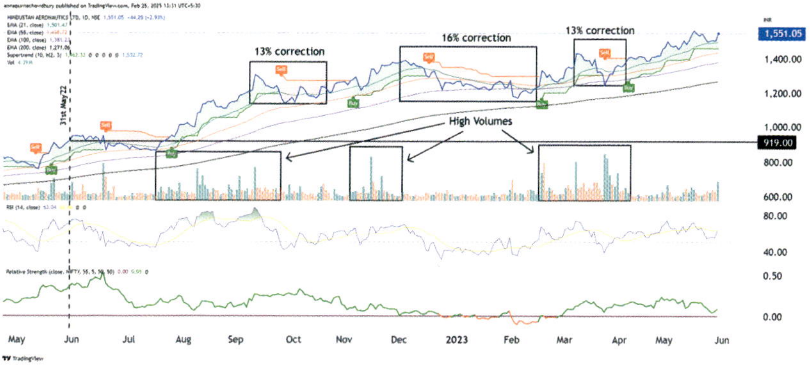

Figure 4.16 Daily chart of HAL

Observe Figure 4.16: the 1-year chart of HAL, a mid-cap stock, where it is trading at the 1551 level as of 30 May 2023, near its 52-week high of 1571. The stock was trading at 919 level on 31 May 2022, at its 52-week high, and increased by almost 70% in the last

52 weeks. The stock underwent a few corrections during this 1 year bull run, but none were more than 16%. Moreover, just look at the high volumes when the stock was in a steep uptrend. HAL was one of the strong stocks and still looks strong trading near its 52-week high.

Figure 4.17 Daily chart of Vodafone Idea

Observe in Figure 4.17 how Vodafone Idea made a low of 5.8, and is trading at 7.1 as of 30 May 2023, i.e., near its 52-week low zone. The stock was trading at the 9.60 level on 31 May 2022, and whenever the stock attempted to break its downtrend, it faced resistance and came back down sharply, making a new low.

There could be a bullish operator in HAL, and a bearish operator in Vodafone Idea who is not letting the stock come out of this 52-week high and low zones.

To reiterate the importance of analysis and data-driven moves, I want to share an instance with you. One of my friends called me to ask if Vodafone Idea was a good buy at 6/7 level with the underlying logic that it has already fallen a lot, so the only way is up now for the stock. His claim was highly flawed. If we were to believe in this theory, then the same could've been said when the stock fell from the 120 level in April 2015 to the 40 level in January 2017, or when it came down to the 15 level in April 2019.

The stock may or may not reverse at this level either and we don't know for certain. We have to believe in price action and technical analysis rather than something we may consider common logic. Believing in such false narratives could have led us to enter at 45, expecting the stock to reverse and ending up in deep losses.

I bring this up as it is a very common thought of most retail investors to buy when the stocks are down and are looking cheap. Be aware and conscious of the same.

Stock selection should be based on technicals and price action and not based on price of the stock, however cheap or lucrative they look.

Cheap stocks always look lucrative to buy. However, there is a reason that this stock is so cheap; it could become cheaper with time. There could be a bearish operator operating in the stock. A stock that is expensive could become more expensive, moving higher up with time and a cheap stock could go down further.

There is always a reason for a stock to be expensive or cheap; we might not know the underlying reason, but we have to believe in the price. Absolute prices do not matter when trading. It is only the price movement that is important. You may invest the same amount of capital in a Rs 100 stock and a Rs 10 stock but make more profits on the more expensive stock if the price increase percentage is higher.

Coming back to the 52-week theory, if we're able to identify stocks that are entering this important zone, then we're halfway there.

Stock Identification

How do we filter out stocks that are in the 52-week high zone?

StockEdge has 52-week scans (refer to Table 4.13). There are 3 scans that you can focus on:

- Close crossing the 52-week high—stocks that closed above 52-week high in the previous trading session.
- Close within the 52-week high zone—stocks that are within 15% of the 52-week high price.

- Close entering the 52-week high zone—stocks that entered the 52-week high zone.

Table 4.13 52-week scans in StockEdge

You can consider all the above-mentioned scans while filtering stocks, and you may find some stocks that fulfil all the criteria.

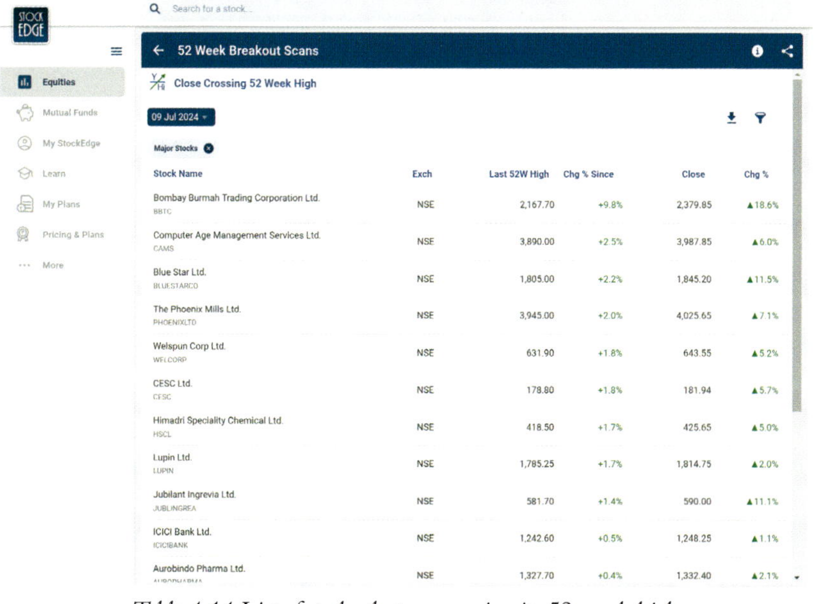

52 Week Breakout Scans

Close Crossing 52 Week High

09 Jul 2024

Major Stocks

Stock Name	Exch	Last 52W High	Chg % Since	Close	Chg %
Bombay Burmah Trading Corporation Ltd. BBTC	NSE	2,167.70	+9.8%	2,379.85	▲18.6%
Computer Age Management Services Ltd. CAMS	NSE	3,890.00	+2.5%	3,987.85	▲6.0%
Blue Star Ltd. BLUESTARCO	NSE	1,805.00	+2.2%	1,845.20	▲11.5%
The Phoenix Mills Ltd. PHOENIXLTD	NSE	3,945.00	+2.0%	4,025.65	▲7.1%
Welspun Corp Ltd. WELCORP	NSE	631.90	+1.8%	643.55	▲5.2%
CESC Ltd. CESC	NSE	178.80	+1.8%	181.94	▲5.7%
Himadri Speciality Chemical Ltd. HSCL	NSE	418.50	+1.7%	425.65	▲5.0%
Lupin Ltd. LUPIN	NSE	1,785.25	+1.7%	1,814.75	▲2.0%
Jubilant Ingrevia Ltd. JUBLINGREA	NSE	581.70	+1.4%	590.00	▲11.1%
ICICI Bank Ltd. ICICIBANK	NSE	1,242.60	+0.5%	1,248.25	▲1.1%
Aurobindo Pharma Ltd.	NSE	1,327.70	+0.4%	1,332.40	▲2.1%

Table 4.14 List of stocks that are crossing its 52-week high

52 Week Breakout Scans

Close Entering 52 Week High Zone

09 Jul 2024

Major Stocks

Stock Name	Exch	Previous Close	52W High	Gap from 52W High	Close	Chg %
Bombay Burmah Trading Corporation Ltd. BBTC	NSE	2,006.70	2,408.00	-1.2%	2,379.85	▲18.6%
Shree Renuka Sugars Ltd. RENUKA	NSE	48.39	57.25	-13.7%	49.41	▲2.1%
Campus Activewear Ltd. CAMPUS	NSE	285.50	338.90	-14.3%	290.40	▲1.7%
Punjab National Bank PNB	NSE	121.36	142.90	-14.4%	122.39	▲0.9%
Indian Bank INDIANB	NSE	526.50	632.70	-14.4%	541.70	▲2.9%
SJVN Ltd. SJVN	NSE	143.02	170.50	-14.7%	145.36	▲1.6%
DCM Shriram Ltd. DCMSHRIRAM	NSE	989.65	1,175.00	-15.0%	999.10	▲1.0%
Eureka Forbes Ltd. 543482	BSE	485.70	588.00	-15.0%	499.90	▲2.9%

Table 4.15 List of stocks that are entering its 52-week high zone

As observed in Table 4.14 and Table 4.15, Bombay Burmah Trading Corporation (BBTC) is common in both the lists indicating that BBTC entered the 52-week high zone and crossed its 52-week high in the same trading session. Let's look at the chart of BBTC.

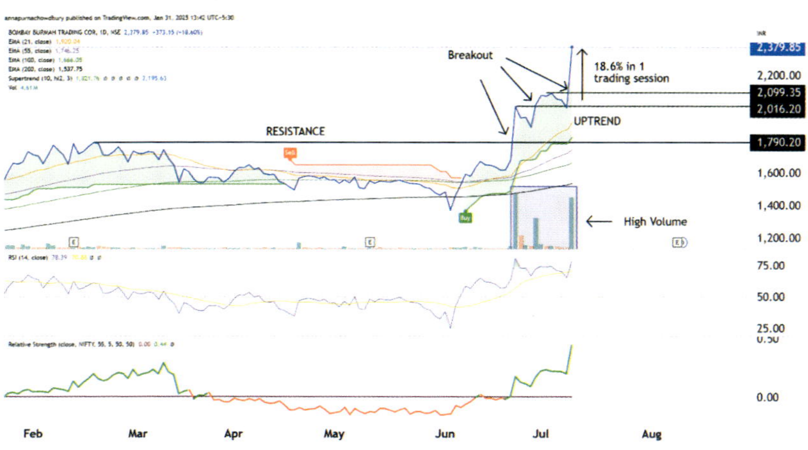

Figure 4.18 Daily chart of BBTC

Observe Figure 4.18: BBTC rallied 18.6% in a single trading session, making a new 52-week high and also entering its 52-week high zone at the same time. Additionally, all the indicators are giving positive signals:

- stock is in uptrend;
- high volume and delivery (refer to Figure 4.18);
- price is above 21-EMA, and all the shorter tenure EMA is also trading above longer tenure EMA;
- supertrend is buy;
- RSI 14>50;
- RS55>0.

The stock fulfils all the criteria, making it the perfect stock to add to the radar. But will we enter the stock now? We could, depending on the risk-reward. If the risk-reward for the stock is favourable then yes; if not, then no. We will discuss more on the right price points to enter in the strategies section of the book.

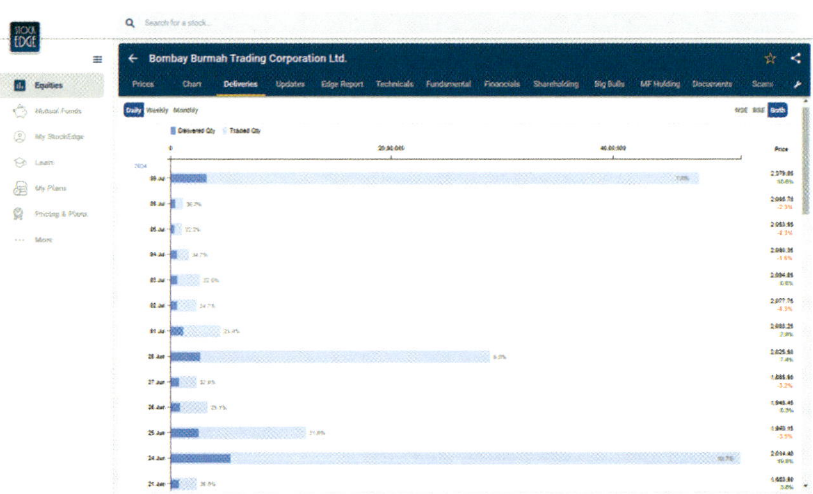

Table 4.16 Delivery data for BBTC

As traders should you consider the stocks that are crossing 52-week high or stocks that have just entered the 52-week high zone?

You can consider both; however, the chances of having a favourable risk-reward in stocks in the former category would be relatively lower than the stocks in latter category. Having said that, you would still want to keep such powerful stocks on your radar. The best way would be to make a list of all the stocks from both categories and add to your watchlist.

Stocks entering the 52-week high zone could be promising candidates for trading, but it's essential to analyse their charts to determine their trading potential. It's advisable to review all the stocks on this list, as you can find a relevant opportunity in any stock. To refine the list, you can create a combination scan. For example, a '52-Week High Plus Delivery' scan can filter stocks by both their 52-week high entry and high trade and delivery quantities.

52-Week High Zone and High Delivery

We now know the significance of delivery to judge the strength of a price movement in a stock. Think about how powerful a stock will be if it is near its 52-week high zone and has had high delivered quantity coupled with strong price action. Let's look at the list of stocks that fulfil both the criteria.

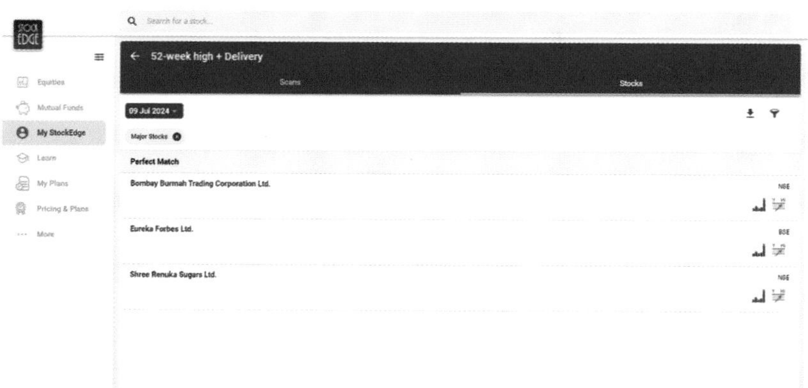

Table 4.17 List of stocks that are entering the 52-week high zone and had a high traded and delivered quantity in the last trading session.

Let's look at the chart of Shree Renuka Sugars.

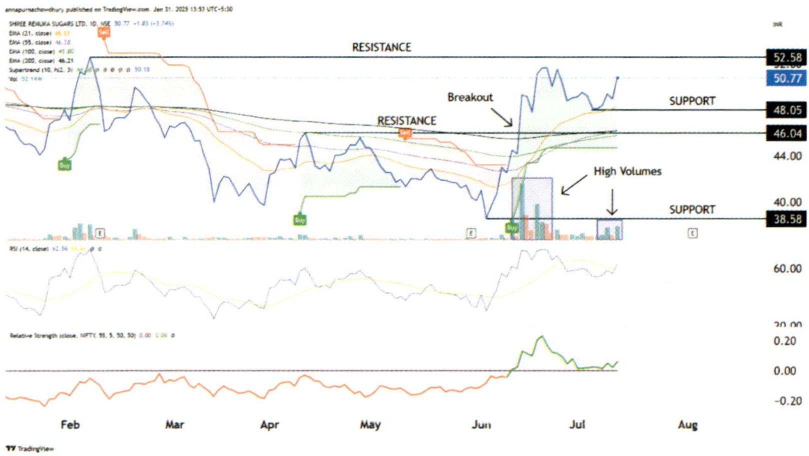

Figure 4.19 Daily chart of Shree Renuka Sugars

Shree Renuka Sugars, as seen in Figure 4.19 is trading at 50.77 as on 10 July, while immediate support is at 48.05 level. The stock gave a reversal from 39 levels, giving a strong breakout supported by high volumes on 13 June 2024, and making higher highs for the past 1 month. The stock is fulfilling the following criteria:

- stock is in uptrend;
- high volume and delivery in recent trading sessions;
- near its 52-week high zone;
- price is trading above all EMAs, however 200-day EMA is still above 55-day EMA and 100-day EMA;
- supertrend is buy;
- RSI 14>50;
- RS55>0.

Except for one, the stock is fulfilling most of the criteria, making us positive on the stock. The stock is trading between its demand zone/ support level and supply zone/resistance level at 52. The stock could either reverse from its resistance or give another breakout. Hence, the risk-reward is 1:1 at the current level. As traders we just add the stock to the radar and just observe the price action. Let's take a look at Eureka Forbes from the list (refer to Figure 4.20)

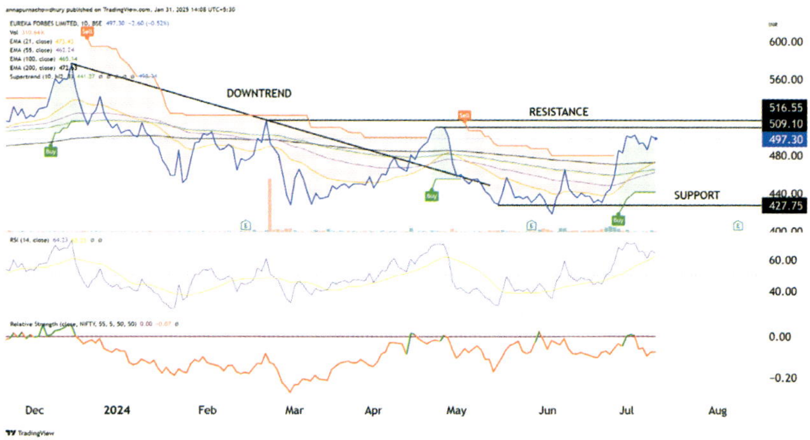

Figure 4.20 Daily chart of Eureka Forbes Ltd

As observed in Figure 4.20, Eureka Forbes is trading at 497.30 as on 10 July 2024. Even though the stock has entered the 52-week high zone and the stock is pushing to make higher highs from past 10 to 12 trading sessions, supported by relatively higher volumes than other trading days, yet the uptrend has not been confirmed by the price action. The uptrend in the stock will only be confirmed once it sustains its upmove and breaks the 509 and 516 levels, which is a supply zone or the resistance level. Moreover,

- price is above EMAs, but 200-day EMA is still above shorter tenure EMAs;
- supertrend is buy;
- RSI>50; and
- RS55<0.

The chart is indicating that the stock is still not strong vis-à-vis Nifty50, making it a less favourable candidate for us to trade.

If the price movement sustains and the stock pushes past the 516 level, and the indicators turn bullish, then it could be a good trading opportunity. Hence, as of now, we will just add it to our tracker and wait for the right opportunity to initiate the trade.

Techno-funda Scans

An experienced trader knows the importance of the art of rejection.

The ability to reject stocks is just as important as the ability to select them. This critical skill can often be the difference between success and failure. Recall that we've covered the difference between investing and trading and how for investing one needs to undertake fundamental analysis of a company. Techno-funda is a powerful approach that combines both technical analysis and fundamental analysis.

Imagine you are the manager of a sports team aiming to win the championship. To build a winning team, you need both talented players (the fundamentals) and effective game strategies (the technicals). Each element is important on its own, but the combination of both is what creates a championship-winning team.

Fundamental analysis is like scouting and recruiting the best players for your team. It involves evaluating a company's financial health, earnings, growth potential and competitive position. Just as talented players are crucial for a strong team, strong fundamentals indicate a company's intrinsic value and long-term potential.

On the other hand, technical analysis is like designing and implementing effective game strategies. It involves studying price charts, trends and patterns to predict future price movements. Even the best players need good strategies to win games.

Every business has a cycle, companies do well in some quarters and can falter in some quarters, or can remain stagnant without growth. For example, an ice cream company does well in the summer months. However, if a company has been consistent with growth of profit and turnover over a considerable period of time, we can presume that the company is fundamentally strong.

The key parameters for techno-funda are:

- financials
- price
- volume
- delivery

I developed my own set of techno-funda filters that has been highly rewarding for me through ample reading and countless trial and error. As a trader, you need not have a 360-degree fundamental knowledge; however, you need to be aware of some crucial parameters that will make your life easier in the process of judging a company.

There are 2 ways to judge fundamentals of a company—qualitatively and quantitatively.

Quantitative analysis involves analysing the company based on its numbers whereas qualitative analysis involves analysing the management of the company, the potential of the business and so on. For a techno-funda approach in trading, we will only look at the quantitative data. Some broad parameters to judge the company are:

- Profitability: How much are they earning?
- Turnover: How much are they selling?
- Solvency: Is it at risk of becoming bankrupt?
- Cash flow: Are they bringing money home?
- Valuation: Is the stock cheap or expensive compared to its earnings?
- Dividend: Is the company distributing its profits to their shareholders?
- Efficiency: Is the company using its assets efficiently?
- Shareholding: Are the shareholders weak or strong and are the strong shareholders increasing their stake in the company?

- Promoter holding pledged: Are the promoters pledging their shares? (Pledging occurs when promoters give their shares to banks or NBFCs in exchange for personal loans. If promoters have pledged their shares, it is a red flag, as they have used their own property, i.e., shares, as collateral against a loan.)

We will focus broadly on 3 out of the above for holistic view of the company:

1. Profitability
2. Turnover
3. Cash Flow

There are various ways to measure each of the above parameters. We will use several accounting terms and formulas for calculations. Do not be overwhelmed; they will become easier if you practice regularly.

Profitability Parameters

Return on Equity (ROE)

Imagine you have 2 friends who each start their own lemonade stands. Both friends ask for your help to decide which stand is doing better. They both tell you how much profit they made and how much money they initially put into their stands. To figure out which stand is making better use of its initial investment, you use a simple but powerful metric called return on equity (ROE). It is a measure of how effectively a company is using the money invested by its owners (shareholders) to generate profits. It's a way to see how good a business is at turning the money put into it into more money.

Example: Imagine you gave Rs 10,000 to each friend to start their lemonade stands. One friend (A) makes a profit of Rs 2,000, and the other friend (B) makes a profit of Rs 1,000. ROE tells you that the first friend is more efficient in using your Rs 10,000 to make a profit.

To calculate ROE:

ROE = (Net Profit/Shareholders' Equity) × 100

So, A's lemon stand's ROE:

ROE = (2,000/10,000) × 100 = 20%

B's lemon stand's ROE:

ROE = (1,000/10,000) × 100 = 10%

This means that A made a 20% return on the money you invested, while B just made a 10% return.

If you're thinking about investing more money, you'd prefer to invest in A's stand which has a higher ROE because it shows that stand is better at turning your investment into profit. In the bigger world of business, a company with a high ROE is often considered healthy and well-managed because it shows they are effectively using their resources to grow and make money.

Return on Capital Employed (ROCE)

Now, imagine your friends (A and B) not only use their own money but also take out a loan to expand the lemonade stand. You want to see how effectively all the money invested in the business (both yours and the loan) is being used to generate profits. Imagine A used Rs 10,000 of their own money and borrowed Rs 5,000, making a profit of Rs 2,000. B used Rs 10,000 of their own money and borrowed Rs 10,000, making a profit of Rs 2,500. ROCE tells you which friend is more efficient in using the total capital (their own money plus borrowed money) to make a profit.

To calculate ROCE:

ROCE = [Earnings before Interest and Tax (EBIT)/Capital Employed] × 100

So, A's lemon stand's ROCE = [2,000/(10,000 + 5,000)] × 100 = 13.33%

B's lemon stand's ROCE = [2,500/(10,000 + 10,000)] × 100 = 12.5%

A's lemonade stand is better at generating profit from all the money invested. If you're thinking about investing more money, you'd prefer to invest in the stand with a higher ROCE because it shows that the stand is better at turning total capital into profit. You'd likely choose to invest in A's stand because it's more efficient and gives you a better return on your money. In the bigger world of business, a company with a high ROCE is often considered healthy and well-managed because it shows they are effectively using all their resources to grow and make money.

Earnings before Interest Taxes, Depreciation and Amortization (EBITDA)

As the name suggests, EBITDA is a measure of a company's overall financial performance helping you see how profitable a company's core operations are before the influence of financing and accounting decisions.

Let's go back to the lemonade stand example. A's lemonade stand generates Rs 10,000 in sales and incurs Rs 3,000 in operating costs (lemons, cups, sugar and wages), while B generates Rs 10,000 in sales and incurs Rs 5,000 operating costs. Their EBITDA would be:

EBITDA = Revenue − Operating Expenses

So, A's lemonade stand's EBITDA = 10,000 − 3,000 = 7,000

B's lemonade stand's EBITDA = 10,000 − 5,000 = 5,000

A's stand is better at generating profit from its operations. You'd likely choose to invest in the A's stand because it's more efficient in its core business activities.

While EBITDA tells us how much profit a business is making in absolute terms, EBITDA Margin tells us how efficient the business is by expressing EBITDA as a percentage of total revenue.

If we use the above example, A's lemonade stand's EBITDA Margin would be 70%, while B's lemonade stand's EBITDA Margin would be 50%.

Now suppose B's EBITDA was 6,000, but the revenue was 8,000, then the EBITDA Margin for B's lemonade stand would be 75%.

Now when we compare, B's business would stand to be more efficient with its core operations.

It's a valuable metric for comparing different businesses and making informed investment decisions.

Turnover Parameter

Sales Growth

To understand how well a business is growing over time, you look at a key metric called sales growth. Sales growth measures how much a company's sales (or revenue) have increased over a specific period. It's an indicator of how well the business is expanding and attracting more customers.

Imagine that in the first month, each friend sells 100 cups of lemonade. By the second month, A sells 150 cups, and B sells 120 cups. Sales growth tells you that A's business is expanding faster. It indicates that there is strong demand for A's lemonade. This could mean they have a better location, a more appealing product, or more effective marketing.

Even if B's lemonade stand has a higher ROE, if their sales are not growing, it might suggest that they have already reached their peak. On the other hand, strong sales growth suggests that the business has potential for even greater profits in the future. If A's lemonade stand has a sales growth of 50% and B's lemonade stand has 20%, the first one is expanding its market presence faster. You'd likely choose to invest in A's stand because it shows greater potential for future growth and profits.

Cash Flow Parameter

Cash from Operations (CFO)

This measures the amount of cash a company generates from its regular business activities. It's a way to see how much actual cash flow the business is creating from selling lemonade, rather than from other activities like borrowing money or selling assets. Let's go back to the lemonade example again and break it down simply:

Cash sales: Your friend sells lemonade and collects Rs 3,000 in cash.

Credit sales: Your friend sells lemonade worth Rs 2,000 but hasn't received the money yet.

Operating expenses: They spend Rs 1,500 on lemons, sugar and other supplies.

To calculate CFO: CFO = Cash Sales − Operating Expenses

So, for the lemonade stand:

CFO = 3,000 – 1,500 = 1,500

This means your friend generated Rs 1,500 in actual cash from operating the lemonade stand.

If a lemonade stand has high profits but low cash flow, it might struggle to pay for lemons, sugar and other expenses. A high CFO indicates that the business can sustain its operations and grow without relying on external financing.

You'd likely choose to invest in the stand with a higher CFO because it shows that the business is generating sufficient cash from its core activities, making it more reliable and less risky. It's a vital indicator of financial health, sustainability and liquidity, providing a clearer picture of the business's ability to sustain and grow its operations.

There are a large number of fundamental parameters that a true fundamentalist takes into account while judging a company, but since our purpose is to trade, knowing only the most important ones is sufficient for us to filter out companies that are doing fairly well. I use some more fundamental parameters, which I will explain briefly as and when I use them.

SUMMARY

- A stock trading within 15% of its 52-week high is considered in its 52-week zone, indicating strength and bullish operator support.
- Empirical studies show that stocks in an uptrend controlled by bulls typically do not fall more than 15% from their 52-week high; a fall beyond this indicates potential weakness.
- Operators drive significant price movements, and strong stocks remain in the 52-week high zone due to bullish operator support, making them ideal for trading.
- Techno-funda approach combines technical and fundamental analysis to filter stocks that are fundamentally strong and meet technical criteria, enhancing trading success.
- Financials, price, volume and delivery are essential for a holistic view of a company in the techno-funda approach.
- Profitability Parameters:
    - ROE (return on equity): Measures efficiency in using shareholders' funds to generate profits.
    - ROCE (return on capital employed): Assesses efficiency in using total capital (own and borrowed) for profit generation.
    - EBITDA: Evaluates core operational profitability before financing and accounting influences.
- Turnover parameters:
    - Sales growth: Indicates how well a company is expanding and attracting customers, signalling future growth potential.
- Cash flow parameters:
    - CFO (cash from operations): Measures cash generated from core business activities, indicating financial health and sustainability.

My Few Combo Scans

Now, let's learn the art of creating combo strategies using the combos I use. You can use this as an illustration and a guide to create your own. Every trader is unique, and we may arrive at the same stocks using different combinations, but what is important is to understand the idea behind the strategy.

Eagle Stocks

Eagle is a symbol of power, strength and courage, with the ability to fly high in the sky unlike other birds. Similarly, this mechanism filters stocks that are outperforming the market, have their own strength and potential to fly higher than all other stocks. The underlying theory of this combo scan is that a hyper momentum stock that behaves like an eagle will keep surprising everyone.

I have created a combo scan that helps me identify the powerful eagle stocks:

Price scans:

- Close within 52-week high zone
- Outperforming benchmark index in both 1 week and 3 months
- Outperforming sectoral index in both 1 week and 3 months

Technical scans:

- Strongly outperforming benchmark index
- Outperforming sectoral index
- Both SRS and ARS above Zero

Fundamental scans:

- High return on equity (ROE>15%)
- Consistent sales growth ratio (annual report) (positive for last 4 financial years)
- Consistent cash from operations (positive for last 5 years and at least 10% growth per year)
- Increase in institutional shareholding

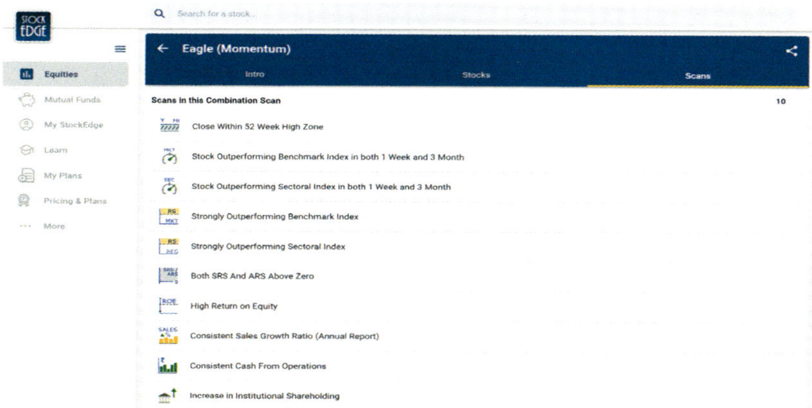

Table 4.18 Eagle scan to identify stocks that are in momentum

Let's understand the individual scans added to the combo. Starting with technical scans:

1. Close within 52-week high zone
2. The relative performance scans:
    a. Stocks outperforming benchmark index in 1 week and 3 months. The theory behind this is if a stock has been outperforming the benchmark index in 3 months and 1 week now, then the stock has been strong for some time and is still in momentum.
    b. Stock outperforming sectoral index in 1 week and 3 months—a strong stock would not only beat the benchmark index, but also its sectoral index.
3. The RS55 filters:
    a. RS55>0 (the one that we've already discussed)—strongly outperforms benchmark index and the sectoral index.
    b. SRS and ARS are types of relative strength (RS) created by one of my favourite RS practitioners, Premal Parekh. SRS stands for static RS and ARS stands for adaptive RS, and both are momentum indicators signalling that when SRS and ARS >0, the stock is in momentum.

Now let's come to the fundamental scans.

The Relevance of Institutional Shareholding

Institutional investors are large entities like mutual funds, pension funds and insurance companies that invest huge sums of money, often influencing the market with their decisions. Whenever a large institutional investor adds their position in a stock, it reflects the confidence of these large, resourceful investors in a company's future. This provides stability to the stock price and often signifies a thorough vetting process that reassures smaller investors about the company's quality and potential, making it a fundamentally good pick. Such institutions would typically increase the shareholding when they're still bullish on the stock.

When we combine all the scans, we get a list of companies that have been fundamentally good with an anticipation of more upside coupled with strong momentum in the stock.

Trading in such powerful stocks can generate high returns; moreover, even if the stock corrects (not attributed to fundamental changes in the company), it would be an opportunity to add to the position.

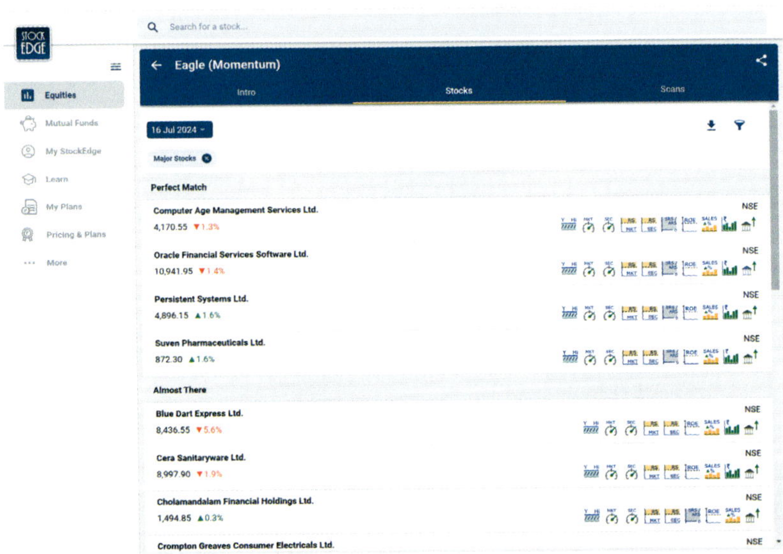

Table 4.19 List of eagle stocks

Let's look at the chart of the first stock in the list (reference Table 4.19), Computer Age Management Services (CAMS).

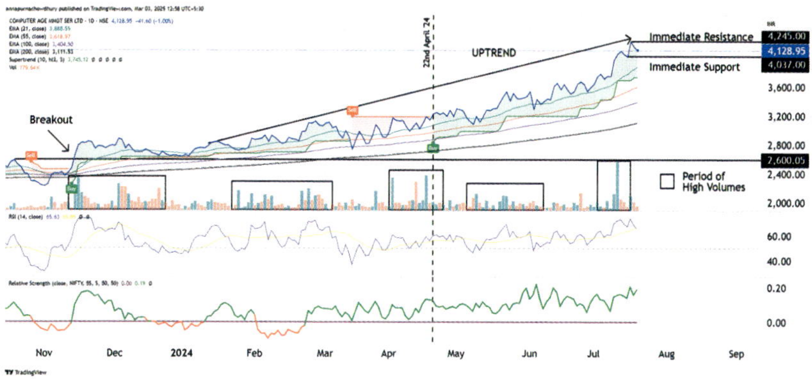

Figure 4.21 Daily chart of Computer Age Management Services (CAMS)

As observed in Figure 4.21, after a brief consolidation, the stock gave a breakout on 22 April 2024, at the 3201 level and the supertrend became positive after 2 trading sessions. The stock has been making new highs and new lows since then. The stock is trading at the 4129 level as on 19 July 2024 while the immediate resistance is at the 4245 level, and immediate support is at the 4037 level. Moreover, the stock is fulfilling the following criterion:

- stock is in uptrend;
- high volume and delivery;
- price is above all EMAs, and all the shorter tenure EMA is also trading above longer tenure EMA;
- supertrend is buy;
- RSI 14>50;
- RS55>0.

This is a perfect stock to add to the radar. Risk would be 4129 – 4037 = 92, while potential reward could be 4245 – 4129 = 120, making the risk-reward ratio 120:92 = 1.30:1. The risk-reward ratio is not favourable, hence we will wait.

The stock has been strong since mid-November 2023 around the 2600 level oscillating in phase 1. Though it did give a correction, it never transitioned into a downtrend, and eventually transitioned to phase 2. Such is the power of eagle stocks; even if the stock corrects, a strong stock should bounce back from its support zone.

Financial Improvement with Price Action (FIPA) Stocks

A company exhibiting improvement in financial performance, supported by price action has high potential of a larger upmove. A good way to filter such potential candidates is by examining the quarterly performance of companies. Stocks show sustainable swings when supported by strong fundamentals. Additionally, price action combined with relative strength further increases the probability of success in identifying promising stocks.

I have created a combo scan that helps me identify FIPA stocks:

Price scans:

- Close within 52-week high zone

Fundamental scans:

- Improved return on equity
- Improved return on capital employed
- Quarterly net profit growth YoY (growth of >=20% from same quarter last year)
- Quarterly EBITDA growth YoY (growth of >=5% than same quarter last year)
- High increase in quarterly sales YoY (results)
- Consistent cash from operations (positive for last 5 years)

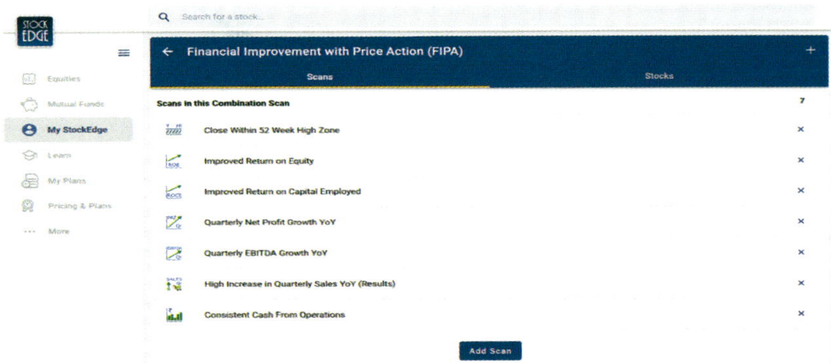

Table 4.20 FIPA scan

Let's look at the list of stocks that we get from the scan.

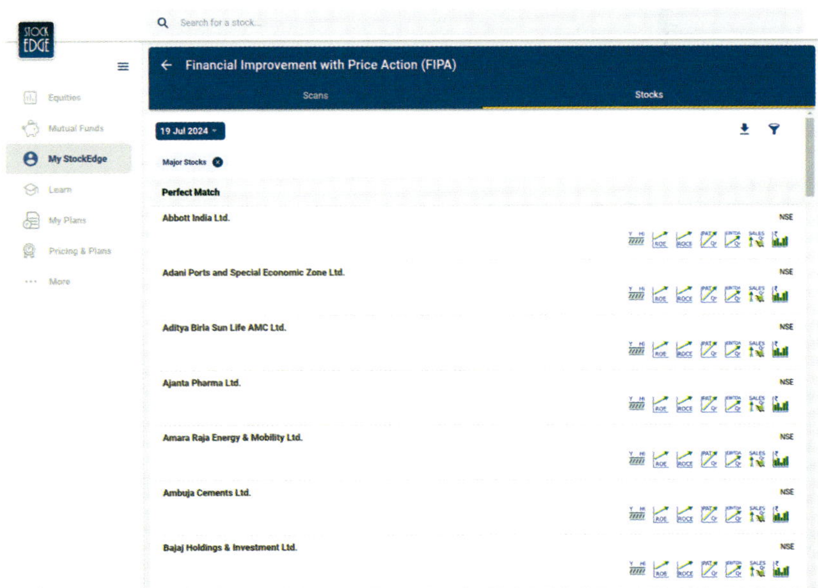

Table 4.21 List of stocks under FIPA scan

Let's look at the chart of the first stock in the list, Abbott India.

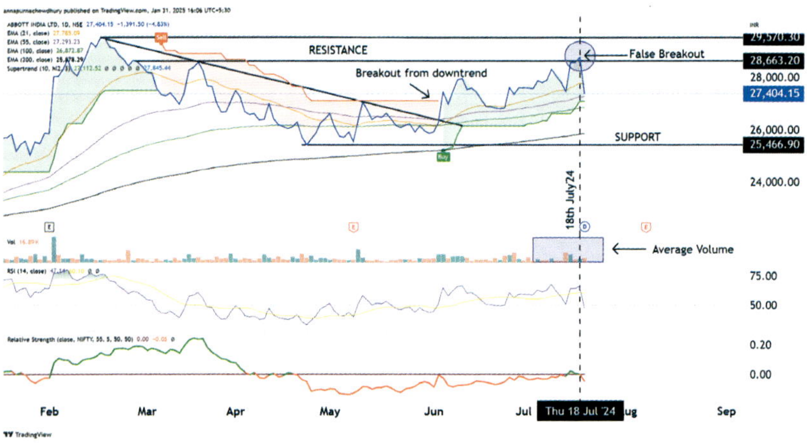

Figure 4.22 Daily chart of Abbott India

As observed in Figure 4.22, the stock transitioned to an uptrend from downtrend in June 2024. Let us evaluate whether the stock is fulfilling all our other criteria:

- stock is in uptrend;
- average volume in the past few trading sessions;
- price is taking support at 55-day EMA;
- supertrend is buy;
- RSI>50 is not met;
- RS55>0 is not met.

The stock is trading at the 27,404 level as on 19 July 2024, even though the stock has taken support near its previous swing low and supertrend is still buy, but RSI is below 50 and RS is not positive as per our setup. Additionally, the recent breakout attempt on 18 July 2024 was not supported by volume, making it a failed breakout, post which the stock moved past its 21-day EMA and took support at 55-day EMA. So as of now, we will not be positive in the stock, till most of the indicators give a green signal.

However, I would like to highlight another scenario. Let's assume that we're seeing the chart on 15 July 2024, when the stock was attempting a breakout above 28,663 level. On that day, the price action was supported by above-average volumes, supertrend was buy, price was above all EMAs and the shorter tenure EMAs were above the larger tenure EMAs, RS55 and RSI were all giving green signals. The stock was fitting into our setup perfectly, making it tempting for traders to punch the trade; however, the risk-reward on that level was equivalent to 1 as there is resistance on 29,570 level. A disciplined trader would have waited till the risk-reward was favourable for him to initiate the trade. The act of being disciplined saved him from getting trapped into a failed breakout setup and incurring a loss. That is the power of discipline.

Let's take another stock from the list, Aditya Birla Sun Life AMC.

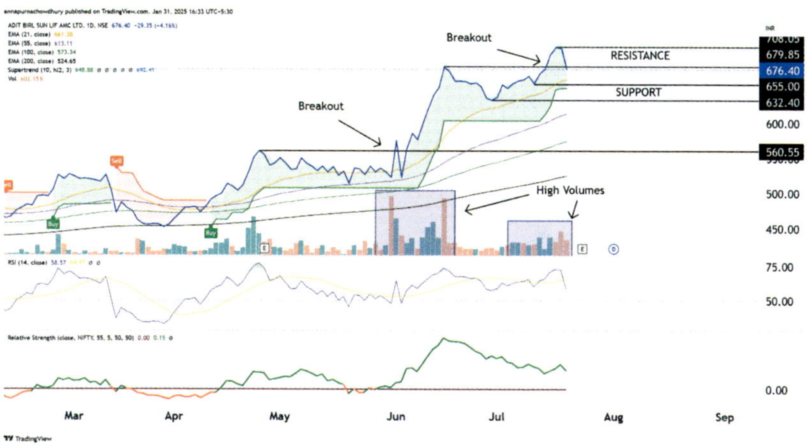

Figure 4.23 Daily chart of Aditya Birla Sun Life AMC (ABSLAMC)

Observe Figure 4.23: the stock is trading at 676 level and:

- stock is in uptrend;
- high volume and delivery;

- price is above 21-EMA, and all the shorter tenure EMAs are also trading above longer tenure EMAs;
- supertrend is buy;
- RSI>50; and
- RS55>0.

As observed in Figure 4.23, ABSLAMC fulfils all our criteria and fits perfectly into our setup, making it the ideal candidate to add to the tracker. The stock is currently retracing and could potentially bounce back from either its 21-day EMA, the supertrend line or its price-based demand zone. The immediate support level is at 655 while the resistance stands at the 708 level, making the risk-reward less than 2:1 but more than 1:1. For now, let's just say that this is a good stock to add to the tracker.

Let's move on to the next scan.

Capital Expenditure (Capex) + Earnings + Price Action (CEPA) Stocks

We're aware of the relevance of earnings to identify fundamentally strong companies. Now let's understand the meaning of capital expenditure or capex.

Capital expenditures (capex) refer to the one-time expenditure that a company incurs to acquire, upgrade and maintain physical assets such as property, buildings, technology or equipment. These are long-term investments that are expected to improve efficiency, increase production or support expansion into new markets.

High capex often indicates that a company is investing in its future growth. Such companies usually have strong financial health and access to capital. Moreover, companies that continually invest in capex can maintain or improve their market position by staying ahead of competitors in terms of technology and infrastructure.

Suppose a tech company like Tata Consultancy Services (TCS) announces it is investing heavily in new data centres and advanced AI technology. This capex investment signals that TCS is preparing for future growth and wants to enhance its service capabilities. For investors, this can be a sign that the company is positioning itself for long-term success and staying competitive in the rapidly evolving tech industry.

Technically speaking, companies with capex plans tend to outperform in the long term, and the last 3 years increase in asset base is a good proxy to identify capex. Additionally, sector-level capex boost can lead to a broader market participation. When supported by price action, such stocks have potential to give a big rally.

I have created a scan to help identify such CEPA companies:

Price scans:

- Close within 52-week high zone

Fundamental scans:

- High return on equity (ROE >15%)
- High return on capital employed (ROCE >15%)
- High EBITDA margin (EBITDA margin >20%)
- Consistently high EBITDA margins (EBITDA margin >15% for last 4 financial years)
- Consistently high ROCE (ROCE >15% for last 4 financial years)
- Consistently high ROE (ROE >15% for last 4 financial years)
- Consistent cash from operations (positive for past 5 years)

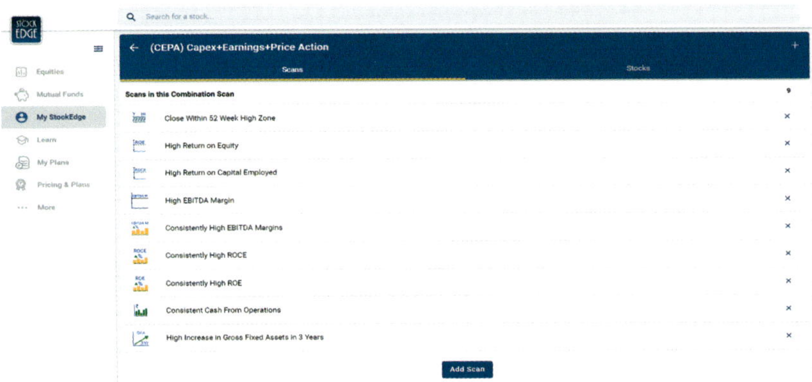

Table 4.22 List of scans under CEPA

Let's look at the list of stocks that we get from the scan.

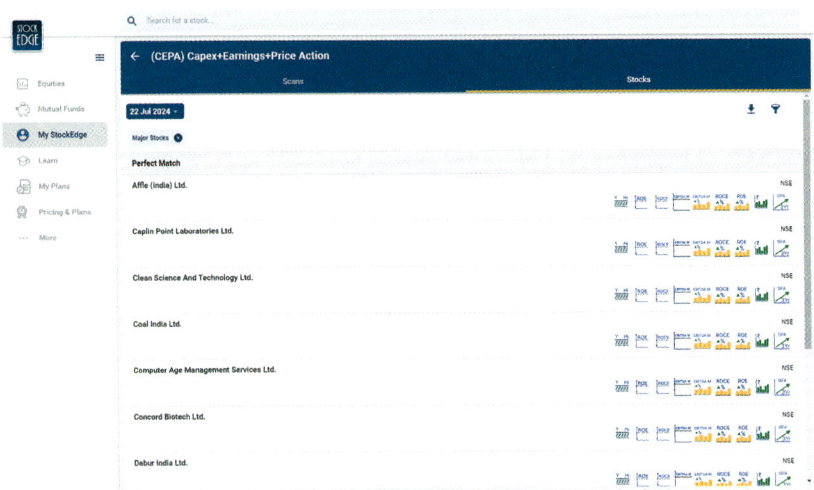

Table 4.23 List of stocks under CEPA scan

Let's look at the chart of Affle India.

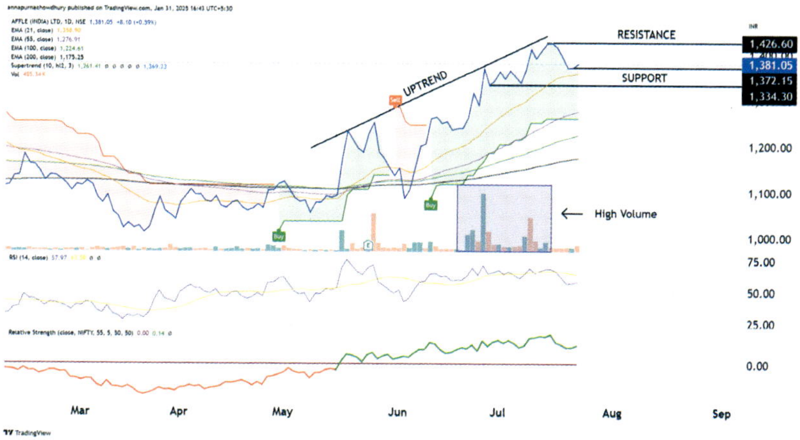

Figure 4.24 Daily chart of Affle India

Observe in Figure 4.24, the stock is trading at the 1381 level as on 23 July 2024 with immediate support at the 1372 level, resistance at 1426 level and

- stock is in uptrend;
- has high volume and delivery;
- price is above 21-EMA, and all the shorter tenure EMA is also trading above longer tenure EMA;
- supertrend is buy;
- RSI>50; and
- RS55>0.

Affle is fulfilling all our criteria and fitting perfectly in our setup. The stock has been in uptrend since 22 March 2024 and after a small correction in June 2024, the stock sustained its swings and went on to make higher highs supported by high volumes and delivery, maintaining its uptrend. The stock faced a resistance at 1426 and came down to take support at the 1372 level. Since the stock is trading near its support zone, the risk-reward is favourable at the current price point making the stock a perfect candidate to trade. The stock can either go up or down from the current level of 1381.

Let's move on to the next scan.

Tiger Stocks

Tiger is symbolic of strength and opportunity. It represents stealth and only attacks at the right time. Similarly, tiger stocks are powerful internally but only move when the opportunity is right. I have created a scan to help identify such tiger companies:

Price scans:

- Stock outperforming benchmark index both in 1 week and 3 months

Fundamental scans:

- Consistently high EBITDA margins (EBITDA margin >15% for last 4 financial years)
- Consistently high PAT margins (PAT margin >10% for the last 4 financial years. PAT stands for profit after tax which measures the profit earned after deducting all taxes, depreciations, interests, while PAT margin is the profit expressed as a percentage of revenue)
- Consistently high ROCE (ROCE >15% for last 4 financial years)
- Consistently high ROE (ROE >15% for last 4 financial years)
- Consistent positive free cash flow/share, i.e., cash left over after the company pays for its operating expenses and capital expenditures. (Free cash flow for last 4 financial years)

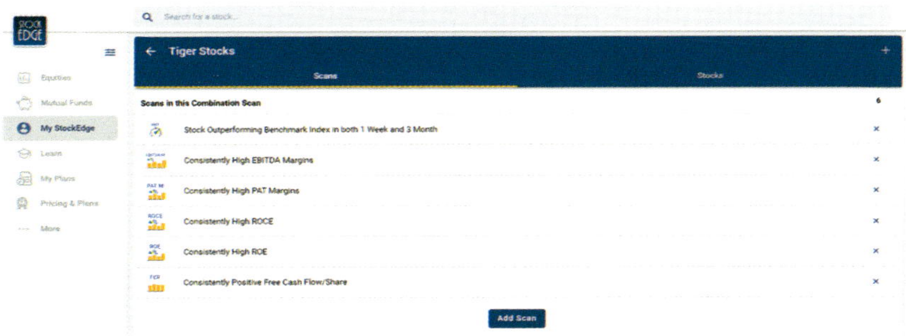

Table 4.24 List of scans to identify tiger stocks

Let's look at the list of stocks under tiger scan:

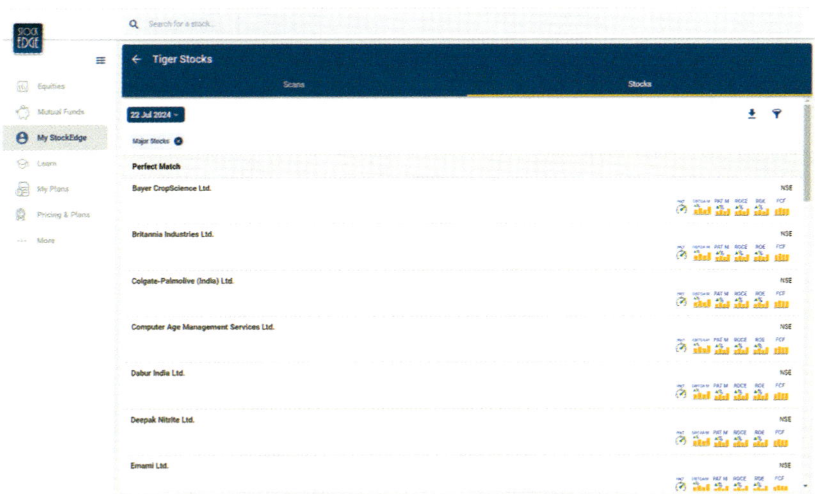

Table 4.25 List of stocks under the tiger scan

Let's look at the chart of Bayer CropScience Ltd.

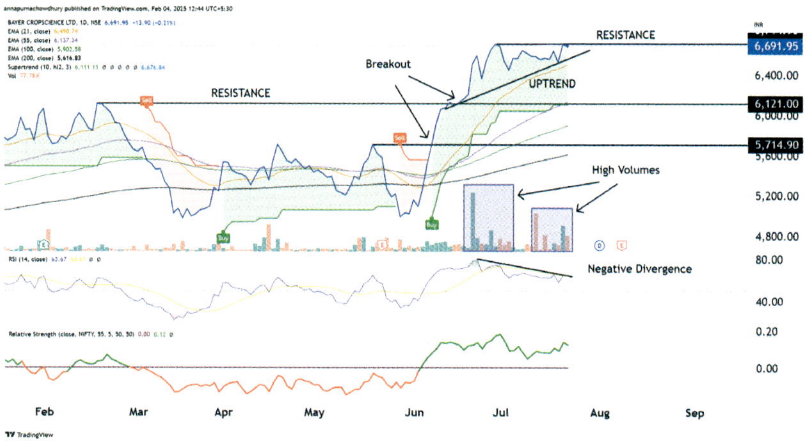

Figure 4.25 Daily chart of Bayer CropScience Ltd

Observe in Figure 4.25, the stock is trading at the 6692 level, its resistance level and immediate support at the 6520 level, while the stock is

- in uptrend;
- has high volume and delivery;
- price is above 21-EMA, and all the shorter tenure EMA is also trading above longer tenure EMA;
- supertrend is buy;
- RSI>50; and
- RS55>0.

All the technical indicators for the stock are positive, and there is strong momentum in the stock. However, there is a resistance formed at the 6700 level, from where the stock has been facing rejection.

Additionally, the RSI is in a downtrend while the price is on uptrend, indicating negative divergence. As traders it's best to avoid stocks that are sending mixed signals. In such cases, we wait for price action to confirm a move, with all indicators aligning. Till then, we wait and observe.

Let's take another stock, Britannia Industries.

Figure 4.26 Daily chart of Britannia Industries

Observe in Figure 4.26, the stock is trading at the 5887 level as on 22 July 2024 at an all-time high level and potential support is around the 5758 level and 5520 level, and

- stock is in uptrend;
- has high volume and delivery;
- price is above 21-EMA, and all the shorter tenure EMA is also trading above longer tenure EMA;
- supertrend is buy;

- RSI>50; and
- RS55>0.

The stock is fulfilling all the criteria and looks to be a perfect stock to add to the radar. Now will we trade in the stock at the current level? No. Even though the stock looks strong and is in momentum, the risk-reward is not favourable. The stock has been making higher highs and higher lows consecutively for the past 12 sessions, which is a very unnatural move for a stock. Moreover, notice that RSI is near 80, entering an overbought zone, some correction could be due in the stock. If the stock still maintains its strength, then it might enter a consolidation phase. To judge the next direction of the stock movement, we have to wait for the price action. Till then, we add the stock to the radar, and enter when the price and the technical indicators are all aligned along with a favourable risk-reward ratio.

High on Life Stocks

Another one of my favourite scans are the stocks that are high on life. A person is high on life when they're very happy in their life and living life to the fullest. Similarly high on life stocks are those stocks who have passed the test of time and are still standing tall, and enjoying high profitability at a good price.

I have created a scan to help identify such high on life companies:

Price scans:

- Close within all-time high zone

Fundamental scans:

- Highest quarterly EBITDA in last 10 years
- Highest annual EBITDA in last 10 years
- Highest quarterly net profit in last 10 years (net profit is the same as PAT)
- Highest annual net profit in last 10 years
- Highest quarterly sales in last 10 years
- Highest annual CFO in last 10 years

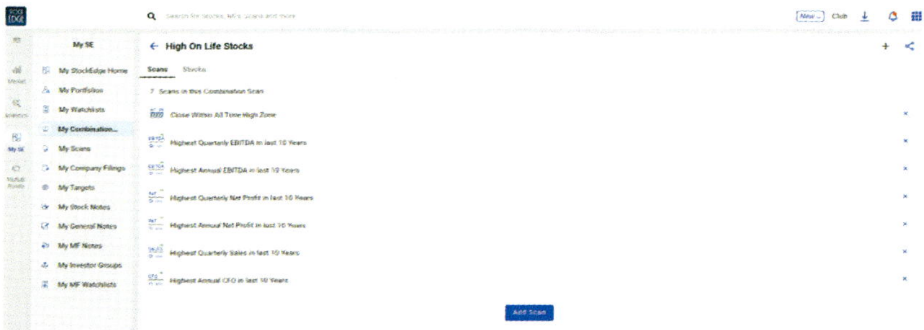

Table 4.26 List of scans to identify high on life stocks

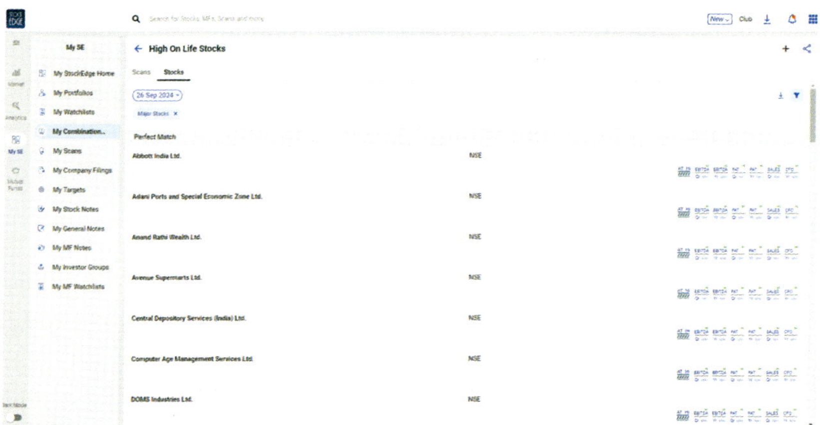

Table 4.27 List of stocks under the high on life scan

Abbott India and Adani Ports are the top 2 stocks in the scan. Recall that these 2 stocks were also identified by the FIPA Scan. Since we've already covered Abbott, let's take Anand Rathi Wealth.

In the Figure 4.27, observe that stock has been in consolidation since the end of April 2024, and has been moving in the range of 3568 and 4200, the levels being support and resistance respectively. The stock

- is in consolidation mode;
- has average volume;
- price is right above 21-EMA, and all the shorter tenure EMAs are also trading above longer tenure EMAs;

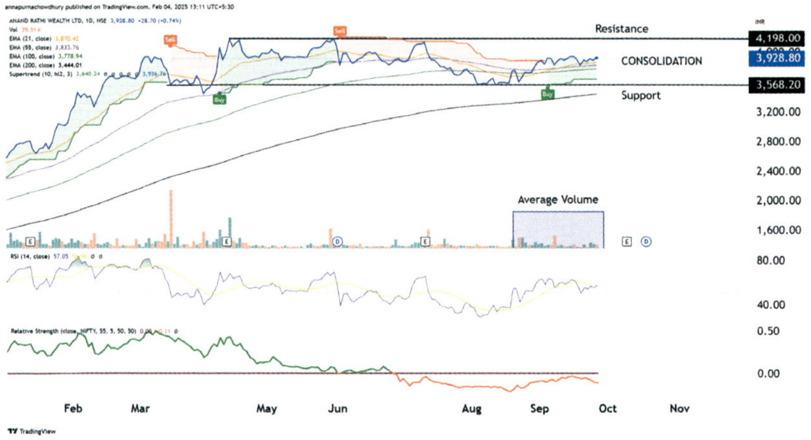

Figure 4.27 Daily chart of Anand Rathi Wealth

- supertrend is buy;
- RSI 14>50; but
- RS55>0 not met.

The stock is not fitting well into our template, making us move on from the stock to another. Let's take the example of Avenue Supermarts now:

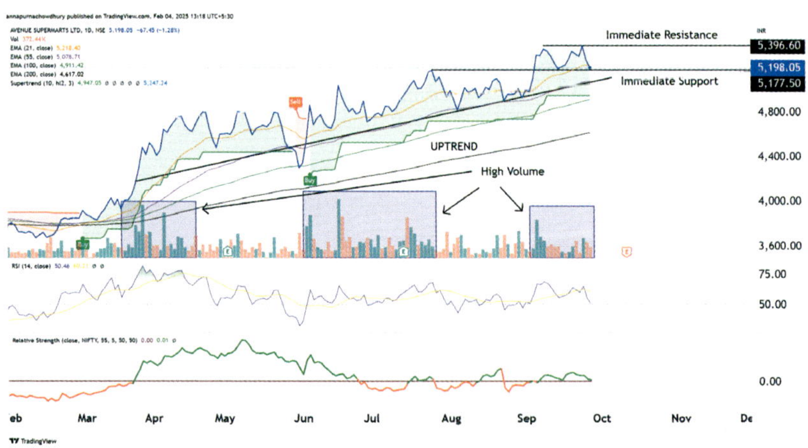

Figure 4.28 Daily chart of Avenue Supermarts Ltd

In Figure 4.28, the stock is trading at the 5198 level as on 27 September 2024, with the immediate resistance being at the 5396 level and support at the 5177 level. The stock is trading right at the support level and

- stock is in uptrend;
- has high volume and delivery;
- price is right below 21-EMA, and all the shorter tenure EMAs are trading above longer tenure EMAs;
- supertrend is buy;
- RSI 14>50; and
- RS55>0.

The stock has been in uptrend since March 2024, almost 6 months as on 27 September 2024. Even though the RSI 14 is just at the 50 level, and RS55 is just near 0, yet the overall setup looks very good in the stock. If the stock is strong, the RSI and RS can reverse anytime showing momentum and fulfilling all our criteria. A very interesting observation in this chart is the cluster of high-volume zones when the stock was in a strong uptrend. Whenever the stock was giving a breakout and making higher highs, it was supported by continuous high volumes, whereas the volumes were average when the stock was range-bound. As a result, the stock was able to sustain its upmove; that is the power of volumes in a chart. With proper volume analysis, you can easily filter out strong stocks. We will definitely keep this stock on our radar, and enter at a favourable risk-reward level.

These are a few of the combo scans that I use in my daily trading journey to identify strong stocks that are in momentum.

I have shared the scans that work for me best, but something else could work for you better than it does for me.

As a beginner, you can start with these combo scans, although I would highly recommend creating your own combo scans. It has taken me a lot of trial and error and experience in the market to create my own combo scans. Till date, I keep changing and updating the scans when I feel the need. There are numerous scans in StockEdge that you can use to create your own winning combo scan. Start tracking the stocks that appear in these scans and making a judgement of its potential move.

When you start practicing this frequently, you will notice that a few stocks appear commonly among most of the combo scans. Conviction to trade in such stocks is naturally higher.

We need to import the entire list of combo scans into TradingView and track the charts of all the stocks to identify the perfect candidate for our trades. Remember that there will be times when all the stocks look tempting to add to the portfolio; that is when we need to reject stocks brutally even for not fulfilling the minutest of parameters, a trait that you need to inculcate to become a pro trader.

You need to give in time and effort on each list of stocks that you get from these scans. There is no shortcut to success. However, there is a tool that can help you identify winning stocks with a lot less effort; that's the one that StockEdge has built using Artificial Intelligence. It is called the Chart Pattern Recognition Tool.

SUMMARY

- Eagle stocks are symbols of power and strength, representing stocks with hyper momentum that outperform the market and have the potential to soar above others.
- Financial improvement with price action (FIPA) stocks are companies with improving financial performance and positive price action, indicating a high potential for upward movement.
- Capital expenditure (capex) + earnings + price action (CEPA) stocks focus on companies with strong capex, solid earnings, and supportive price action, indicating potential for long-term growth and strong market performance.
- Tiger stocks are fundamentally strong but wait for the right market conditions to make significant moves.
- High on life stocks have endured market challenges, proven their resilience and continue to maintain high profitability while trading at good price levels.
- Take the list of the stocks that fulfil the criteria of either of the combo scans, import the list in TradingView and track the charts.
- If a stock appears in most of the combo scans, then the conviction to trade in such stock will also be higher.
- We will only trade in stocks that fulfil our criteria and has a favourable risk and reward.

LEARNER'S CORNER

Are there any other fundamental parameters that I should consider while making a techno-funda scan?

You may consider any other fundamental parameter that suits you. I have created my combo scans as per what I feel is important to identify fundamentally strong companies. Feel free to add parameters that you feel are reflective of a fundamentally strong company. However my advice would be to keep a limit to the number of fundamental parameters you add. We cannot have 15 parameters and expect a company to fulfil all of them. No company is perfect. Hence, keep around 4 to 6 fundamental parameters and 4 to 6 technical parameters, making it 10 parameters in total. This balance ensures that your scan is both effective and manageable.

Can I just create a combo scan with the technical parameters?

Yes, you may create a combo scan with only technical parameters. However, I would recommend that you trade in such stocks for a shorter trade tenure. Longer trade tenures need some fundamental backing for it to sustain the uptrend.

How many scans should I have in a combo?

A good number would be between 5 and 10. Any number less than 5 would give you a very long list of stocks, both bad and good, making it an inefficient and a very time-consuming affair, whereas any number more than 10 would give you a very limited stock list to work on, making you miss other good opportunities. You would want a decent number of stocks to track on a daily basis.

Chart Pattern Recognition Tool

There is a pattern in everything around us, including the stock market. The price actions are symbolically identified through chart patterns and is a science comprehensively used by successful traders as a part of their strategy. They provide insights into market trends and potential price movements. When used correctly and in conjunction with other analytical methods, they can significantly enhance a trader's ability to make informed and strategic decisions. However, only knowledge of chart patterns is not enough. While tracking the charts, we need to identify if there is any pattern being formed, and if yes, then which one. Additionally, the right method to draw such patterns is crucial to ace this study. Just this study could take weeks to perfect, making it highly effortful and time-consuming.

To simplify this further, there is a tool that automatically identifies if there is any chart pattern being formed in any of the listed stocks. As traders, you can make a separate list of the stocks where a bullish chart pattern has been formed. Some traders trade solely based on chart patterns; however, I feel that chart patterns should be used just like other technical indicators to build conviction in a stock. For example, if National Aluminium Company Ltd (NALCO) is appearing in most of our combo scans, supported by high volume and delivery and fits perfectly in our setup with favourable risk-reward, moreover a bullish chart pattern has been recently formed in the stock, then it builds the conviction to trade in the stock.

As traders you cannot trade in all the stocks that fulfil your criteria and fit perfectly in the trade setup; you will need to pick and choose stocks with higher conviction. Such a tool helps the traders to build conviction in the already filtered stocks.

How Does It Work?

StockEdge has this tool. I'm not sure which other analytics platforms provide this, but you're free to use any other tool.

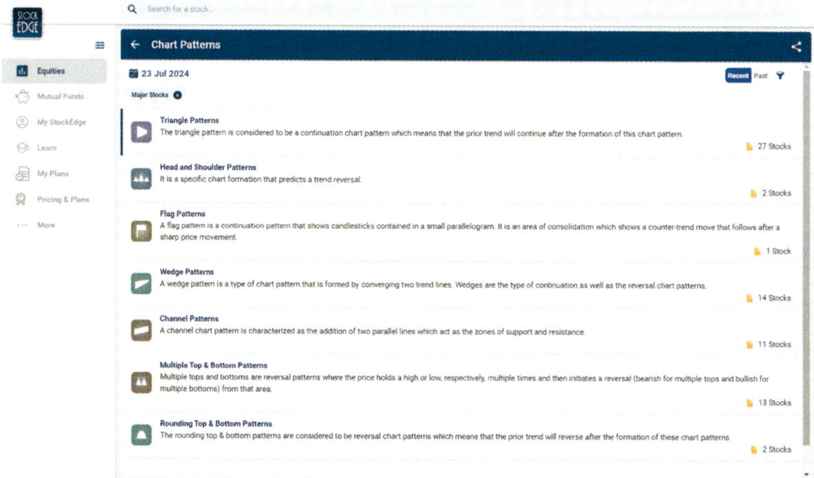

Table 4.28 List of chart patterns that StockEdge can identify in stocks

In Table 4.28 we have the list of the chart patterns that StockEdge can automatically identify when one is formed. Let's take the first one, triangle patterns, as an example.

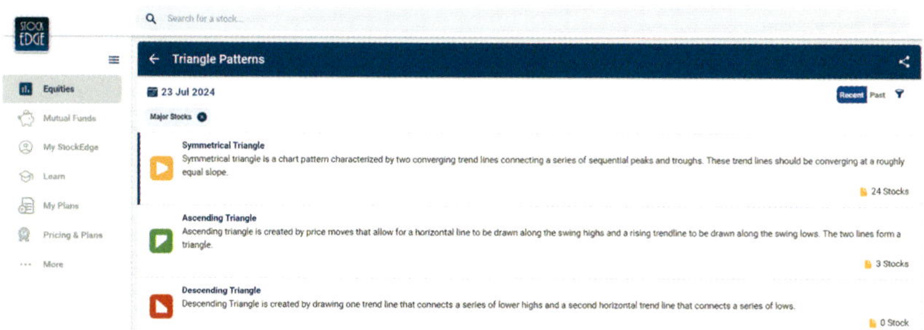

Table 4.29 Types of triangle patterns in StockEdge

In Table 4.29, we have the list of the different types of triangle patterns that StockEdge can identify when formed in a listed stock. There are 3 triangle patterns:

- Symmetrical Triangle: Indicates a continuation pattern till the price moves above or beyond the pattern. If the price breaks the pattern at the upper right corner with an upmove, it hints at a bullish breakout, whereas if the price breaks the pattern by moving below it at the bottom right corner, it hints at a bearish breakdown.

- Ascending Triangle: Indicates a bullish continuation pattern formed when the stock is in uptrend. As soon as the price breaks out from the top right corner, the stock gives a breakout indicating another rally.
- Descending Triangle: Indicates a bearish continuation pattern formed when the stock is in downtrend. As soon as the price breaks down from the bottom right corner, the stock confirms another breakdown, indicating further downtrend in the stock.

Let's look at the stocks where such chart patterns have been identified:

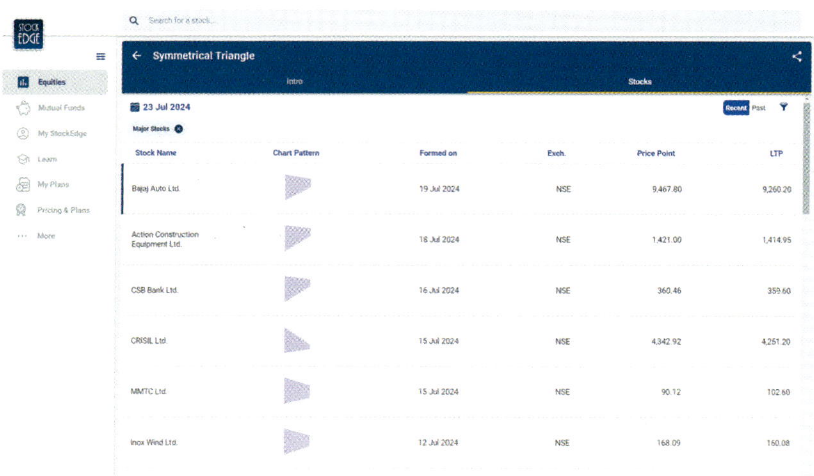

Stock Name	Chart Pattern	Formed on	Exch.	Price Point	LTP
Bajaj Auto Ltd.		19 Jul 2024	NSE	9,467.80	9,260.20
Action Construction Equipment Ltd.		18 Jul 2024	NSE	1,421.00	1,414.95
CSB Bank Ltd.		16 Jul 2024	NSE	360.46	359.60
CRISIL Ltd.		15 Jul 2024	NSE	4,342.92	4,251.20
MMTC Ltd.		15 Jul 2024	NSE	90.12	102.60
Inox Wind Ltd.		12 Jul 2024	NSE	168.09	160.08

Table 4.30 List of stocks where symmetrical triangle has formed

Let's look at the chart of Bajaj Auto.

Figure 4.29 Symmetrical triangle being formed in Bajaj Auto on 19 July 2024

Observe Figure 4.29; there was a symmetrical triangle identified in Bajaj Auto on 19 July 2024. The stock was range-bound, till the price broke the pattern from bottom right corner, hinting at a bearish breakdown in the stock. Let's look at the chart of MMTC.

Figure 4.30 Symmetrical triangle being formed in MMTC Ltd on 15 July 2024

Observed in Figure 4.30, MMTC was in a long consolidation phase till the price broke the pattern at the top right corner with a strong upmove, indicating a bullish breakout above the 90 level on 15 July 2024. The stock is trading at the 102 level as on 24 July 2024, an upmove of more than 10%, in roughly 6 trading sessions. Let's look at the chart on our setup:

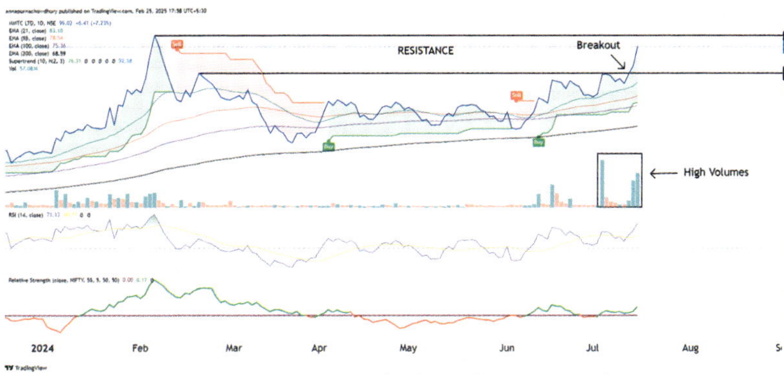

Figure 4.31 Daily chart of MMTC Ltd

Observe the daily chart of MMTC Ltd in Figure 4.31; the stock has been in uptrend since 18 June 2024, giving a price breakout above the 80 level, supported by tall volume bars and

- price is above 21-EMA, and all the shorter tenure EMA is also trading above longer tenure EMA;
- supertrend is buy;
- RSI>50; and
- RS55>0.

The stock kept making higher highs and higher lows with each new swing, supported by high volumes with each big price upmove, demonstrating the strength in the stock. The stock had already given a breakout on 12 July 2024, the prior trading day, a Friday, above the 86 level, making it the perfect stock for trading.

The idea was to show you how the chart pattern recognition tool works and can be used to reject/select stocks to trade. In case a stock was filtered through the eagle scan, but you see a bearish chart pattern being formed, then it's best to avoid that stock, and rather focus on a stock that's common across most of your combo scans; a bullish chart pattern at that moment will be a bonus and add conviction to trade in the stock.

Like food is a primary need for any being, so is identifying stocks for a trader. Identifying and trading in the right stocks is just like having a balanced meal. Turtles understand the need of different types of food and use appropriate scavenging styles. Similarly, as a trader, depending on various external factors, you can choose trades and align your strategies to them.

You need to develop a hunger to identify stocks to get a step closer to getting the turtle mindset. Just like turtles display different scavenging styles, from actively hunting to grazing, as a trader, you need to develop your own hunger for identifying the right stocks. Whether you're actively searching for high-potential opportunities or patiently waiting for the right conditions, your approach should align with your trading style. This hunger for spotting the best trades drives your success, just as the turtle's instincts guide it to the best food sources.

The most important part of stock selection is to build conviction in the stocks. A trader needs to adapt their art of selecting stocks as per the market conditions. In case of a bull run in the market, you will face a problem of plenty when most stocks fit perfectly into the setup supported by high volume and delivery, but there's a limit to the number of stocks that you can participate in. As traders, you need to be ruthless and reject stocks in such a case, even for what may seem as the smallest of reasons. On the contrary, during the bear market, you will face a market condition when none of the stocks perfectly fit into your setup. Such market conditions compel traders to trade in stocks that fulfil most if not all of their filters.

That being said, you will only learn how to adapt to the different market conditions with experience and trial and error. As a professional mentor, I can teach you when to be cautious and when to go all in, but *to make big money from the market, you need to be prepared to lose some, and that will be your learning cost to the market.*

SUMMARY

- Chart patterns are a deep and lengthy study that takes months to master.
- An automatic tool to identify chart patterns takes minutes and helps build conviction in stocks to trade.

5

Strategies That Work

> 'You have to be willing to adapt your strategy as market conditions change. Rigid systems will eventually fail.'
>
> —*Bruce Kovner*[1]

Strategies are crucial, not just in trading but in any business or employment. Everything we've covered so far are tools that traders need to understand and use effectively. However, without the right strategy, i.e., knowing when to enter and exit a trade with the appropriate capital, you could still lose money, even in winning stocks. This is why having a strategy that suits your risk appetite and helps you make money is essential for success in trading and in life.

Moreover, a well-defined strategy provides consistency and discipline, helping in mitigating emotional decisions that can lead to costly mistakes. It allows you to set clear goals, measure performance and adjust your approach based on market conditions. In essence, a robust strategy acts as a roadmap, increasing your chances of achieving long-term success. To bring your strategy to life, you need a trading system.

A trading system is a guideline made of certain rules a trader sets for themselves to help navigate the different market conditions. One may choose to have different strategies for different market conditions, and these strategies make up their trading system. These may change over time with experience and market conditions but broadly define how he/she would react to situations so as to keep emotions at bay.

This is where adopting the turtle mindset plays the most important role. Turtles are known to survive and adapt in varied conditions: deserts, forests, rivers, oceans. Moreover, they exhibit slow, methodical persistence when navigating obstacles, rarely giving up. Your trading system should be such that it is able to adapt to different market conditions—whether bullish, bearish or sideways. The key is to remain persistent and patient, adjusting your approach as needed.

> The best traders aren't afraid. They aren't cocky either. They are confident and disciplined.
>
> —Mark Douglas, author

Let's start with strategizing how to apply the most important tool in trading—stop loss.

Stop Loss and Capital Allocation

To reiterate the concept of stop loss, let us remember that it is a powerful tool where you decide a pre-set level to exit a stock. It helps you limit your losses and in turn saves your capital from bleeding out when your trades go wrong. If you wish to become a successful trader, the most important thing is to respect the stop loss (SL), i.e., accept the loss when it's triggered, exit the stock and move on. While it may sound simple in theory, applying this principle is much more difficult. If you've been trading with real capital, you know exactly what I mean. Respecting a stop loss is something that no guru can teach you, but yourself, and discipline is the key to respecting your stop loss.

There are different methods of setting a stop loss. I'm going to share all the methods that should work, but in the end, you need to practice and apply the ones that help in keeping your mental peace intact.

You can use the following methods to keep a stop loss:

- Capital-based stop loss
- Price-based stop loss
- Indicator-based stop loss

Capital-Based Stop Loss

Let us assume that your trading capital is Rs 10 lakh and you decide you are comfortable with 1% loss per trade (that is, Rs 10,000 per trade). Now, if you take 10 trades and all go wrong, your total loss would be 10% of your capital (which is Rs 1 lakh).

Suppose you set 0.5% as the maximum loss on one trade, i.e., Rs 5,000 on a capital of total 10 lakh. Then it will take 20 consecutive loss-making trades to lose that 1 lakh.

Changing the percentage of stop loss per trade gives you an opportunity to take more trades with your capital.

Stop loss = (Capital allocated in a stock – amount stop loss you can bear)/number of shares.

Let us consider:

Parameter	Value	Formula
Total capital (Rs)	10,00,000	
Loss percentage per trade (%)	0.50%	
Amount of loss per trade (Rs)	5,000	Total capital * loss % per trade
Total loss tolerance (%)	10%	
Total loss tolerance (Rs)	1,00,000	10% of total capital
Number of consecutive losses that will exhaust the total loss tolerance	20	Total loss/loss per trade
Example (MMTC):		
Capital allocated per trade (Rs)	1,00,000	
Share price (Rs)	120	
No. of shares	833	Investment per trade/share price
Amount of loss per trade (Rs)	5,000	Investment per trade * Loss percentage per trade (0.50%)
Stop loss level (Rs)	114	(Investment per trade-loss per trade)/no. of shares
or, simply:		
Amount of loss per trade (Rs)	5,000	
Loss per share we can bear (Rs)	6	Loss per trade/no. of shares
Therefore, stop-loss level (Rs)	114	Stock price-loss per share

Table 5.1

In this approach you fix a loss percentage of the total capital per trade that you can bear without losing your confidence or taking a hard financial hit, and calculate stop loss in each trade accordingly.

Price-Based Stop Loss

This stop loss is purely based on the price action of the stock. A price movement of the stock that makes you uncomfortable and makes you lose your confidence in the stock could be the stop loss. It could be a crucial support level, previous swing low, day's low, week's VWAP, day's VWAP or any other important price level.

A stock that's in uptrend makes new highs and new lows with each new swing. During this phenomenon, the highs and lows of the previous swings become crucial for traders. The stock is expected to at least take support at previous swing low, if not make a higher low to continue to be in uptrend. When the stock breaks the previous swing low, that could be an indication of the break in the uptrend, as retail traders who have participated in the stock could lose their confidence in the stock and drive it further down. It could be an onset of either a sideways trend or a downtrend. Hence, the previous swing low could be a good stop loss.

Similarly, you can consider the following price points as stop loss:

- Day's low
- Week's low
- Day's VWAP
- Week's VWAP
- Fibonacci levels

Figure 5.1 Daily chart of Zomato

Suppose you bought Zomato on 2 August 2024 at the closing price of Rs 262, then a potential stop loss could be the low of the candle on the same day, i.e., Rs 243. You exit the trade as soon as the price breaks this level.

The most commonly used stop loss is generally the high and low of the candle in which you enter.

If you feel that breaking day's low is okay for a stock and cannot be a stop loss, then you can choose any other price action-based stop loss. Seeking comfort and confidence is most important while setting stop loss. Any price-based movement that makes you lose your confidence in the stock could be your stop loss.

Indicator-Based Stop Loss

The third approach is the indicator driven stop loss. Levels defined by each indicator are also important price levels and more often than not act as strong support and resistance levels for the stock. Let's consider the exponential moving averages (EMAs). We've covered 21, 55, 100, 200 period EMAs, and as we're well aware that these EMAs also act as support level, so you could keep the level of 21-day EMA as stop loss. You can also choose to keep one of the following as stop loss:

- supertrend level;
- when RSI 14 goes below 50;
- when RS55 goes below 0;
- lower band in bollinger band.

Let us take another example: Hindustan Unilever.

Observe in Figure 5.2: the supertrend is giving a buy signal and if you have bought this stock at the 2711 level, the current market price (CMP) as on 26 July 2024, then the stop loss can be the 21-day EMA, i.e., 2634, or 55-day EMA at Rs 2526 level. If you consider the RS55>0 as stop loss, then you have to wait till it goes below 0. We follow the RS55>0 indicator to validate whether the stock is strong vis-a-vis Nifty50. If RS55<0, it is an indication that the stock is becoming weak relative to its benchmark index, implying that Nifty50 is giving better returns than the stock in the 55-day period. As traders, you would always want to outperform the returns of Nifty50 when you're putting in so much time and effort to be on the right side of the market. In such a case, it's best to exit the stock and enter another stock that is outperforming Nifty50.

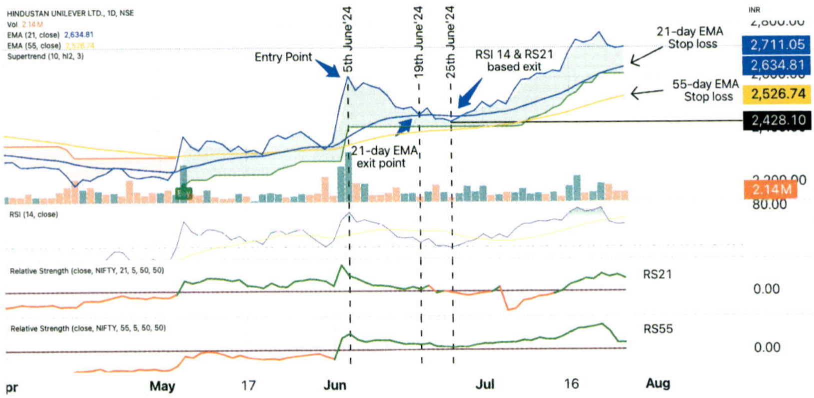

Figure 5.2 Daily chart of Hindustan Unilever

You can also choose to reduce the time frame of the indicators. For example, you can choose to follow RS21 to exit the stock for an early exit. Let's take the example of Hindustan Unilever again. Imagine you entered the stock at the 2600 level on 5 June 2024 (refer to Figure 5.2), then the exit as per the indicator stop loss would have been:

- 21-day EMA: exit at 2,454 on 19 June 2024 as it minutely touched 21-day EMA, resulting in a loss of 146 per stock (2,600–2,454);
- 55-day EMA: no exit yet, with an unrealized return of 111 (2,711–2,600), even if the stock melts down now and the stop loss is triggered, the loss would be 74 (2600–2526);
- supertrend: still holding the stock, with an unrealized profit of 111;
- RSI 14>50: exit at 2,432 on 25 June, with a loss of 168 (2,600–2,432).

- RS21>0: exit at 2,432 on 25 June, with a loss of 168 (2,600–2,432);
- RS55>0: still holding the stock, with an unrealized profit of 111.

Each indicator gave an exit at different price points and different timelines. Following the 21-day EMA would have resulted in an early exit with a loss of 146, while the 55-day EMA still holds the stock, offering a potential unrealized profit.

So, the farther you set the stop loss, the more time you get to spend in the trade. The closer you set the stop loss, the higher the possibilities of your trade hitting the stop loss.

The larger the stop loss, the greater the risk but also greater the possibility of higher returns.

Trailing Stop Loss

Trailing stop loss refers to changing the stop loss of the stock to a higher price as the stock continues to rise. To ride a larger rally, you can choose to trail your stop loss with every new high that the stock makes. The entry price can be set as the potential new stop loss. In this case, even if the stop loss is hit, you do not incur any loss. Trailing stop losses are very widely used by traders who are in the trade for a long period of time.

When you opt to go for the indicator-based stop loss, your stop loss is automatically trailed, as it is not fixed to a specified price point. If you consider the example above, if you considered the 21-day EMA as a stop loss, then the stop loss kept changing as and when the stock rose.

Actual Stop Loss

Your stop loss should actually be different from an obvious stop loss. In the previous example, observe how the stock reversed after taking support at 21-day EMA, and how the RSI bounced back after just crossing 50. Following this, the stock made a higher high, breaking its previous swing high of 2600. Such instances are very common in the market, these key levels act as demand zones and people wait for the price to drop down to such levels to enter the stock.

Professional traders and advanced robots trading in markets understand these psychological levels of the retail traders and purposely drive the prices down to such key levels to fool the weak participants and drive them out of the stock. Meanwhile, these professionals enter or add to their positions at these low levels, only to push the price back up.

If you set your stop loss at these obvious levels, the chances of it being triggered is high. To avoid being trapped; it's best to keep the stop loss at a price slightly below these critical levels, where the chances of manipulation is low.

For example, most people set the stop loss at the 50-day moving average, but you can set it at the 55-day moving average and yours will be different. You will learn how to not get fooled by such tricks over a period of time as you gain maturity while trading in the market and after multiple stop loss hits.

Which One Should You Follow?

Each trader has a different characteristic; knowing yourself and your characteristic would help you define your own method of stop loss. Your approach to stop loss typically depends on 3 things: capital size, risk appetite and personal characteristics (such as patience level and emotional resilience).

1. Capital size: A large capital base provides more flexibility in terms of risk-taking. Smaller the capital, lower the risk that you can take, and vice versa. A larger capital base allows you to risk more on each trade without jeopardizing your overall financial health. Let's consider 2 traders:

Trader A with a capital of 1 lakh, and
Trader B with a capital of 10 lakh.

Both traders put a 0.5% stop loss per trade. Stop loss per trade for Trader A is Rs 500, whereas for Trader B it is Rs 5,000, giving the latter more room to stay in the trade for a longer period of time.

To avoid running out of capital when the trades go wrong, Trader A will have to put smaller stop losses with a small capital allocation per stock, giving them limited room to make mistakes. Whereas, Trader B can afford to put wider stop losses allowing them to spend extra time in the trade, which also comes with higher chances of risk and profitability.

For Trader A, a capital-based stop loss is more appropriate, as it helps manage risk effectively with a smaller account size, while Trader B can opt for indicator-based stop loss, as it is more suited for larger capital base and potentially higher risk-reward opportunities.

2. Risk appetite: Defining stop loss is also dependent on your risk appetite. For someone who is averse to taking large risks, it's better to keep small stop losses, but you also have to be okay with smaller returns, opting for capital-based stop loss. On the other hand, if you're someone who is okay with a big loss, you can opt to keep a bigger stop loss in anticipation of higher returns, opting for indicator-based stop loss or price-based stop loss.
3. Personality traits and characteristics: Someone who has a high emotional resilience along with high patience level, indicator-based stop loss would be the right approach, as you are emotionally immune to high market fluctuations. It allows you to ride out volatility and gives your trades more time. On the other hand, for someone who gets agitated with even small market fluctuations or events and cannot bear to hold positions

for long, it's better to go for a capital-based stop loss, where you don't give much room for large price fluctuations and have more control over risk management.

Hence, to define your own stop loss, firstly consider your capital size; secondly your risk appetite; and lastly your characteristics. If you're an intermediate level of trader, assess yourself as per the above, and choose which approach is more suited for you. However, as a beginner, focus on getting into the habit of setting stop losses. Start with a capital-based stop loss approach to build that discipline. Once you gain experience, you can transition to price-based or indicator-based stop losses. Even with a larger capital base and higher risk appetite, I'd still recommend starting with capital-based stop losses to avoid emotional decision-making, which could lead to frequent stop loss hits.

Losses—Friend Not Foe

Let me tell you this harsh truth—some of your trades will hit stop loss, and you will have to book the loss. You can never make money without incurring loss. Loss is a part and parcel of not just trading, but also life. We, as intelligent humans, have to accept the loss.

You will be surprised to know that even the most successful traders in the markets have a win rate of 50 to 60%. So how are they minting money by being right only 50% of the time? The secret lies in cutting your losses quickly and allowing your winning trades to run. The key to success is not about being right all the time but about making sure your losses are small and your gains are large. One of the crucial rules of money management is that *the stop loss should be small and take-profit should be high* for you to make money. It takes only one bad trade without a stop loss to bleed out all your hard-earned gains.

Did you know that Jesse Livermore, a legendary stock trader, made over $100 million dollars in his trading career despite having a low win rate. His approach was not about winning on every trade but about making sure that his winning trades were large enough to outweigh his losses. Despite a low win rate, Jesse Livermore's ability to manage risk and ride major trends helped him become a legendary figure in the world of trading. His approach was based on the idea that making money in the markets is about getting on the right side of a trend, rather than trying to predict every market move perfectly.

Capital Allocation

How many stocks should be there in our portfolio at a given point in time? Can we put all our money on a select few stocks that we are highly convinced about?

Before I address the questions above, I would like to highlight that there is nothing right or wrong in the world of trading. It is all about your trading style and temperament. These things define your trading system. My approach to the markets might not be as rewarding for you as it is for me. However, one thing that I know will bear results is being consistent with your practice.

Position Size in Each Stock

Should each stock have an equal weightage in your portfolio, i.e., should your capital be evenly divided in each stock? As beginners, this is a good approach to start with, but eventually you would want to *give higher weightage to your winning stocks and lower weightage to your losing stocks*.

One way to do that is to enter a trade with a proportionate amount that you would want to allocate per stock rather than enter with a full amount. For example, your capital size is such that it permits you to take Rs 1 lakh position per stock. In that case, instead of buying a full 1 lakh worth of shares, you can choose to initiate the trade with 20%, i.e., Rs 20,000, and then keep adding additional 20% with every new breakout (more about entry in the next section). That way, even if your stock fails to perform, your loss is limited to just that Rs 20,000, rather than complete stock allocation.

With this approach, you end up giving more weightage to your winning stocks and low weightage to your losing stocks, eventually increasing your overall portfolio returns. Your portfolio will always consist of a few outperformers, a few average performers and a few low performers. Hence, by increasing the weightage on winning stocks, the positive returns from such stocks outweighs the losses from losing stocks or the underperforming ones.

Portfolio Diversification

Coming back, the number of stocks in your portfolio depends on your capital size. A small capital will naturally allow you to take limited positions. Although I would still suggest having at least 10 stocks, irrespective of your capital. Holding fewer than 10 stocks in a portfolio significantly increases the risk of concentrated exposure. With a small number of holdings, the portfolio is highly susceptible to the performance of each individual stock, meaning that a significant drop in just 1-2 stocks can heavily impact the overall portfolio's value. This lack of diversification leaves us vulnerable to unsystematic risk, i.e., the risk tied to specific companies or industries which could be mitigated by spreading the capital across a broader range of stocks.

Moreover, with fewer than 10 stocks, it becomes challenging to cover different sectors and industries adequately, leading to potential gaps in exposure and missed opportunities in the market. The lack of diversification increases volatility in the portfolio, and the potential for significant losses becomes much higher. Maintaining a broader, well-diversified portfolio is a more prudent approach for traders.

Diversifying does not mean we add 50 stocks if we have a large capital base. A well-diversified portfolio typically contains 15-30 individual stocks across various sectors and industries. This range is supported by modern portfolio theory[2], which suggests that beyond

20-25 stocks, the marginal benefit of diversification decreases significantly. Instead of reducing risk, over-diversification can lead to a portfolio that mimics the market index, reducing the chances of outperforming the market and potentially leading to subpar returns.

Moreover, managing a portfolio with more than 30 stocks can become cumbersome and time-consuming. Each stock requires analysis and monitoring. As the number of stocks increases, so does the complexity of maintaining the portfolio, potentially leading to oversight or suboptimal decision-making.

It is just like a game of probability. The higher the number of stocks in your portfolio, the more diverse is the risk. Let's say you have 4 stocks in your portfolio, the probability of the stocks giving good returns is 50-50. That means probability suggests that 2 will work and 2 will not work. Now if the odds are against you, then you run a risk of all 4 not working. When you increase the base count of the total stocks in your portfolio, you increase your chances of getting better odds. You could be wrong 4 times in a row, but can you go wrong 10 times in a row? If you are going wrong that many times at a stretch, then maybe it's time to rework on your stock selection or your trading strategy. On the contrary, the higher the number of trades you take, the chance of success becomes more like a coin toss possibility with the impact of each win significantly reduced in the overall portfolio. Hence, it's best to have an optimum number of stocks in your portfolio to enjoy the benefit of diversification.

Capital Size	**Up to 5 lakhs**	**10 lakhs**	**25 lakhs**	**50 lakhs**	**1 crore & above**
No. of stocks in portfolio	10	15	20	25	30

Table 5.2 Optimum number of stocks in the portfolio as per the capital size

SUMMARY

- There are 3 approaches to creating a stop loss: capital-based, price-based, indicator-based.
- A capital-based approach is when you decide a percentage loss on your total capital and percentage loss per trade.
- Price-based stop loss is when you fix a price as per the chart as your stop loss. A very commonly used price-based stop loss is the entry day candle low.
- Indicator-based stop loss is when you follow an indicator and as soon as the indicator gives a negative sign, you sell.
- Trailing stop loss refers to changing the stop loss to a higher price as the stock continues to rise.
- Your actual stop loss would be below the obvious stop-loss level.
- Your approach to stop loss depends on: capital size, risk appetite and personal characteristics.
- As beginners, it's best to use capital-based stop loss to inculcate the habit of putting stop losses.
- As beginners, it's best to equally divide the total capital by the number of stocks you wish to have in your portfolio to decide the position sizing in each stock.
- When you initiate the trade, you can start off by putting a proportionate amount rather than trade with the full amount that you wish to allocate to the stock.
- For a well-diversified portfolio, it's best to have 15-30 stocks depending on your capital size.

LET'S PRACTICE

Following are some problems on capital allocation and stop loss. Try to apply the concepts we've learned to solve them:

1. You have a trading capital of Rs 5,00,000 and decide to risk 0.5% per trade. If you invest Rs 50,000 in Zomato Ltd at Rs 200 per share, what should be your stop-loss price?

2. You have Rs 10,00,000 in trading capital and plan to take 10 trades, risking an equal percentage of capital in each. You take a trade in SJVN at Rs 250 per share, and your total risk across all trades is capped at 10% of capital; what should be your stop-loss price for this trade?
3. Instead of a fixed percentage, you decide to set your total loss limit at Rs 80,000 across 10 trades. If you buy Rs 1,20,000 worth of PVRINOX Ltd shares at Rs 300 per share, calculate your stop-loss price for this trade.
4. Rohan and Kunal are 2 friends who have recently started trading in the stock market. Both have different capital sizes, risk appetites and personal characteristics, which influence their approach to setting stop losses.
   - Rohan has a trading capital of Rs 1,50,000 and prefers to take minimal risks. He is highly disciplined but gets anxious when market fluctuations occur. He often exits trades early due to fear of losses.
   - Kunal has a trading capital of Rs 15,00,000 and is comfortable with market volatility. He has a high-risk appetite and does not mind holding onto losing trades for a longer period in anticipation of a rebound. He is emotionally resilient and patient.
   - Both traders decide to invest in ITC Ltd, currently trading at Rs 300 per share. They both allocate 10% of their capital to this trade.

   They need to decide between a capital-based stop loss and an indicator-based stop loss.

   a. What should be Rohan's approach to set a stop loss?
   b. How many shares of ITC should Kunal add when entering the stock, considering he wants to increase the weightage of winning stocks in his portfolio?
   c. How many stocks should Kunal hold in his portfolio at a time?

d. Considering Rohan allocated the full amount that he wanted to in ITC at Rs 300 and ITC shares moved up, should he allocate to ITC stocks?

LEARNER'S CORNER

My stop loss keeps getting hit very frequently, what to do?

It is very normal for stop losses to be hit, but if all your trades are hitting the stop loss, then it needs a deeper introspection. You need to analyse each trade to see what went wrong. The first thing to check is whether you followed your own devised process or not. If you didn't then the answer is simple, but if you did and yet your stop losses get hit frequently, then track if the broader markets look strong or not (we will cover this later in the book). If the broader market in itself is weak, then the chances of your stocks performing well is very low to nil. It's best to stay away from the markets in this case. However, if the broader markets are strong and yet your stop losses are getting triggered, then you need to revise your stop-loss strategy.

What is the ideal percentage of loss per trade that I should fix?

It depends on your risk-taking appetite. To start with, it's better to be conservative and keep a 1 to 2% stop loss per trade of your entire capital.

What if I don't keep a stop loss?

Then you will bleed out more money than you make. One bad trade without a stop loss is good enough to lose all your hard-earned money, even if the other 9 out of 10 trades were profitable.

My stop loss was triggered but by the end of the day, the stock recovered. Should I sell real-time or at the end of the day?

Your stop loss is there to protect you. Once it's triggered, you should exit the trade immediately. If the market recovers and you're still positive on the stock, you will always have the opportunity to re-enter. On the flip side, if the market goes down further, you will thank yourself for booking a smaller loss and being disciplined.

When my stop loss is hit, can I average down instead of booking loss?

(Average down is when you add shares to your existing loss-making position to reduce the average cost of the stock in your books.)

> 'Losers average losers.'
>
> —Paul Tudor Jones

Averaging down a losing trade is a pathetic way of doubling down on your loss. To break it down, a logical person would average down when they know that the stock will definitely reverse and go up. How can anyone know that for sure? What is the guarantee for this? What if the stock goes further down? In this case now you have a higher weightage of a losing stock in your portfolio. It's better to be out with a small loss, and re-enter the stock if it reverses, than doubling down on your loss.

How can I add to my existing small position if the stock moves up by more than 15 to 20%?

Just because a stock has moved up 15 to 20%, it does not mean that it could not go up further by another 15% or more. Having said that, a strong stock can give crazy returns even after moving up by 15 to 20%. I will cover this deeply later in the book. It is okay to add more as long as it is as per your pre-defined process.

How do I put a stop loss order? How do I put a stop loss on the trading system?

There are different types of stop-loss orders you can use to manage risk in trading. It will depend on your broker account. But the following are the most widely used methods:

- Stop-Loss Market Order: Triggers a market order when the price reaches your stop level, ensuring execution but with possible slippage.
- Stop-Loss Limit Order: Triggers a limit order at a set price, preventing execution at a worse price but risking non-execution.
- GTT (Good Till Triggered) Stop-Loss: Valid until the stop price is hit, ensuring the order remains active without daily renewal.

To place a stop-loss order in any trading system, first select the asset you're trading. Then, choose the appropriate stop-loss type based on your risk strategy—market, limit, trailing or GTT. Set the stop price at which you want the order to trigger, ensuring it aligns with your risk tolerance. Once set, confirm and place the order in your trading platform. Most trading systems allow you to modify or cancel the stop loss if market conditions change.

What Is the Right Price to Enter?

Choosing the right price point to enter the trade is one of the trickiest and most crucial decisions that a trader has to make. Even if we are tracking the strong stocks, entering at wrong price points can go the other way, making us lose money even while trading in winning stocks. Let's address the million-dollar question: What is the right price to initiate a trade?

Once we have zeroed down on the stocks that we want to trade, we will then assess the risk-reward ratio. Evaluating risk infers to calculating the potential upside and potential downside. The potential upside has to be higher than the downside; only then will you make money in the markets.

Recall the 4 different phases of the cycle that a stock movement has.

Entry at the start of the stage 2 of a stock has the capacity to generate super returns in a smaller time frame, relative to the benchmark index. How do you catch the early move in stage 2? *Price breakouts*. When a stock breaks out from previous swing high, or from a long consolidation, it is a sign of potential upmove.

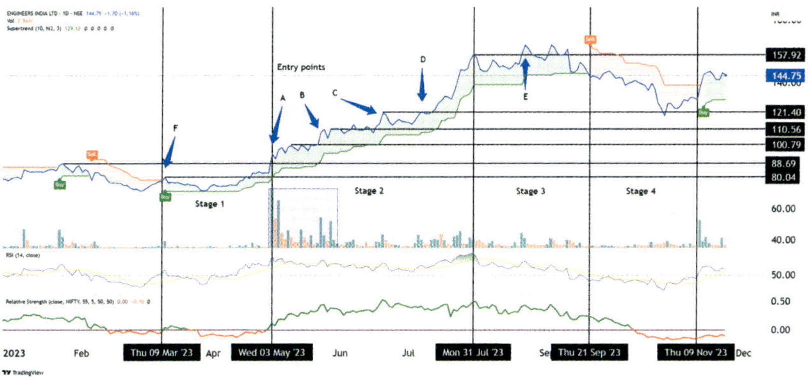

Figure 5.3 Daily chart of Engineers India

Let's say that Engineers India came under your tracker on 9 March 2023, when the stock gave a breakout from previous swing high at the 80 level. Observe Figure 5.3; the stock went through all the 4 stages of the cycle in 9 months:

Stage 1: 9 March 2023 to 2 May 2023: 2 months

Stage 2: 3 May 2023 to 30 July 2023: 2 months

Stage 3: 31 July 2023 to 20 September 2023: 2 months

Stage 4: 21 September 2023 to 8 November 2023: 3 months

The right time to enter the stock is when:

- The stock is in an uptrend
- All the indicators in your template give a bullish sign
- Price action is supported by high volume and delivery
- Price is giving a breakout from previous swing high
- The risk-reward ratio is at least 2:1

A trader can choose to either enter at the breakout level or retracement levels. For super returns, the right entry point is when the price is giving a breakout at the beginning of stage 2. Observe in the chart that stage 2 of Engineers India typically started on 3 May 2023, when the price gave a breakout above the 88 level at point A. The stock had already started making higher highs and higher lows since 18 April 2023, while the RSI 14 was above 50, but RS55 was below 0, indicating weak performance of the stock relative to Nifty50. RS55 became positive on 3 May 2023; the stock gave a strong breakout, and just look at the tall volume bar on that day. That was the best entry point for traders.

Breakout Entry

When a stock is in an uptrend, all indicators are bullish, and the stock gives a breakout from previous swing high, that's your cue to enter the stock if it is trading at a favourable risk-reward ratio. At point A in the chart, the stock gave a breakout above the 88 level; the potential fall of the stock can be the previous swing low, which is at the 82 level, the risk being of Rs 6 or 7%. As per the Fibonacci extensions, the first resistance would have been around 103, making the reward of Rs 15 or 17% (refer Figure 5.4), making the risk-reward of 2.5, which is extremely favourable.

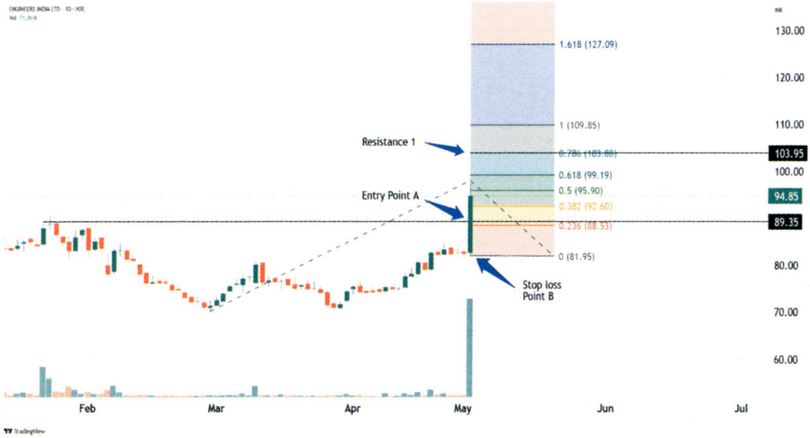

Figure 5.4 Fibonacci extensions on Engineers India

Retracement Entry

What if you miss entering at point A (refer to Figure 5.4)? In case you missed entering at point A, we can wait for the price to retrace. Remember: 'what rises must fall, and what falls, rises again'. The magnitude may be different for stocks of different characters.

Observe how the stock closed at the 95 level on 3 May and came down to the 91 level on 4 May 2023. That could have been a potential retracement entry provided the stock is trading at a favourable risk reward ratio.

What if the stock never retraces back to its breakout level?

The stock is going to go higher; so what if I buy at an expensive price than the breakout level?

It is very common for traders to get major FOMO. Such questions creep into the mind of traders, driving them to make wrong decisions, driven by emotions rather than logically. How do you deal with the FOMO? The strategy to avoid FOMO is to enter with 25% capital when the stock retraces after a breakout, and with every new retracement, keep adding 25% capital. What if the stock never retraces? Observe how the stock was consolidating between point A and point B; this was the zone of accumulation. We accumulate the stock between point A and B, and then go all in when the stock gives another breakout above previous swing high.

In this case, point B. The stock gave a breakout above 100 level, supported by high volumes, while all the other indicators were also giving bullish signals. The next resistance as per the Fibonacci level at this point was at 127 (refer to Figure 5.4), being the potential resistance while the previous swing low or the support level was at the 95 level, making the risk-reward ratio 4.4, which is making it an extremely favourable entry point.

What if we missed buying at point B? This time, after the breakout, the stock retraced back to the 104 level, the risk-reward being 1.8 at this level, making it favourable to enter the stock; we either add at retracement or we wait for another breakout. There is a buying opportunity at every breakout point.

Which Approach to Take—Breakout Entry or Retracement Entry?

Although both approaches are okay, experience has taught me that if you decide to enter at retracement levels, then be prepared to be stuck in the stock with no returns for a while, which is okay if you can be patient. For example, in the aforementioned chart, observe how the price oscillated between the 95 and 100 levels from 8 May 2023 to 24 May 2023. It is common for traders to feel negative about the stock when it does not move for a while, building frustration which drives them to exit the stock just before a big upmove. Sometimes, the stock can even go below the support zone and transition into a downtrend after a long consolidation.

Though the risk-reward at retracement levels will always be more favourable than the newer breakout points, it is best to let the stock come out of consolidation and give another breakout for you to enter the stock.

Another approach is to enter with 50% capital that you would allocate on the stock at the breakout level and accumulate with the rest at every new retracement level that it makes. This way you at least have some positive returns even when the stock is range-bound or consolidating for a while. This way you will have the mental satisfaction of having positive returns, even if it is minute.

The market will give you multiple chances to enter the stock before it's too late. You cannot miss this opportunity if you want to make good returns in the market. Entering at point A has generated 82% returns in 4 months, highly outperforming the market.

What if we missed the stock at point C, would entering at point D, when the stock gave another breakout at 120 level, be okay? The answer is both yes and no. The stock at this point has already given a return of more than 35% in just 2 months; moreover, observe how the volumes were relatively lower with each subsequent breakout. The chances of the stock topping out or moving towards the end of stage 2 is higher in such a scenario, making it riskier to enter. In this case, the stock did move up to make a high of 164; taking the chance would have generated 36% returns if the exit was at 164, the high that the stock made before entering the stage 4.

In this case it's important to define your trade duration. For short-term to medium-term swing trading, this is still a decent point to add, but for long-term swing, the risk-reward is not favourable. The stock was however good to add for short-term, medium-term and long-term swing trading at points A, B and C. I would suggest that instead of adding the stock at point D, look for other stocks that are entering stage 2, or are at the initial phase in stage 2.

Moving on, is the stock good to enter beyond point D? It is okay to add to the existing position at the breakout point above 122, but too risky to enter with a fresh position beyond that level. Observe how the slope of the line became too steep after the breakout above 122 level. Additionally, the RSI entered the overbought zone, making it highly overvalued.

Whenever the stock makes an abnormal upmove, some correction or consolidation is inevitable. The angle is important. I prefer the degree of the price slope to be between 45 degrees and 60 degrees. I am not comfortable to trade aggressively in stocks, showcasing price movement between 60 and 90 degrees.

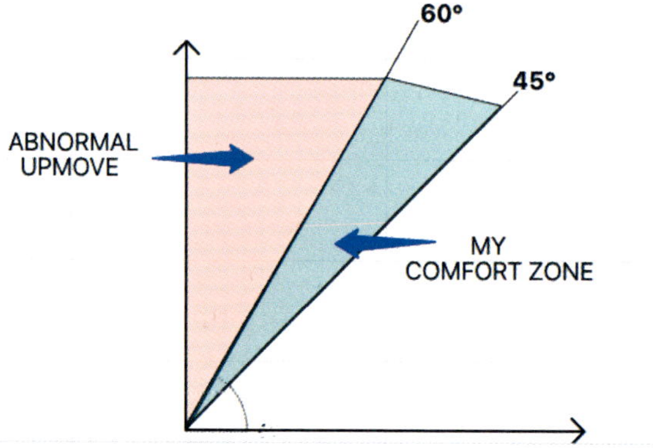

Figure 5.5 Comfort zone as per the movement of the stock

Let's go back to the earlier chart. The theory behind the stock transitioning from the uptrend of phase 2 to a decline in phase 3 is because the start of the phase 2 is driven by operators, but subsequently the stocks change hands from strong players to weak players in the market in the later stages of phase 2, who are unable to handle market fluctuations and eventually exit driving the stock down, which is exactly what happened when the stock peaked at the end of phase 2 at the 160 level. The stock gave a sharp upmove making a steep incline with relatively lower volumes as compared to former breakouts; moreover, the RSI went up to 87 at this point entering a highly overbought zone. Entering at any level during this phase is highly risky.

Trickiest Points

Point E

Be cognizant of the fact that the 4 stages are much more obvious when we look at it retrospectively. For example, it is easier to mark stage 3 after the stock has topped out and post the decline of the stock. When trading real time, such stages are not very obvious; the stock could have given another upmove after consolidation between July 2023 and September 2023, continuing its uptrend. Observing point E in the chart, the stock gave a breakout above the 157 level supported by good volumes. Additionally, the stock still fulfilled all the criteria of our trading template. So, should we not have entered at the breakout level? The answer is yes.

While trading real time, at that point, it seemed like the stock was coming out of the consolidation phase, breaking out above the 157 level and preparing for another upmove with favourable risk and reward ratio, making it a very valid and justifiable trade. Unfortunately, our stop loss would have been triggered entering at this level.

Point F

Observe how the stock was trying to come out of the downtrend at point F early on before entering stage 1. It gave a breakout at the 80 level, supported by good volumes, RSI 14 went above 50, RS55>0. Although the price just came above its EMAs, while all the EMAs converged at that point (although EMAs are not visible in the chart, but in case you open and check, you will see this), the potential risk was of Rs 10 and the potential reward was also of Rs 10, making the risk-reward 1:1 and unfavourable to take the trade. In this scenario, we would have been saved as eventually stock did hit the stop loss. Assume that the risk-reward was also in favour, then would you have entered the trade? The answer is yes, if the risk-reward was favourable, it was a valid and justifiable trade. Unfortunately, we would have hit our stop loss. Point F was a typical case of a false breakout. No matter how much you're good at your analysis, being trapped by such false breakouts is a common occurrence for traders. False breakouts are used for market manipulation driven by the operators. The only way to protect yourself from a large loss in such cases is to keep your stop losses intact.

The reality of the stock market is that 4 out of 10 trades will not work and stop losses will be hit.

This statistic is the logic of take profit being twice your stop loss, so that even if 5 of your trades do not work, you are still at break-even point and do not lose your capital. This is why risk management in every trade is equally important.

To summarize the concept, when a stock falls in our radar that fits perfectly into our trading setup, we enter when the stock gives a breakout above its previous swing high supported by high volume and delivery, and with a favourable risk-reward ratio. If we missed adding at the breakout level, then we enter when the stock retraces, adding 25% of allocated capital per stock at each new retracement level that the stock makes.

Once we've defined the entry point, we enter with the capital that we allocate per stock.

SUMMARY

- Ideally, you should enter at the early stage of phase 2 in a stock.
- It can be identified when the stock is coming out of a very long consolidation or when the stock has been making higher highs and higher lows with each new swing in the past few trading sessions.
- You can either enter when the stock is giving a breakout or when the stock is retracing after giving a breakout.
- Entry has to be when the risk-reward is favourable, i.e., 2 or more.
- Avoid adding the stock if it has given a very steep rally or a very unnatural move, as it is bound to consolidate or give a correction.
- Assess at any given point whether you want to keep the stock for short-term, medium term or long term.
- You can choose to enter with a proportionate amount at the breakout and add up at retracement level.

LET'S PRACTICE

Some charts have been provided below as per our template. Analyse the graphs, and mark whether the stock is good to enter at its last traded price (LTP) on the chart.

Additionally, I would highly suggest that you start taking positions with small capital by applying the concepts discussed in this chapter, and in case you get stuck, feel free to head to stockedge.com and join my community StockEdge Club.

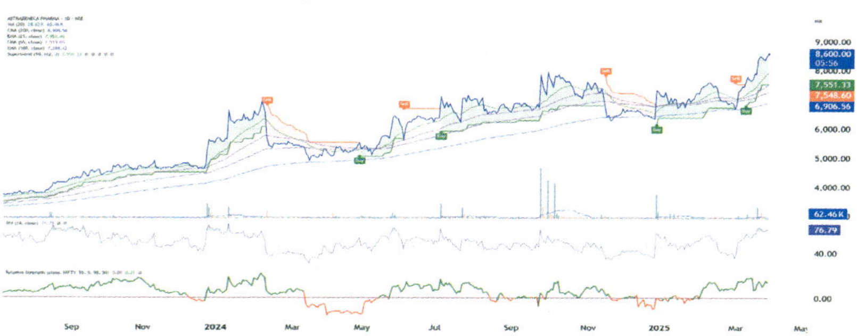

Figure 5.6

Figure 5.7

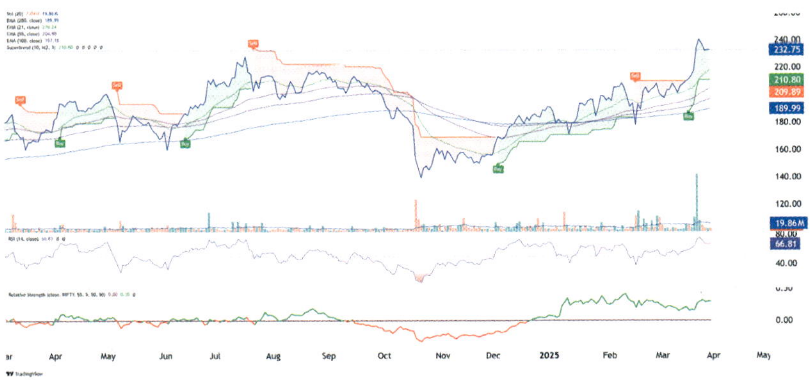

Figure 5.8

Figure 5.9

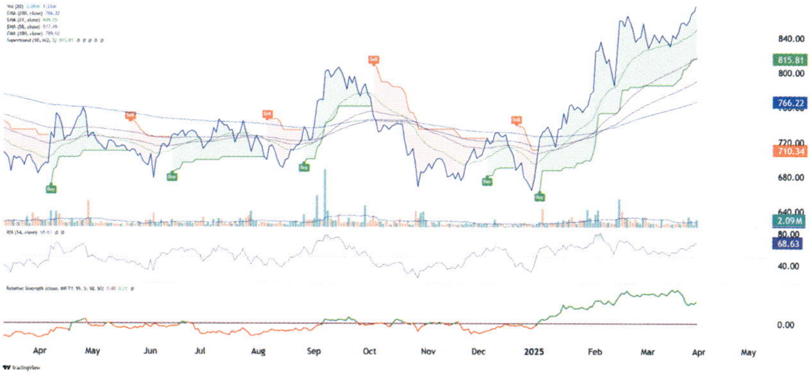

Figure 5.10

LEARNER'S CORNER

I want to be a breakout trader, but the risk-reward is generally not favourable at breakout points. What should I do?

While not all breakouts will have this issue, there will always be some breakout points where the risk-reward is not favourable. In such cases (where the stock gave a rally of >10% at breakout), it's okay to wait for the price to retrace and then either enter at retracement levels with a small position or wait for the stock to give another breakout at a favourable risk and reward level. However, if this is a very common occurrence (even in stocks that give a rally of <10% at breakouts), then your method of calculating risk and reward might need revisiting, or maybe your risk appetite is not large enough to become a breakout trader. In such a case, it's okay to become a retracement trader. As beginners the idea is to become comfortable with charts and experiment with different trading styles. You can start by becoming a retracement trader and always switch to breakout trading when you're mature in the markets.

If I missed entering at breakout point, can I enter a few points above the breakout level?

It will depend on the risk-reward at that level. If it is still favourable to you, then it's okay to enter. However, if the risk-reward is not favourable at that point, then you will not add. It's okay to feel

FOMO, but dealing with FOMO is better than dealing with loss due to stupidity. It's better to wait for the stock to give another breakout for you to enter, or there will be more opportunities in some other stocks that you can consider instead.

How do I get stocks that are going to give a breakout?

The different combo scans and sector rotation explained in chapter 4 will help you make a list of stocks that are strong. Typically, these strong stocks have a higher probability of giving a breakout. So, I would highly suggest making a watchlist of such stocks, and add alerts (TradingView feature) at breakout levels to participate.

I take retracement entries with the anticipation that the stock will reverse; however, it does not. What should I do?

Such cases could be a typical case of false breakouts. All you can do is trigger your pre-set stop loss. However, there are different ways to reduce the probability of such instances. One way could be to use the Fibonacci Retracement tool to be more sure of the potential reversal levels from retracement. Another way could be to enter once the stock starts moving up again after retracement. If it bounces back, then the chances of it sustaining its uptrend is higher.

Should I always wait for the breakout above all-time high to make the entry?

A stock that is giving a breakout above its all-time high is likely to be a very strong stock to go beyond such a key level and is the ideal point to enter. Wait for the confirmation of the breakout by letting the candle close above the breakout level to enter. However, it's not possible to wait for the stock to give a breakout above its all-time high to make an entry. The stock might have already rallied too much by then. So, if the stock is fulfilling all our criteria and fits into our template/setup, then you may enter when the stock breaks its previous swing high.

What Is the Right Time to Exit the Trade?

Your trades can go horribly wrong if you don't exit the stock on time. Let me share a story with you.

In my initial years of trading, I took a position in a stock as it was in an uptrend, fit perfectly in my setup and was at a favourable risk-reward ratio. Moreover, one of my friends owned that company, doubling down on my conviction of the stock.

Not that it mattered, but potential future growth of that company was doing the rounds in the news, and naturally that made me want to speak to him about it. During the conversation, his body language made me pretty confident in his words. Moreover, he was very excited about the future business potential. The stock went up by 20% after that; my trading system told me to book some of my position, but because of my high conviction in the stock, I held onto it. Soon after, the stock started falling down and my stop loss was triggered. My confidence in the stock clouded my judgement and being optimistic that the stock would eventually go up, I held onto the stock.

The stock fell further and my losses widened to 40%, shaking my confidence and making me very anxious about my decision. To seek validation, I decided to have a chat with that friend of mine. Without being able to identify any major reason for the downfall, as the fundamentals of the company remained intact, I decided to hold on to the stock. Unfortunately, it went further down and my losses widened to 70%; this is when I squared up my trade. Later, on further investigation, it was found out that there was an internal family issue that became the cause of the massive downfall.

Booking 70% loss on a trade that could have been booked at 20% profit took a big toll on me mentally. However, I took it as a learning from the market. The market taught me 2 things that day—respect your trading system and make data-driven decisions, not emotion/bias-driven decisions.

Even though I had initiated a trade on a winning stock, not exiting it at the right time bled my capital. Since then, I have worked on my exit strategy. Now I exit my positions as per my pre-defined system, come what may.

As beginners, when is the right time to exit?

For a losing trade, whenever the stop loss is hit you exit the stock. *Period*. You do not keep holding and waiting for it to recover to exit at a lower loss percentage.

Now, the more bewildering question is when to exit in case of a winning trade? Again, each trader is different and has a distinct characteristic that defines their exit strategy. The different methods you can use are:

1. When the target price is achieved
2. Partially exit when the stock is showing overbought signs (abnormal rally)
3. When the stock is showing weakness

Let us understand these better.

Exit As per Target Price

Before entering a trade, you need to set a target price for the stock. There are various methods and tools to define the target price.

Price-based targets can be set before entering a trade. In case you enter a stock that is not at an all-time high, then the historical resistance level of the stock could be the potential target, as it is very likely for a stock to respect its resistance and reverse from there.

In case you enter a stock that is trading at an all-time high, there are multiple tools that can be used to measure the potential target price. One of the tools that you could use is Fibonacci extensions. We've already covered it in detail earlier in the book. A more simplistic approach is to keep the target price at twice the distance of the stop loss from the entry price. For example, if the stock is trading at 170 and the stop loss is at 155, then the target price should be 200, and as soon as the target is met, you book the profit and close the trade.

Partially Exit When Stock Is Overbought

Another way to protect your profits and to exit timely is to partially book your profits when the stock has given an abnormal rally entering the overbought zone. As mentioned earlier, if a stock is giving a steep incline (more than 80 degrees) then some profit booking by retail traders post this rally leading to correction or consolidation in the stock is inevitable. How do we know when the stock is entering the overbought zone?

One way is by judging the steepness of the upmove, as already discussed. Another way which I use is if RSI touches or crosses 90, it is an indication that the momentum of the stock movement is abnormally higher than its historic movement. Hence, booking at least 20 or 50% of your trade is a smart move of protecting your profits. Now even if the stock goes for a toss and you have to exit at your entry level, you can at least be mentally satisfied that you made some profit from the trade.

Exit When Stock Shows Weakness

Another method is to keep riding the stock till it loses its momentum (becomes weak). In such cases, whenever the stock gives a fresh breakout, you keep trailing your stop loss till the stock is strong to maximize your profits. How do you judge the stock's weakness?

Price-Based judgement

Just like how you define a stop loss when entering a trade, you could trail the stop loss with every new price movement that the stock makes.

- The new support levels created by the stock in a continuous uptrend could be a potential stop loss.
- With every new swing that the stock makes, the previous swing low could be potential stop loss.

- With every new candle the stock makes, the previous candle's low could be a potential stop loss.

Indicator-Based judgement

Another way is to set indicator-based trailing stop loss. If you're someone who's following an indicator-based stop loss, then you are automatically trailing your stop loss, as you exit when the indicators are not working in your favour.

One of the caveats to the indicator-based exit is that there are chances of the profits getting wiped out till the indicator gives a sell sign. A way to overcome this challenge and protect our profits is to reduce the time frame of the chart or the indicator for an early exit.

For example, in case of EMAs, if you consider the price going below the 21-day EMA, or 21-day EMA going below the 55-day EMA as a potential sign of weakness, then instead of waiting for the crossover of 21-day EMA, and 55-day EMA, you can use the crossover of 9-day EMA and 21-day EMA. In case of a supertrend, you can reduce the chart time frame. If you entered the stock looking at the daily chart, then you can exit when the supertrend gives a sell signal in the 2-hourly chart. Similarly, you can use RSI 12<50, or RS21<0 for early exits in the stock.

Which Approach Should You Follow?

Again, know your risk appetite first, and then decide the course of your action. Just as there are 2 faces of a coin, there are pros and cons both of following either approach. When you choose to trail your stop loss the chances of getting a higher return increases, but also it comes with a possibility of booking at a lower profit percentage than your initially set target.

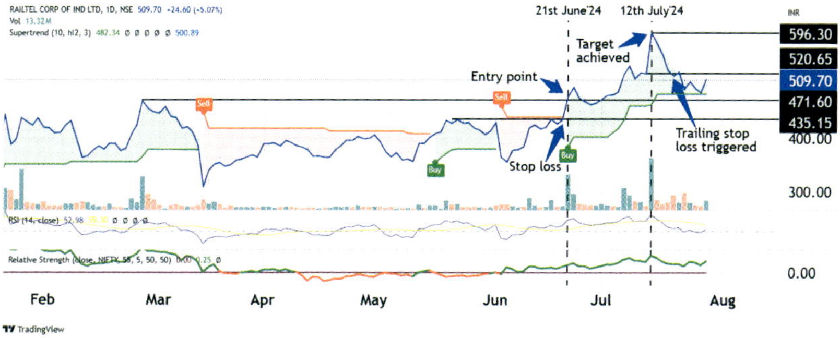

Figure 5.11 Daily chart of Railtel Corporation

As observed in Figure 5.11, the stock gave an all-time high breakout on 21 June 2024 above the 471 level. The stock was fulfilling all our criteria and fit into our trading setup perfectly, making you initiate a trade at 472. Let's assume that we kept the stop loss at 431, Rs 4 below 435, which was an important resistance level, making it the new support; moreover, it is also very close to the supertrend level, making it an important level. Now if the stop loss is at 431, then the take profit should be 551 [471 + (40*2)]. The stock made a high of 596 on 12 July 2024, exceeding my target price. As per the process, I trailed the stop loss. Let's assume that I trailed the stop loss to the previous swing low, which would be 520, i.e., 31 lower than my target price. Observe how the stock hit the trailing stop loss, making me exit the trade at 520 on 19 July with a profit of 48, i.e, roughly 10%, when the potential was much higher.

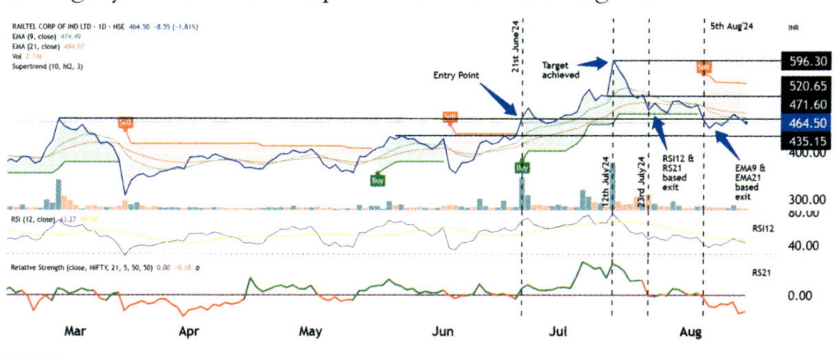

Figure 5.12 Daily chart of Railtel

In case we followed the indicator-based trailing stop loss, observe in Figure 5.12, the exit would have been at

- 9-day EMA & 21-day EMA crossover: 471, making it a no profit, no loss trade;
- RSI 12>50: 491, with a return of merely 4%; and
- RS21>0: 491, same as above.

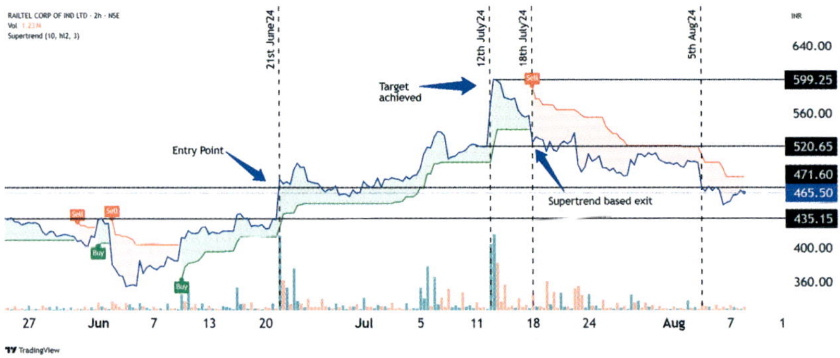

Figure 5.13 2-hourly chart of Railtel

In the case of supertrend-based exit, the trailing stop loss would have been hit at the 524 level at a 2-hourly chart, the profit being roughly 10% for the trade.

However, in case of larger rallies, the potential upside is also bigger. Let's take another example:

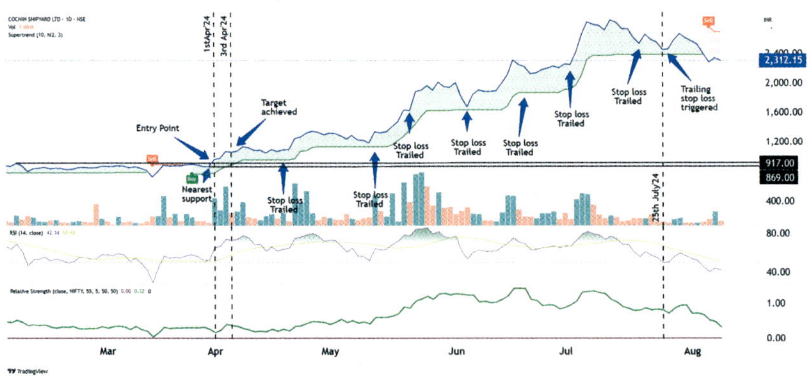

Figure 5.14 Daily chart of Cochin Shipyard

As observed in Figure 5.14, the stock was fulfilling all our criteria as on 1 April 2024, and fit into our trading setup perfectly, making you initiate a trade at 917 when it gave an all-time high breakout. The stop loss was kept at the nearest support at 869 level, making the target price 1013 [{(917 – 869)*2 + 917]. The stock gave a very good rally, and the target price was achieved on 3 April 2024 itself. We thought it best to ride a larger rally and hence trailed our stop loss. Assume we follow price-based stop loss, and we kept the previous swing low as the stop loss. Observe how with every fresh breakout, the stock made higher lows, and the stop loss was trailed to previous swing low. The trailing stop loss was triggered on 25 July 2024 when it broke the level of previous swing low, generating a whooping return of 178%.

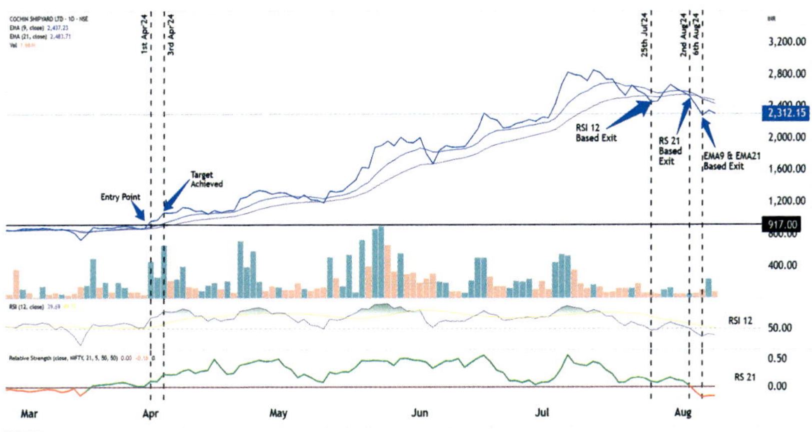

Figure 5.15 Daily chart of Cochin Shipyard

In case we followed the indicator-based stop loss, the exit would have been a:

- 9-day EMA and 21-day EMA crossover: 2290, with a return of 150%;
- RSI 12>50: 2461, with a return of 168%;
- RS21>0: 2357, with a return of 177%.

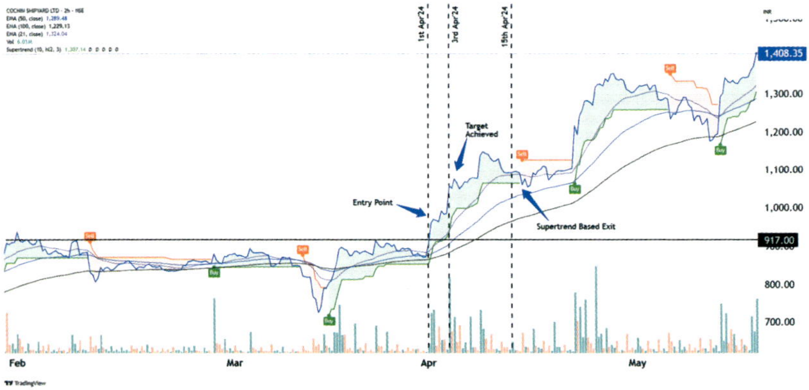

Figure 5.16 2-hourly chart of Cochin Shipyard

In case of a supertrend-based exit, our stop loss would have been triggered at the 1066 level, generating a return of 16%, which is also a generous return one can generate in 15 days. However, the chance of riding a potential big rally would have been missed if we trailed the stop loss as per supertrend signal in the 2-hourly chart.

A trailing stop loss gives an opportunity to ride a large rally, but it comes with its associated risks, as observed in the above examples. Another very common question in the mind of the readers—

How to book the trade when the stock is at its peak?

It is impossible to identify a certain price as the peak until it starts falling. So, while it can be coincidental that you exit at the peak, you would not know it is the peak until it starts to fall. Even in the above case, observe how the stock made a high of 2863, yet the highest exit that we could get as per our process was at the 2546 level, i.e., 11% lower than the high. While trying to book at a peak price, you run a chance of missing out on a bigger rally. The stock gave an upmove of 13% on a single day on 23 April to close at 1093, assuming it to be a top and booking the profits would have made you miss the larger rally. *An experienced trader is always mentally convinced to exit at a lower level from the top to avoid missing out on potential rallies.*

Mixed Approach: For Mental Peace

Trailing the stop loss without booking profits has both pros and cons. It can make you exit a winning trade with losses, as observed in the case of Railtel, while it also has a potential of giving you larger returns as observed in the case of Cochin Shipyard. Another way to protect your profits is to go for a mixed approach where we book 50% of the profits when the target is achieved or is overbought and ride the other 50% till trailing stop loss is triggered. This approach helps in protecting the profits if the stock reverses after reaching its target. Let's go back to the example of Railtel.

Let's calculate the percentage return in case we had booked 50% of the profits when our target was achieved, i.e., 551. Recall that we entered the stock at 472 with a target of 551. Assuming that we bought 100 shares of Railtel, i.e., took a position of Rs 47,200, let's calculate the returns.

No. of shares	100				
Entry price	472				
Capital allocated	47200				
	PARTIAL EXIT 1 (book 50%)	**COMPLETE EXIT 2 (book rest 50%)**			
	Target price	**Price-based stop loss**	**RSI- & RS-based stop loss**	**EMA crossover-based stop loss**	**Supertrend-based stop loss**
	551	520	491	471	524
Profit/loss per share	79	48	19	-1	52
Profit/loss on 50%	3950	2400	950	-50	2600
Total profit		6350	4900	3900	6550
Profit %		13.45%	10.38%	8.26%	13.88%

Table 5.3 Potential returns in Railtel

Had we booked 50% of our position, i.e., profits for 50 shares in this case, we would have already booked the profit of roughly 8% of the position allocated to Railtel. When we trail the stop loss for the rest 50%, we ride on the opportunity of a larger rally. Table 5.3 gives a picture of the percentage return we would generate for each different stop loss approach. The highest returns that we would have generated in the case of Railtel would have been through following the supertrend-based stop loss. Recall that the returns generated by just trailing the stop loss was 10% at the max, and returns at completely booking at our target would be just 8%.

Hence, through this approach, even if the stock reverses, and our stop loss is hit, our returns would be relatively better than the earlier scenario when we trailed our entire position, and our stop loss was hit. Another approach to partially book is when the stock enters overbought signs. In the case of Railtel, there were no overbought signals given. However, partially booking at overbought signs is also another approach that helps maximizing returns while lowering your risk of losses.

This is the power of risk management. When we trail our stop losses we extend our risk in anticipation of higher returns. When we book 50%, we reduce the risk of losing a higher amount while trailing the stop loss in anticipation of higher returns. However, in the end it boils down to anxiety management, when we book 50% at our desired price, it gives mental satisfaction, making us less anxious to ride the rest 50%. Now even if we exit at cost for the remaining 50%, at least we can be content with the small profit that we booked earlier.

Remember that *you only realize your profit or loss in any trade once you exit it*. Truth be told, you never really exit the market, which means you don't truly close out the master trade, rather you keep switching from one trade to another. It's similar to a relay race where you're just passing the trade from one stock to another. It's that one race you need to complete, with the turtle mindset, where ensuring that the baton does not fall is more important than the speed of the running. The race is more about having the mindset of consistency and steadfastness.

In markets, not everything will work as per your wish and desire. It's important to make an attempt to optimize the returns while ensuring mental stability. More than that, it's important to be consistent with your practice, adopting the turtle mindset. What works for me might not work for you, and vice versa. I know so many traders who have a very different style of trading than me and generate amazing returns. Repeating again that every person has a different characteristic and approach. I can teach you the fundamentals of trading and the different strategies, its advantages and disadvantages, but unless you try it yourself, you will never know what works for you. Trading is exactly like any professional sport. You can observe other traders, learn the rules, know what the game is about—but you only get better with time, experience and consistency.

SUMMARY

- In case of a losing trade, exit as per your defined stop loss.
- In case of a winning trade, you can exit when the target is achieved, or partially exit when the stock shows overbought signs and completely exit when the stock shows weakness.
- Target prices can be historical resistance level, and in case of a stock trading at an all-time high – the target price could be measured through Fibonacci extension tool, or keep keeping it at twice the distance between the entry price and the stop loss.
- Overbought signs can be identified by assessing the steepness of the upmove, or when the RSI of the stock is around 90 or beyond.
- Even if the stock reverses and goes for a toss, partially booking the stock gives mental satisfaction.
- A stock's weakness can be assessed using 2 approaches: Price based trailing stop loss and Indicator based trailing stop loss.
- Price-action based trailing stop loss could be altering your stop loss to previous swing low, or new support levels, or the previous candle's low.
- Indicator-based stop loss could be whenever an indicator gives signs of weakness or changing trends in the stock.
- No trader can book the stock at its peak without it being accidental. A peak in a stock can only be identified when it starts falling.
- To protect your profits, you can also go with a mixed approach, where you partially book the profits when the target is met and ride the larger rally with the other half.
- The mixed approach gives a mental satisfaction of booked profits to ride the other half of the capital peacefully.

LET'S PRACTICE

Some charts have been provided as follows. Analyse the graphs, and mark what should be the exit level, if any, on the chart. Consider both price-based as well as indicator-based exits to mark the exit:

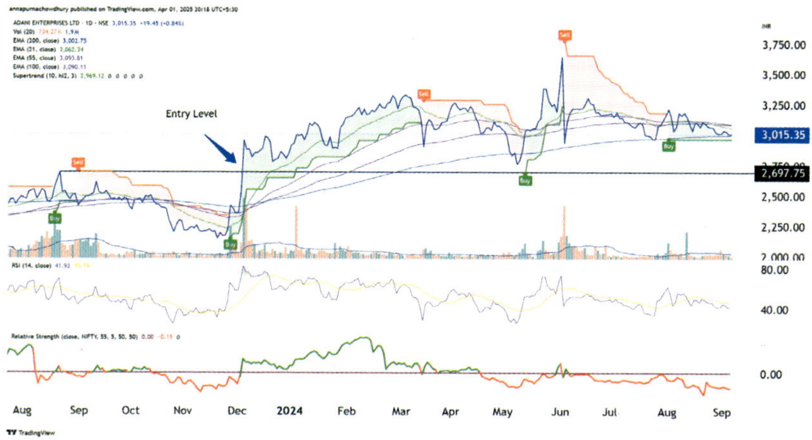

Figure 5.17

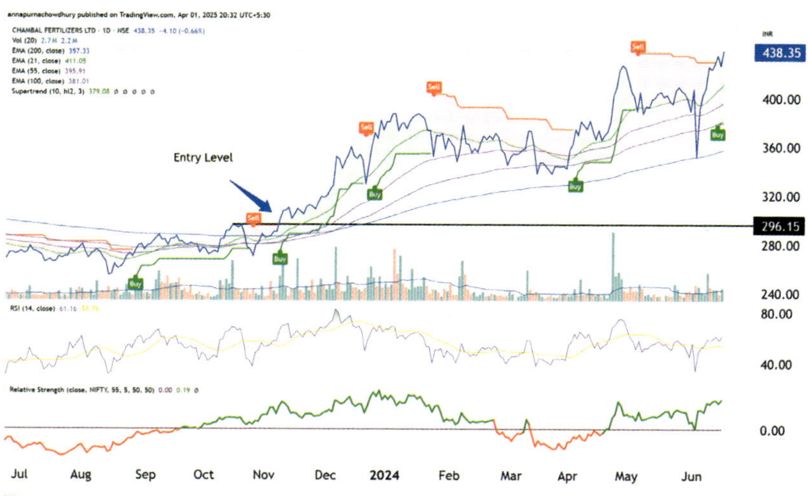

Figure 5.18

Figure 5.19

Figure 5.20

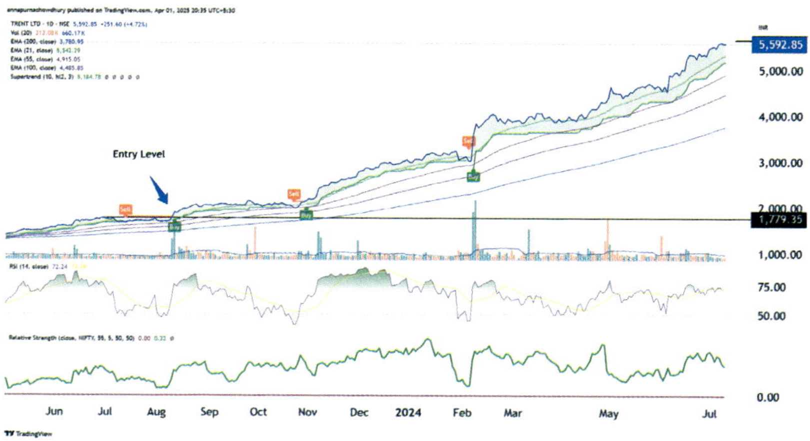

Figure 5.21

LEARNER'S CORNER

I entered the stock as per the criteria, but then the stock started consolidating. Now there are other stocks that are giving good rallies, but I feel that my capital is stuck in an average stock. Should I exit, even if my trading system does not ask me to?

These are very common situations that any trader faces. It is normal for stocks to behave this way. Hence, I keep stressing about entering with a small position in any stock, and to double up, or add more once it has already given a good upmove. This way at least only a limited amount of capital is tied with an average performing stock. You will only exit once your setup asks you to. Till then you will maintain your position. If you follow the price-based stop loss and the stock ends up being in consolidation for a long period of time, then it might get difficult to exit. However, in case of indicator-based exit, the indicators will start acting up and give a bearish sign for you to exit.

For example, in case of RS, the RS will eventually go below 0 if the stock has lost its momentum.

As soon as I entered a stock, it gave a small upmove. I trailed my stop loss at cost, but my stop loss was triggered. The stock went up to give a generous return later. Should I not have trailed my stop loss?

Firstly, it's okay for the stop loss to be triggered. As I keep saying, stop losses are the best tool that you can adopt in your trading journey to protect your capital from large losses. However, the approach towards stop loss should also be such that it gives some time to your trades to make a move, and not so tight that it keeps getting triggered with small fluctuations in the market. If it was triggered by a small fluctuation, then maybe it's time for you to revisit your stop loss approach. If it was triggered by a somewhat large price fluctuation, then it's better to be out of the stock for the time.

The stock that I have is currently at a resistance, so should I book my profits and exit?

When a stock is nearing its resistance then some profit booking is likely, retracing from that point. However, if it's a strong stock, then it could bounce back and go on to give a fresh breakout. Hence, designing your system plays a crucial role here. If at this resistance level, the stock is giving overbought signs, then partial booking would be ideal. If you're following price-based exits and have a low emotional resilience, even in that case booking at least 25% of your position would be suggested. This will help in your anxiety, as if the stock gives a complete reversal from its resistance, then at least you will have the mental peace that you booked some profits at the high level. If you're someone who follows the indicator-based exits, then I would suggest you hold on to it till it shows weakness and double up your capital if it gives another breakout.

Multi–Time-Frame Trading: Mother Daughter Trading Template

Now you know when to enter and when to exit a trade. Theoretically, it seems pretty simple that when the indicators are all giving a green signal, and the stock fits perfectly into our trading setup with favourable risk and reward then we enter the trade. However, in practice it is a tad bit more complicated than that. If you've already started trading, then you would know the challenges that a trader faces while making the entry and exit decisions. It is so common for the stock to go down when you enter the trade and reverse as soon as you hit stop loss.

One of the most important traits of a professional trader is to build conviction in a stock before you enter a trade. When we look at the same chart in different time frames, and if all the time frames are indicating the same thing, that's when your conviction is high. This is the concept of *multi–time-frame trading*.

Figure 5.22 Weekly chart of Eicher Motors

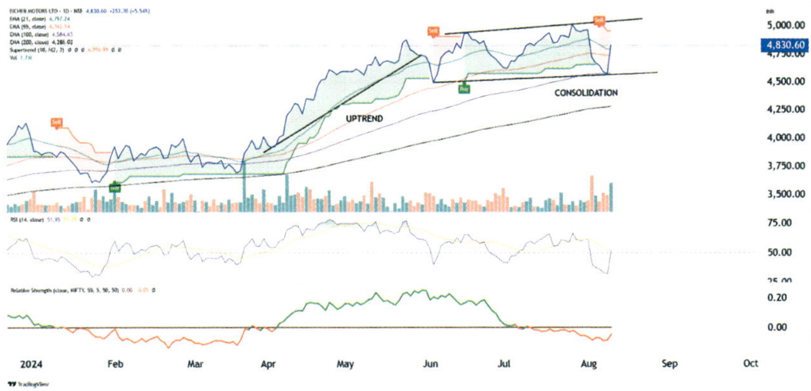

Figure 5.23 Daily chart of Eicher Motors

Figure 5.24 2-hourly chart of Eicher Motors

Observe the weekly chart of Eicher Motors in Figure 5.22; each plotted price depicts the closing price at the end of 1 week. The stock is in uptrend, and all the indicators in our template are giving bullish signals. Now observe the daily chart of Eicher Motors in Figure 5.23, after a big upmove from April 2024 to end of May 2024, the stock has been moving sideways and there has been a recent correction in the stock. Moreover, supertrend and RS55 is hinting a break in the momentum of the stock. This is in contrast to the weekly chart of the stock.

In the 2-hourly chart the stock is showing strength (refer to Figure 5.24) and trying to reverse from its corrected levels and move up higher.

In the 3 scenarios, the weekly chart is showing strength and momentum, the daily chart is showing weakness and consolidation, while the 2-hourly chart is showing regained strength and bounce back. Each chart portrays a different story of the same stock.

Your trade tenure will decide the time frame of the chart that you should be tracking to take trades.

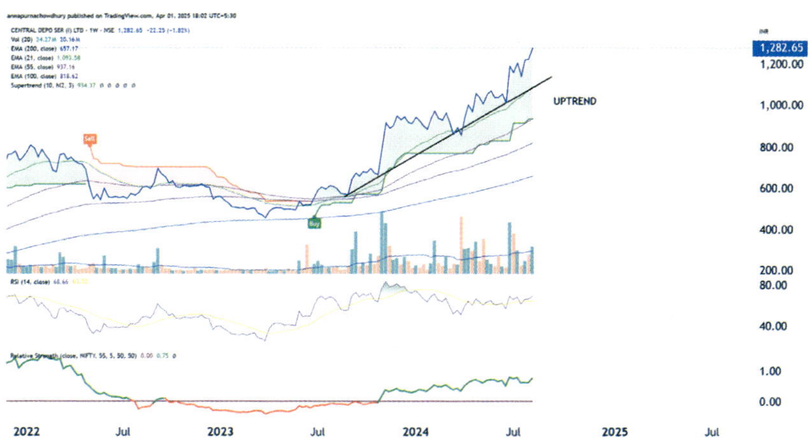

Figure 5.25 Weekly chart of CDSL

Figure 5.26 Daily chart of CDSL

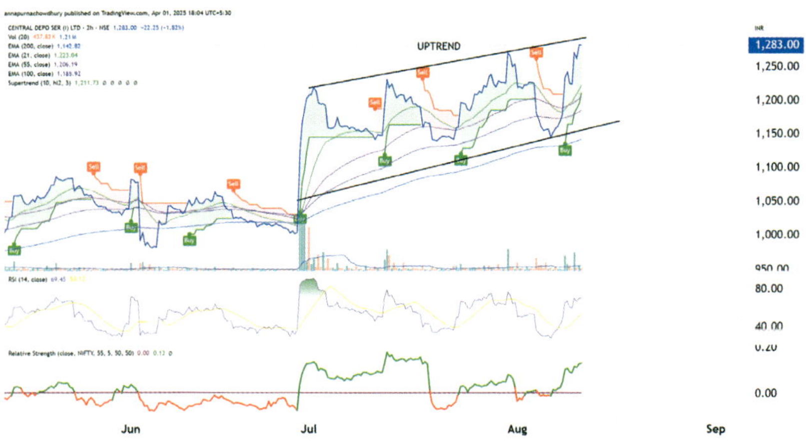

Figure 5.27 2-hourly chart of CDSL

In the weekly chart as per Figure 5.25, the stock has been in an uptrend for a while and all the indicators are giving bullish signals. Now observe the daily chart in Figure 5.26, the stock is reflecting a similar uptrend with a recent price breakout, while all the indicators are bullish too. Coming to the 2-hourly chart in Figure 5.27, the overall trend of the stock is still up with a recent price breakout. Although the stock witnessed 2 corrections, it bounced back to make a higher high, along with the bullish support of all the indicators indicating strength in the stock.

Now if you have limited capital and you have to choose between a stock that is showing bullish strength in daily chart, while still being in downtrend in the weekly chart vs a stock that is showing strength in both daily and weekly chart, which one are you more likely to trade in? Remember, the art of rejection is extremely crucial in the markets, especially in a bull market when you'll be faced with a problem of plenty. A synchronous trend across multiple time-frame charts builds higher conviction while trading a stock.

Having said that, we cannot follow all time-frame charts and expect it all to be synchronous. For example, if I change the time frame of a CDSL chart to 10 seconds, it will probably show a different picture. Tracking 2 different time frames that suit your trading tenure at the same time is good enough for building conviction, the larger tenure being the mother and the shorter tenure being the daughter of the mother-daughter template. A few commonly tracked chart time frames are:

- Long-term swing trading/momentum investing: monthly and weekly
- Medium-term swing trading: weekly and daily
- Short-term swing trading: daily and 2-hourly/75 minutes
- Intraday trading: 2-hourly/75 minutes and 15 minutes

When using the multiple time-frame template, we use the longer tenure template or the mother template to form judgement of the stock, and a shorter time frame or the daughter template to decide the entry and exit levels of the stock. Suppose we decide to do medium-term swing trading, we track the weekly chart for overall trend confirmation, and use the daily chart to decide the entry and exit levels.

Figure 5.28 Weekly and daily chart of CDSL in a multi–time-frame layout

When you look at 2 time frames together, you get a clearer picture of the stock. In Figure 5.28, we use the multi–time-frame available in TradingView; weekly is on the left side of the chart, while daily is on the right. On the weekly time frame or the mother template:

- the stock is in uptrend;
- there are high volumes and delivery;
- RSI 14>50;
- RS55>0;
- price is trading above all EMAs, and shorter tenure EMAs are above longer tenure EMAs.

They are all confirming the trend. On the daily time frame or the daughter template, the stock is resonating the same momentum as in the weekly time frame with a recent price breakout supported by a favourable risk-reward ratio, the entry point being perfect for us to initiate the trade. Let's take another example:

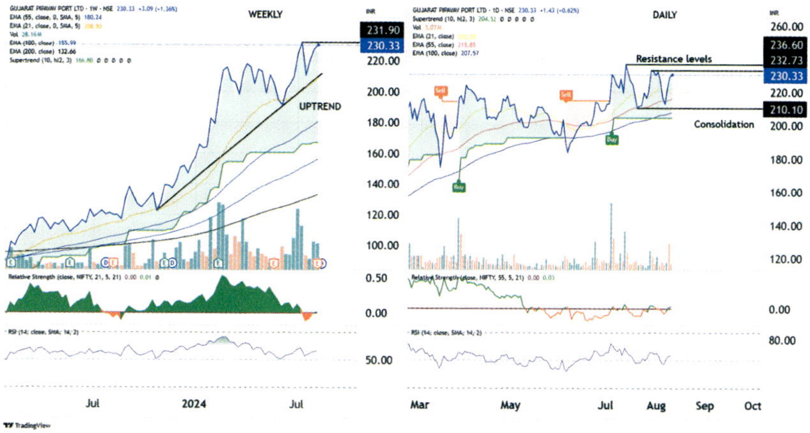

Figure 5.29 Weekly and daily chart of Gujarat Pipapov Port Ltd (GPPL)

In the weekly chart or the mother template, the stock has been in uptrend supported by high volume and delivery while all the indicators are looking bullish too, making us positive on the stock. However, on the daily time frame or the daughter template, the stock has been in a sideways consolidation, struggling to come out of its resistance levels in the past 1 month. Moreover, observe how RSI 14 and RS55 have also been fluctuating along the 50 line and the 0 line respectively, indicating the struggle of the stock to be in momentum. In such a scenario, we will wait for the stock to break the resistance level supported by high volume and delivery in the daily chart before we initiate the trade.

Observed in Figure 5.30, the stock has given a very strong breakout in the daily chart or the daughter template making higher highs and higher lows, supported by high volumes and delivery, while all the technical indicators are giving bullish signals. However, the weekly chart or the mother setup is indicating a sideways movement. Till the stock moves past the resistance level in the weekly chart and sustains, making higher highs and higher lows hinting towards the shift in the trend, we will not enter the trade. Even if the stock fits perfectly into our daily chart, we will avoid taking the trade. Can you ever get convinced to trade in a stock that is giving such confusing signals?

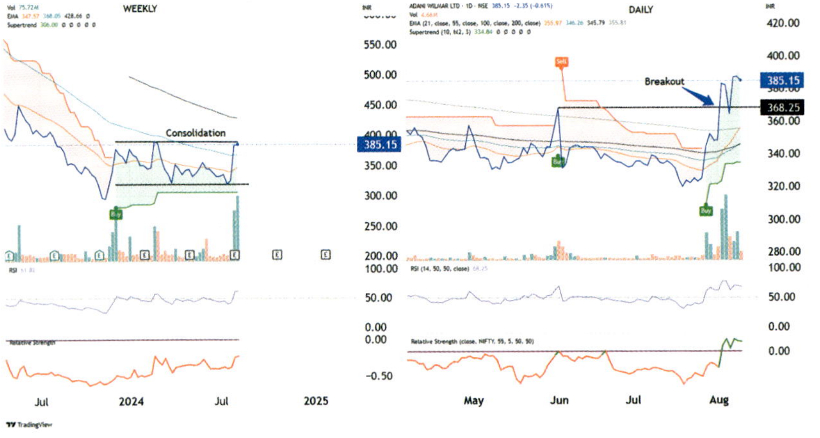

Figure 5.30 Weekly and daily chart of Adani Wilmar Ltd (AWL)

Why take a trade where the longer duration chart is not supporting the shorter duration chart, when there are multiple other options available that fulfil our criteria, and where the charts are synchronous to each other? *Look for reasons to reject stocks to trade.*

SUMMARY

- Chart trends vary when looked at on different time frames.
- If all the different time frames indicate the same, then there is higher conviction in the stock.
- Multi–time-frame charts help you check the same chart in different time frames.
- A longer tenure time frame is to form a judgement on the stock, and the shorter tenure time frame is to decide the entry and exit levels in a stock.
- We will only take the trade if the stock movement is aligned in both the mother and the daughter chart setup.

My Formula for Success in Momentum Investing

Until now this book has given you tools and concepts which I felt are important for you to know as a stock trader, regardless of whether I follow them or not. As a guru/teacher, it is my responsibility to impart knowledge about all the tools that a trader should be aware of. Even the template that I've shared is very similar to what I follow but not exactly the same. The objective of this book is not to make you blindly follow my way of trading but to equip you to create your own trading system—one that suits your characteristics and personality.

I have my own trading system and a template that has evolved over years. I still keep altering it as per my comfort and as the market evolves. This chapter presents my formula for success which has taken multiple trial and errors to create and is one that works best for me.

My trading setup follows these stages:

1. Evaluation: My combo for stock list
2. Validation: My own stock template
3. Execution: My trading strategy that includes stop loss and take profit

I feel price is the most important parameter to be included in evaluation. There are some very important theories which I have derived from stock prices. Before we discuss these theories, I want to talk about another important skill that has given me success in trading—having a trading habit that enabled me to build the turtle mindset.

Developing effective trading habits from the early stages of my career has been essential in cultivating a sustainable and rewarding trading practice. Establishing a routine that includes diligent market research, disciplined risk management and reflective journaling has helped me build a solid foundation. In the initial phases, these habits required conscious effort and commitment, but the consistency added to the compounding effect of my growth and success in the markets, paving the way for confidence in my decision-making. By cultivating patience and mindfulness early on, I minimized impulsive actions driven by emotions, leading to a more peaceful trading experience. This proactive approach not only enhanced my skills but also ensured that I'm better equipped to take on any challenges that the market throws at me and to develop the turtle mindset.

> 'Never ever argue with your trading system.'
>
> —Michael Covel, author[3]

Coming back to the trading system, I want to share the inspiration and the foundation behind my system with you.

My participation in the stock market is the function of my life experiences. In fact, the stock market is nothing but a cumulation of everyone's life experiences. The concepts of life introduced by scholars and scientists have as much application in financial markets as elsewhere.

The Foundation of the RS Strategy: The Laws of Motion and Relativity

My success in the market is purely based on my mastering one strategy—the RS strategy. The foundation of this strategy is based on the law of motion introduced to the world by Sir Isaac Newton. The first law of motion states: 'Every object in a state of uniform motion tends to remain in that state of motion till it is stopped by an external force.'[4] A simple yet extremely powerful concept, and not just for physics. Momentum as defined by Newton can be applied to stocks as well. Stocks that show strong momentum are likely to continue their move in the same direction until an external force (e.g., market conditions, economic events, fundamental change, sentiment shift) interrupts it. The measurement of momentum can differ based on asset class and markets.

An outstanding research paper by Jagadeesh and Titmant[5] states that stocks that are strongest 3–12 months in retrospect are also the strongest over comparable future periods. A very important statement implying that any stock that is stronger than other stocks for a period of 3 months and 12 months has a higher chance of remaining strong for some period of time.

The above theories helped me build the foundation of my strategy while another amazing scientist, Albert Einstein[6] gave me direction to build my core trading model through his theory of relativity. The theory is that there is no absolute frame of reference. Every time you measure an object's velocity or its momentum, it's always in relation to something else.

The theory of relativity is crucial. In academics, a person may be considered a top performer because others are ranked lower. In a broader sense, when we define success, it often comes in comparison to others. Simply measuring my wealth in isolation may not lead to feelings of satisfaction or achievement. I only feel successful in relation to others. This idea underscores the significance of relativity in various aspects of life, including the stock market.

The deeper I went into the theory, the more I was able to connect it to the stock market. It changed the way I looked at the following 3 important components:

- Time: I realized when trading, the time duration of the stock greatly influences how one judges the stock performance. While a stock can do well in a week, it might not in a year. Hence, my trading tenure mattered a lot when deciding which time frame of the chart to track.
- Expectation: Another important insight was that every individual is unique and has different expectations from the market. Maybe someone expects to win a race quickly, while another is happy just to finish. This difference exists due to unique personal backgrounds—family, monetary and mental. I had to set my own expectations as per my traits and characteristics.

- Risk-weighted opportunities: Every individual has their own way of assessing risks. Some people like to take big jumps, like jumping from a high swing, while others like to stay low where it's safer. I started to understand my risk-taking capacity and used that to manage my trading habits.

Patterns: Your Guide to the Market

Over time, I have noticed that the market behaves in patterns, much like the cycles of nature; think of the Earth's rotations and seasons. The stock market too follows patterns that can help identify the right time to enter or exit a trade. Additionally, long-term patterns turn out to be more accurate. Recall that we discussed the 4 stages of a stock earlier in this book.

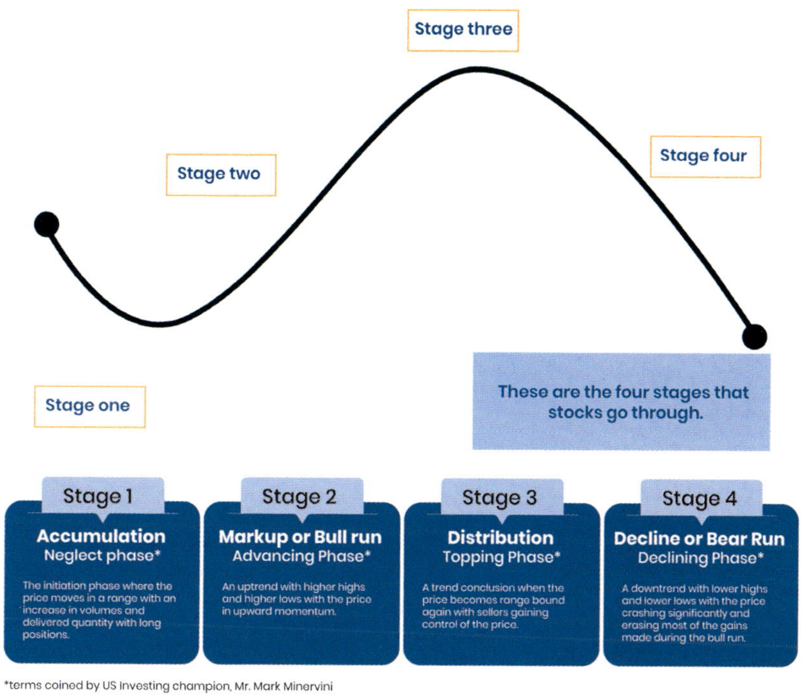

Figure 5.31 Market cycle

The Role of Time and Relativity in Stock Cycles

Understanding time relativity helps us navigate the stock market swings—big, medium and small (refer to Figure 5.32). As a trader I learned that an operator or a resourceful person typically starts the bull run or enters the stock at stage 1 and exits at stage 3, ending the bull run. Retail participants like you and me typically enter the market during stage 2 of a stock and attempt to exit post stage 3. With each new swing created in the later part of stage 2, the stocks change hands from operators to the weaker participants of the market, who do not have the capacity to maintain the bull run, eventually entering the stage 3 of the stock. You would want to enter the trade at the start of stage 2 and ride the momentum when the operators are still in control of the stock. You will still not be able to exit at the top until your take profit is coincidentally set at the same price that you later realize was the top. Even if you exit below a certain percentage from the top, you will still make money and that percentage is dependent on the market capitalization and free float available.

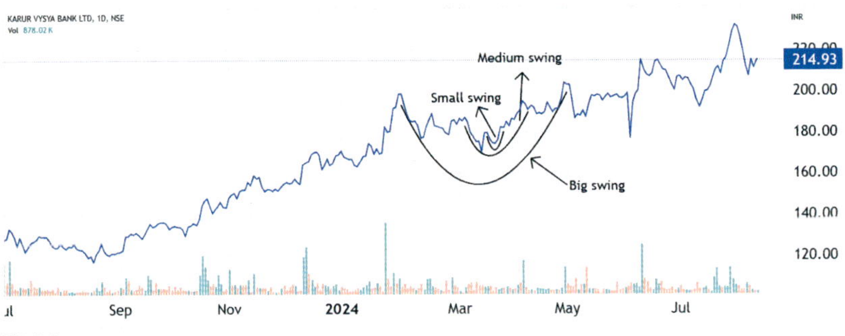

Figure 5.32 Small, medium and big swing of a stock

The Relative Strength Approach

In the end, it's about money—an ongoing race to find winning stocks. To gauge which stock has the advantage, one should consider relative performance vis-à-vis itself and the benchmark, thereby employing the relative strength index (RSI) and relative strength (RS).

We've already discussed these 2 concepts in the indicators section of the book, and how you can use a combination of the 2 to judge the strength in the stock. Personally, I find this methodology effective and continue to enjoy the journey of exploring momentum investing. Now let me break down the entire process of trading for you.

Step 1: Defining Your Tenure

The most important part is to define which tenure of trade you want to take. The different time frames that you can trade in are:

Sl. No.	Trading Type	Trade Tenure	Minimum Risk-Reward Ratio
1	Intraday	1 day	6/4 = 1.5
2	Swing:	2 to 120 days	
2a	Short-term swing	2 to 20 days	10/5 = 2
2b	Medium-term swing	20 days to 60 days	20/8 = 2.5
2c	Long-term swing/momentum investing	60 days to 120 days	30/10 = 3

Table 5.4 Different trade tenures

It's important to first define the duration of the trade as that would direct you to the duration of the chart that you'll have to track. The shorter the duration of the trade, the shorter the duration of the chart that you will track. Each duration of trade will have a different risk-reward ratio associated with it. With intraday the number of trades will be higher in a month while the risk-reward in each trade will be lower, whereas in swing trading the frequency and the number of trades will be lower but the risk-reward will be higher (refer to Table 5.4 for different risk-reward as per the time frame). A longer time frame requires fundamental scrutiny; no big waves can be created without any sound reason, hence for larger returns on a longer time frame, fundamentals of the company play a crucial role.

I use the multi–time-frame template or the mother-daughter setup to track charts of the stock.

Intraday Trading Template

I would like you to avoid intraday trading until you are a full-time market participant and are trading futures and options. Intraday is a different ball game altogether and demands a considerable amount of time and dedication. It is like a full-time job just like a wage earner. You need to be involved all day. The biggest problem is that you become too dependent on the market. Suppose you fall sick and are unable to work for 4 days, then you cannot earn on those days. Similarly, you'll have to trade even when you're on a holiday to earn. There's no point in taking such holidays. I will not recommend getting into intraday trading. It is better to focus on swing trading because you will earn a similar return but you will be saved from the pressure of tracking the market all the time.

Short-Term Swing Trading Template

Short-term swing trading is for positions between 2 and 20 days with a target profit of around 10 to 15% and a stop loss of 3 to 5%. I use the following setup for the same:

- Time duration: 2 to 20 days
- Stop loss: 3 to 5%
- Target profit: 10 to 15%
- Trade setup:
  - Mother chart setup - Daily chart:
    - RS55>0
    - RSI 14>50
  - Daughter chart setup - 2-hours chart:
    - RS55>0
    - RSI 14>50
    - Supertrend = Buy
- Mother chart setup is used to build conviction in the stock

- Entry/exit levels are taken as per the daughter chart setup:
    - Entry at price breakout/retracement in the daughter chart setup
    - Exit as per indicator-based stop loss/price-based stop loss

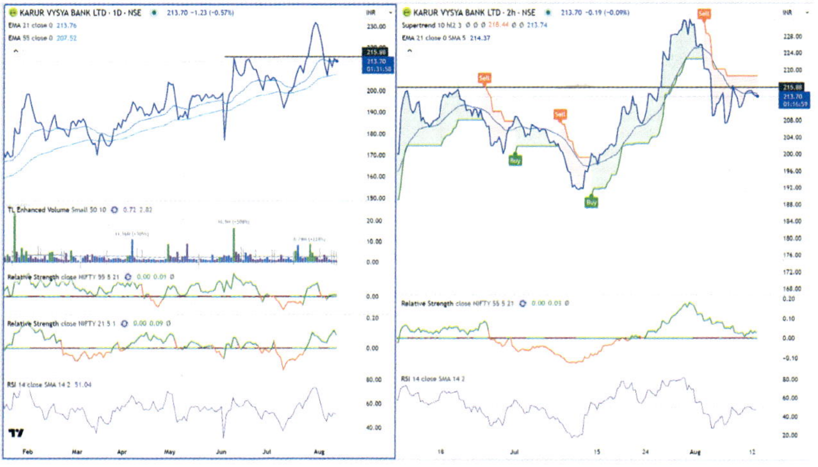

Figure 5.33 Short-term swing trading template

You may use a 2-hourly or a 75-minutes chart depending on your temperament and availability of time.

Medium-Term Swing Trading Template

Medium-term swing trading is for positions between 20 and 60 days with a target profit of around 20 to 25% and a stop loss of 7 to 10%.

- Time duration: 20 to 60 days
- Stop loss: 8 to 10%
- Target profit: 20 to 25%
- Trade setup:
    - Mother chart setup - Weekly chart:
        - RS21>0
        - RSI 14>50
    - Daughter chart setup - Daily chart:
        - RS55>0

- ➤ RSI 14>50
- ➤ Supertrend = Buy

- Mother chart setup is used to build conviction in the stock
- Entry/exit levels is taken as per the daughter chart setup:
  - Entry at price breakout/retracement in the daughter chart setup
  - Exit as per indicator-based stop loss/price-based stop loss

I take the RS21 instead of RS55 in the weekly setup. The logic being that 21 periods in the weekly chart is roughly 6 months, which becomes a more relevant time frame for medium-term swing trading than for 55 periods, which is over a year. The template of this setup is:

Figure 5.34 Medium-term swing trading template

Long-Term Swing/Momentum Investing Template

Long swing trading/momentum investing is for positions beyond 60 days with a target profit of minimum 35% and a stop loss of 10 to 15%. I use the following setup for the same.

- Time duration: more than 60 days
- Stop loss: 10 to 15%
- Target profit: >= 30%
- Trade setup:
  - Mother chart setup - Monthly chart:
    - RS12>0
    - RSI 12>50
    - Revenue growth
    - Stable/growing EBITDA margin
    - Stable P/E ratio
    - Stable P/B ratio
  - Daughter chart setup - Weekly chart:
    - RS21>0
    - RSI 12>50
    - Supertrend = Buy
- Mother chart setup is used to build conviction in the stock
- Entry/exit levels is taken as per the daughter chart setup:
  - Entry at price breakout/retracement in the daughter chart setup
  - Exit as per indicator-based stop loss/price-based stop loss. If the risk profile is lower, we can opt for RS55<0 for exit as per the daily chart for early exit.

A must need is good fundamental (sales and EBITDA) growth in the company for any position here. I change the time frame of RS and RSI for the sole reason that when considering a monthly chart, 12 periods give us one year of data, which is more relevant than 14 months or 21 months.

P/E (price-to-earnings) ratio is calculated by dividing stock price per share by its earnings per share (EPS). It tells us how much people are willing to pay for each rupee a company earns. The P/B (price-to-book) ratio is calculated by dividing stock price per share by its book value per share. It compares a company's market value to its book value.

A high P/E or P/B are both indicative of an overvalued stock, while a low P/E or P/B are indicative of an undervalued stock as per its potential.

While it's common advice to be cautious of stocks with high P/E or P/B ratios, a strong company with solid earnings or valuable intangible assets may adjust its P/E or P/B ratio over time, particularly after earnings reports. Adding these fundamental parameters helps me in avoiding stocks that hint at overvaluation.

The template I use for this setup is here.

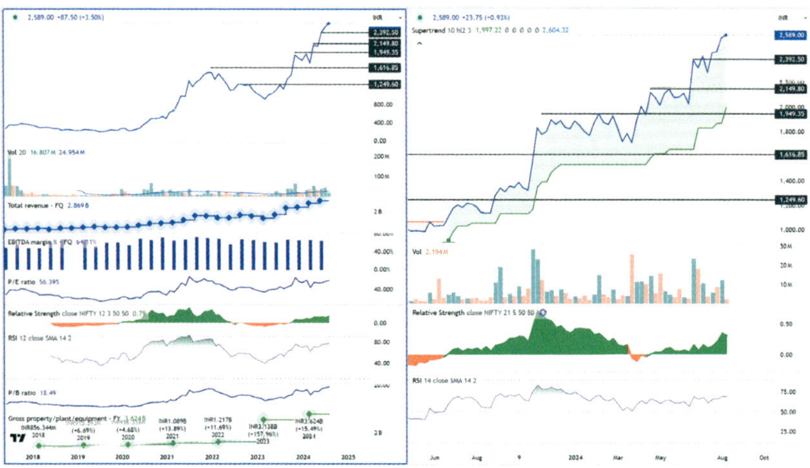

Figure 5.35 Long-term swing/momentum investing template

Long-term swing trading demands fundamental scrutiny. Large market moves need to be backed by some fundamental strength of the companies, or the chances of sustaining such large moves are low; the reason being that tracking earnings data becomes extremely crucial for long swings. TradingView gives us the power to track this data in the chart along with the price movement. Now that our template is ready as per the defined time frame, we can move on to the next step.

Step 2: Stock Selection

Once you've decided the tenure of trade, we add stocks to the watchlist and keep a close eye on the ones that fit perfectly into our template. You can use all the different combo scans that we covered to make a watchlist. We track the charts of all the stocks in the watchlist and mark the ones that fulfil the following criteria:

- Stock is in uptrend
- High volume and delivery
- Fits in our trading template

Sector rotation: This method of stock selection is ideal for medium-term trading setup.

Techno-funda scans: These scans are ideal for medium-term to long-term swing trading as it is supported by strong fundamentals. You may find some short-term swing opportunities too through these combo scans.

Trending stocks (Volume shockers): This is another method you can use to identify stocks on a real-time basis. This list consists of stocks in which there has been a large price movement, or/and there has been higher than average volumes in the stock for the day. These stocks are ideal to catch short-term swings in the stock. Please note Trending Stocks is a StockEdge feature. You may find stocks with high volumes in a day on other platforms too under some other feature name.

Momentum score: Another approach that I take is to use momentum scores on my watchlist. Being a momentum investor, analysing momentum in a stock is crucial for me while selecting stocks. To judge the momentum, I use the momentum score. It is a proprietary algorithm developed by StockEdge, and I'm not sure if any other stock analytics platform provides this analysis.

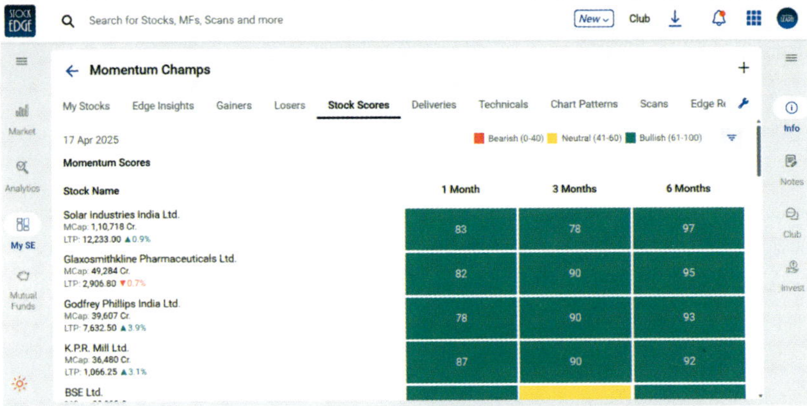

Stock Name	1 Month	3 Months	6 Months
Solar Industries India Ltd. MCap: 1,10,718 Cr. LTP: 12,233.00 ▲0.9%	83	78	97
Glaxosmithkline Pharmaceuticals Ltd. MCap: 49,284 Cr. LTP: 2,906.80 ▼0.7%	82	90	95
Godfrey Phillips India Ltd. MCap: 39,607 Cr. LTP: 7,632.50 ▲3.9%	78	90	93
K.P.R. Mill Ltd. MCap: 36,480 Cr. LTP: 1,066.25 ▲3.1%	87	90	92
BSE Ltd.	[illegible]	[illegible]	[illegible]

Table 5.5

I take out the list of stocks from all the combo scans, create a watchlist and then check the momentum score on those stocks, and naturally I prioritize tracking stocks that are in the green zone (have the highest momentum score).

The above chart shows the momentum score for 1 month, 3 months, and 6 months of the stocks on my watchlist. For:

- Short-term swing trading: I consider stocks that are in bullish zone in 1 month
- Medium-term swing trading: I consider stocks that are in the bullish zone in 3 months
- Long-term swing trading: I consider stocks that are in bullish zone in 6 months

When a stock is in the bullish zone across all time frames, it indicates that the stock has been strong for a while now. Let's see the chart of the first stock in the list—Solar Industries.

Short-Term Swing Trading

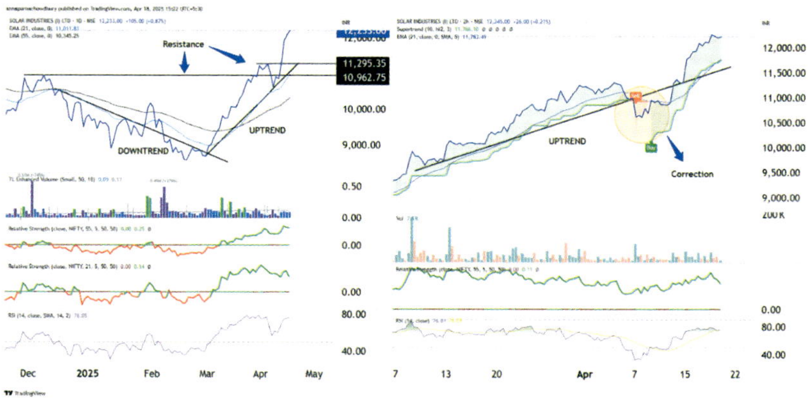

Figure 5.36

The stock is trading at the 12,233 level. Moreover:

- In the mother setup daily chart:
  - RS55>0
  - RSI 14>50
- Daughter chart setup for the 2-hours chart:
  - RS55>0
  - RSI 14>50
  - Supertrend = Buy

In the mother setup, the stock has transitioned into an uptrend after facing a downtrend, while in the daughter setup, the stock has been in a continuous uptrend. Although it did face a correction in between, it bounced back strongly, maintaining its uptrend, making me positive on the stock.

Medium-Term Swing Trading

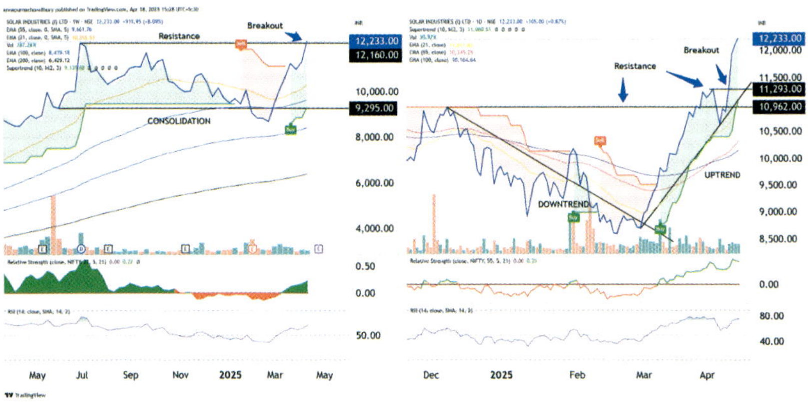

Figure 5.37

The stock is in uptrend in all time frames, trading at the 12,233 level. Moreover:

- Mother chart setup - Weekly chart:
  - RS21>0
  - RSI 14>50
- Daughter chart setup - Daily chart:
  - RS55>0
  - RSI 14>50
  - Supertrend = Buy

In the mother setup, the stock was in consolidation for long and has just given a breakout above its all-time high price of 12,160. While in the daughter chart setup, the stock has given a sharp upmove. Although the stock is in momentum, and all the indicators are hinting towards it, the risk-reward ratio at this level is not favourable for me. However, I will track it closely.

Long-Term Swing Trading

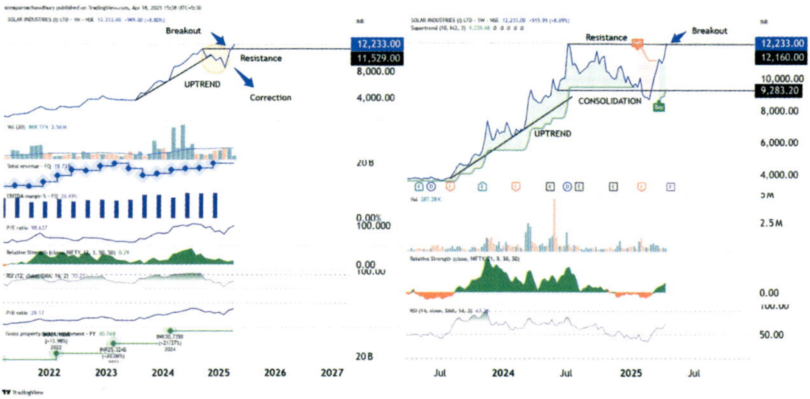

Figure 5.38

The stock is trading at the 12,233 level. Moreover:

- Mother chart setup - Monthly chart:
  - RS12>0
  - RSI 12>50
  - Revenue growth
  - Stable/growing EBITDA margin
- Daughter chart setup - Weekly chart:
  - RS21>0
  - RSI 12>50
  - Supertrend = Buy

In the mother setup, the stock has been in an uptrend for a while now; although it did face a small correction, it bounced back strongly and has given a breakout above the 11,529 level. Moreover, the uptrend is backed by strong fundamental growth giving me conviction. In the mother setup, the stock was in consolidation after an upmove and has just given a breakout above its resistance level, which could mark a beginning of a new rally. I am very positive on this stock and will add this to my tracker.

Once we have identified the stock, the next step is to identify the price we should enter at.

Step 3: Enter at the Right Price Point

We've heard the saying 'Buy low, sell high' multiple times, but let me complete the sentence for you: 'Buy at a lower current price and sell at a higher future price.' Buying low does not mean that you buy when the stock is at its lowest, although it does look tempting since it's trading at a very cheap price. However, just because the stock is trading at its lowest, it does not mean it cannot go lower than that; similarly, when the stock is trading at its highest, it does not mean that it cannot go higher than that. There's a reason for a stock to be trading at its lowest or its highest. The law of motion is very much applicable for stock movements too. If the stock is at its lowest and creating a low with every new swing, then it is most likely to be in that motion. The same logic is applicable when the stock is creating a high with every new swing; it is most likely to be in the same motion.

When momentum investing, identifying such stocks that are in the upmove plays a crucial role, and price breakouts are a way to identify such stocks. As a momentum investor, you can choose to be a:

- Breakout trader
- Retracement trader

Breakout Trading

A price breakout is an indication towards fresh buying interest in the stock, especially when supported by high volumes and delivery as it is very likely that the stock has piqued the interest of an operator, the market movers. Breakout trades are like adding acceleration to the existing speed of the stock making it drive further up, adding momentum to the stock. Trading in a stock momentum has higher chances of giving larger returns in a shorter period of time.

Retracement Trading

For someone who is not comfortable to enter a stock at its breakout point, you can always choose to enter when it retraces. As a retracement trader, you would ideally look to enter when the stock retraces near its support zone, or its previous swing low, as it is very likely to reverse from that point. Even as a retracement trader it's best to add after the stock has reversed after creating a new swing low, rather than adding it when it is retracing (refer to Figure 5.39).

Figure 5.39 Ideal retracement entry

Although there will always be a few exceptions. Some stocks just do not retrace after a strong breakout for a very long time, not giving you an opportunity to enter the trade.

In the chart of Ajanta Pharma in Figure 5.40, the stock gave an all-time high breakout on closing basis above the 2538 level on 31 July 2024, and that's when the RS55 went above 0, but the potential downside was more than 10%, not making the risk-reward favourable to enter at that point. Since then, the stock never retraced back, giving 25% returns in just 9 trading sessions, or 13 calendar days. In such cases, it's very common to feel FOMO, making us make mistakes such as entering at a high level even though risk-reward is not favourable. This is when you need to be highly rational and harsh with yourself to let go of the stock. We will lose out on some of such alpha generating stocks, and we have to be okay with it, and focus on other high potential stocks.

Figure 5.40 Daily chart of Ajanta Pharma

To summarize, you need to decide who you are—a breakout trader or a retracement trader. If you're someone who can be aggressive with trades, then you can choose to be a breakout trader; however, if you're someone who needs a higher safety margin, then you can choose to be a retracement trader.

Short-Term Swing Trading

Figure 5.41 Daily and 2-hourly chart of NTPC Ltd

In the daily time frame, or the mother setup, the stock is in an uptrend and currently facing a slight correction from its all-time high, RS55>0 and RSI 14>50, making me bullish on the stock. However, in the shorter time frame or the 2-hourly time frame, the stock broke its support level, which is also the current supertrend level of 409, indicating some profit booking in the stock, RS55>0, but RSI 14 is below 50, indicating loss of momentum in the 2-hourly chart, not making it a good candidate for the short-term swing trade. I will only enter this trade when the 2-hourly chart speaks the same language as the daily chart, i.e., when the stock transitions back to uptrend, supertrend is buy, RS55>0 and RSI 14>50. Once the stock fulfils all my parameters, then I will wait for the stock to break out of its previous swing high to enter the trade, with a return expectation of at least 10% and a potential downside of not more than 5%.

Medium-Term Swing Trading

Figure 5.42 Weekly and daily chart of NTPC

In the weekly chart, the stock is in uptrend, RS21>0 and RSI 14>50, making me bullish on the stock. In the daily chart, the stock is retracing and is trading at the previous resistance level, which could also be the new potential support level. Moreover RS55 = 0 and RSI 14 = 50, making me neutral on the stock in the daily time frame. It is currently at a crucial zone, where a breakdown from this level could mean more downside in the near future; however, a price reversal would mean that the bullish sentiment in the stock is still intact. A breakout trader will wait till it reverses and gives a breakout above the 423 level on a closing basis to enter the trade. However, a retracement trader will wait till it reverses and gives a closing above 396 level to enter the trade.

Never be in a hurry to enter or exit a stock as soon as the stock breaks out, always wait for the confirmation of the price. The breakout is only confirmed once the price closes above its breakout level, so wait for the closing price to enter a trade, be it 2-hourly or daily. In case of breakouts in the 2-hourly chart, wait for the completion of the 2-hourly candle, and in case of breakouts in the daily chart, wait for the completion of the daily candle before entering the trade.

Long-Term Swing/Momentum Investing

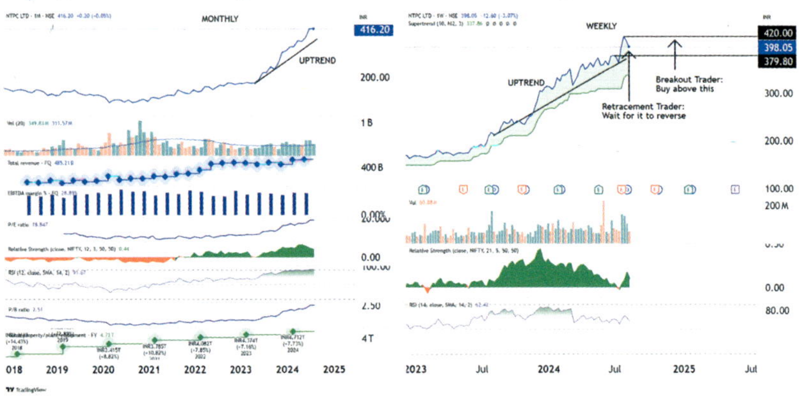

Figure 5.43 Monthly and weekly chart of NTPC

The monthly chart of the stock is in an uptrend, supported by growth in the fundamental parameters of the company, revenue growth, good EBITDA margins, along with a capex growth; moreover, it is supported by technical indicators; RS12>0 and RSI 12>50 is making me bullish on the stock. In the weekly chart, the stock is in uptrend, retracing from its all-time high breakout, RS21>0, RSI 12>50. A breakout trader will wait for it to reverse and cross its previous swing high above the 420 level to enter the trade. However, a retracement trader will wait for it to reverse after creating a new swing low to enter the trade. Till then we will wait.

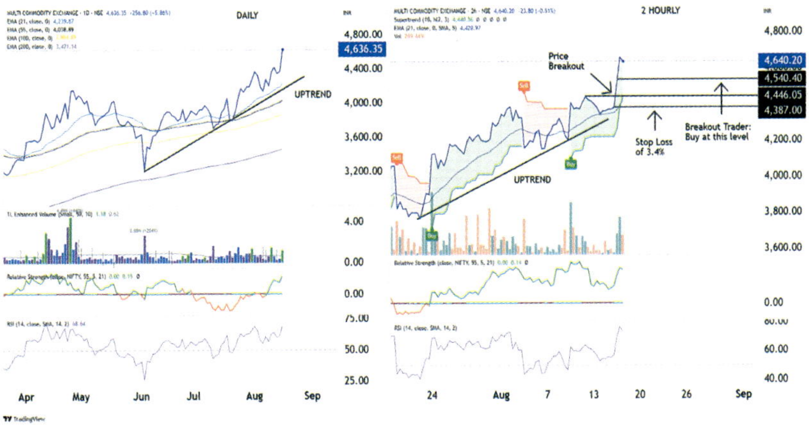

Figure 5.44 Daily and 2-hourly chart of Multi Commodity Exchange (MCX)

Short-Term Swing Trading

In Figure 5.44, the mother setup or the daily chart of MCX is in an uptrend, RS55>0 and RSI 14>50, making me bullish on the stock. Coming to the daughter setup, or the 2-hourly setup, the stock is in uptrend, RS55>0, RSI 14>50, and supertrend is also buy; moreover, the stock gave a breakout above the 4446 level, which was the previous swing high. A breakout trader will wait for the closing of the candle above the breakout level to enter the trade. The 2-hourly candle closed at 4540, making the breakout traders enter the trade, with a stop loss of 3 to 5%. I like to keep my stop loss at the previous swing low, so my stop loss would be 4387, i.e., 3.4% below the buy price. A retracement trader would wait for the price to come down and then reverse again to enter the stock.

Medium-Term Swing Trading

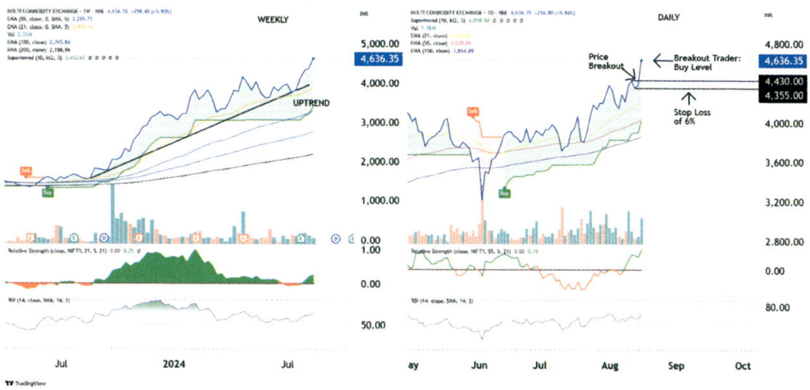

Figure 5.45 Weekly and daily chart of Multi Commodity Exchange (MCX)

In Figure 5.45, the mother setup or the weekly chart of MCX is in an uptrend, RS55>0 and RSI 14>50, making me bullish on the stock. In the daily chart, or the daughter setup, the price is in an uptrend, RS55>0 and RSI 14>50. The stock has just given a breakout above its previous swing high, which was the 4430 level. A breakout trader would wait for the closing price to go above the breakout level for the confirmation of the breakout to enter the trade. The price closed at 4636, which became the buy price for the breakout trader, with a stop loss of 6%. The stop loss being the previous swings low, i.e., the 4355 level. A retracement trader would wait for the price to come down and then reverse again to enter the stock.

Long-Term Swing Trading/Momentum Investing

Figure 5.46 Monthly and weekly chart of Multi Commodity Exchange (MCX)

In Figure 5.46, just observe the monthly chart of MCX, the stock has been in an uptrend for a while now and just look at the steep incline of the stock from roughly the 1600 level to the 4600 levels in a year, generating 187% returns in a year and still looking strong. Looking at the fundamental parameters of the stock, the revenue has been rising each quarter, with EBITDA margins of 60% and 65% the last 2 quarters. A very interesting thing to note is how the PE has adjusted itself with the earnings result. When the price was on a steep incline, the PE kept rising exponentially from the 360 level and now it's back to the 200 level, a sign of a fundamentally strong company, making me more convinced about the stock. Coming to the technical parameters in the monthly chart, or the mother chart, RSI 12>50 and RS12>0, making me bullish on the stock. Coming to the weekly chart or the daughter setup, the stock is in a continuous uptrend, and gave a breakout above its previous swings high level of 3986 to close at the

4140 level on 22 July 2024, but a quick observation will show you that the RS21 on that day was still at borderline 0, even though RSI 14>50, the RS was not making me comfortable to enter the stock. I waited till RS21>0 on a closing basis to enter the stock, hence being a breakout trader, my entry price would be 4330 when RS21>0. Moreover, at this price point, the stock gave an all-time high breakout, making my conviction about the trade stronger. My stop loss would be the previous swing low, which is the 3775 level, i.e. 12% from its breakout level. Again, a retracement trader would have to wait for it to retrace and then bounce back up to enter the trade.

The above examples were given to help you understand my method. I would suggest you experiment with the same.

Step 4: Decide Allocation per Stock and Stop Loss

We've already covered the allocation of capital per stock. The simplest way is to divide your total capital amongst the number of stocks in your portfolio. With proper risk management in place, you will generate good returns following this approach to start with. The returns of a well-diversified portfolio often follow a bell-shaped curve, known as normal distribution. This implies that if you have 20 stocks in your portfolio, then it is very likely that 10 out of those 20 stocks will give you average returns, while 5 of them might give you very high return, and the other 5 will give you a low return. To increase your overall portfolio return you would want to give higher weightage to the winning stocks in your portfolio and lower weightage to losing stocks. I'll show you what I did to increase the weightage of a winning stock in my portfolio.

Central Depository Services Limited (CDSL) was one of my beauty picks in the portfolio.

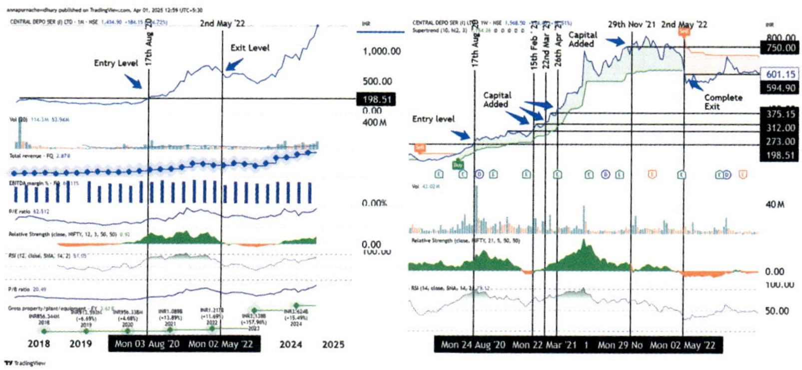

Figure 5.47 Monthly and weekly chart of CDSL

I went in for long-term swing trading in CDSL when it fulfilled all my criteria to enter the trade. I entered with 20% of the capital that I was supposed to allocate to the stock at the 201 level during the week of 24 August 2020 (refer to Figure 5.47). The stock went on to make a higher high, and gave a fresh breakout at the 275 level, supported by high volumes; I added another 20%. CDSL turned out to be one of those hero stocks that kept making higher highs, and giving fresh breakouts. So, this was one of those stocks where I'd keep adding my capital unless it shows weakness.

I added 20% at the 312 level, another 20% at the 375 level and another 20% at the 750 level at breakout level, allocating 20% more in the stock than I usually would. The average price came down to 383. This concept of adding at higher levels is also called pyramiding.

A common question would be why did I not add at the 500 level breakout. Simply because the risk-reward was not favourable at that price point. Observe how the rally became too steep, making me jittery to take any new positions at that price point. There were more breakouts given by the stock, but the risk far outweighed the reward till the fresh breakout given on 29 November 2021.

I sold my entire holding when the super trend changed to sell, and RS21 went below 0 at 595 level during the week of 2 May 2022 as per the daughter setup of the chart (I will cover how I take exits in the next section). The return generated was 55% in 1.5 years, which is more than what most stocks could give. Remember that since the stock price is going up, the profit on the previous trade is also going up giving you more room to add more quantities at higher levels. You may adjust this 20% based on your comfort. Some will start from 10%. Some may like to do 50-50, some like to do 20-40-40. The amount you want to invest in any stock should be predefined for your clarity in action. Eventually the stock will have a higher proportion of your portfolio.

Stop Loss

When we are doing momentum trading or investing, we would want to ride the stock till the momentum dies off. This is my mantra when riding momentum. Being a professional trader, I have a good risk appetite that gives me room to keep a larger stop loss, which also comes along with a higher return anticipation. Momentum trading or investing has the power to give you large returns if you can be strong enough to hold the stock for a longer period of time.

Trading Tenure	Stop Loss	Take Profit
Short-term swing	3% to 5%	10% to 15%
Medium-term swing	8% to 10%	20% to 25%
Long-term swing/momentum investing	10% to 12%	>=30%

Table 5.6: Stop loss and take profit

The above table defines the take profit and stop loss that I keep when entering a trade. For example, short swing trading my stop loss is typically 3 to 5%, while the take profit is 10%.

Initial Stop Loss

When entering a stock, the stop loss that I use is the price point that is a bit below the previous swing low, which should be within the reasonable range as mentioned in the table for me to consider entering the trade. It is based on a simple logic that if the stock is going to make a higher high and higher low, confirming the uptrend, it'll give me room to generate higher returns without my stop loss getting triggered; and if it does get triggered, then maybe my stock selection or my entry was not right, or maybe it was a bear trap—it could be anything.

Trailing Stop Loss

Being a professional trader, I choose to follow the indicator-based stop loss (which automatically trails my stop loss) and hold the stock till my pre-defined indicators hint towards a weakness in the stock. The indicator-based stop loss that I follow are:

Short-term swing trading

- Daughter chart setup (2-hourly/75 minutes chart):
  - RS55<0
  - Supertrend = Sell
- Mother chart setup (Daily chart):
  - Daily RS21<0

Medium-term swing trading:

- Daughter chart setup (Daily chart):
  - RS21<0
  - Supertrend = Sell

Long-term swing trading:

- Daily chart:
  - RS55<0
  - Supertrend = Sell

This approach gives me more time than the price-based stop loss to confirm that the momentum has been exhausted in the stock. This works well for me; being in the market for over 20 years, I'm not much bothered by stock fluctuations as long as my setup is still intact. Such emotional resilience, a high-risk appetite and a large capital base allows me to keep the indicator-based stop loss.

It also comes with a disadvantage that the indicator takes some time to confirm the weakness in the stock. Hence, if I was someone who did not have as much risk appetite or a strong emotional resilience towards fluctuations, then I would opt for a price-based stop loss.

I would probably opt for the previous swing low as the trailing price-based stop loss; the simple logic being that the previous swing low should ideally be the demand zone of a stock. If the stock goes below that demand zone, then the stock could be losing its strength.

Empirical studies suggest that when an operator is dominant in a stock, one should try to filter out the weak retail investors from the stock, by purposely driving the stock below its demand zone. The operators know how most of these retail investors operate and try to shake them out of the stock before driving it further up. During this stage the stock is capable of falling 15 to 20% from the top and can consolidate at this lower level for a while, creating a perception that maybe the momentum has died in the stock, and the stock is entering the distribution or the fourth phase of the market cycle, when in reality the strong stocks are actually just creating another base before moving up further. Hence, if my risk appetite was low, I would prefer to exit a stock early on with higher profit, than holding on to it further along with the risk of a lower profit.

Which Stop Loss Is Ideal for the Time Frames?

The approach that makes you least anxious is the approach that you should choose to follow for your stop loss.

Step 5: Right Time to Exit

An exit strategy is as important as an entry strategy or right stock selection. Without a proper exit strategy, you could end up losing even in winning stocks. An ideal exit from a strong stock is when the stock has lost its strength. A professional trader can feel the stock scream 'Sell' through the charts. I am very ruthless when it comes to exiting a stock, be it loss or profit. Your take profit and stop loss level should have already been well-defined while entering a stock. I would:

- Completely exit when my stop loss is triggered
- Partially exit when my take profit is achieved (stock enters overbought zone)
- Completely exit when stock hints weakness

	Price-Based Exit		Indicator-Based Exit	
	Stop Loss	**Take Profit**	**Stop Loss**	**Take Profit**
Short-term swing trading	3% to 5%	2 times of your stop loss	2-hourly RS55<0 Daily RS21<0 Supertrend = Sell	RSI>90
Medium-term swing trading	8% to 10%	2.5 times of your stop loss	Daily RS21<0 Supertrend = Sell	RSI>90
Long-term swing trading	10% to 12%	3 times of your stop loss	Daily RS55<0 Supertrend = Sell	RSI>90

Table 5.7 Defining take profit and stop loss based on your tenure of trade

Let's dive deeper into the above table.

Completely Exit When My Stop Loss Is Triggered

If my stop loss is triggered without giving any upmove, then I completely exit from the stock no matter what.

Partial Exit When My Take Profit Is Achieved (Stock Enters Overbought Zone)

If the stock gives an upmove, then I book 50% of my position when my take profit is achieved. Take profit too can be defined in 2 ways:

Indicator based: When following indicator-based stop loss, you should book partial profit when the indicator gives you overbought signs, indicating that the stock has given an abnormal rally. I book 50% of my trade when the RSI goes above 90 in the daughter chart setup, as it is indicative of stock entering an overbought zone, and you can choose to exit when the RS model tells you to sell. Indicator-based exit can offer an opportunity to ride larger rallies.

Price based: When opting for the price-based stop loss, I book 50% of my position when my take profit is achieved as per Table 5.7. So, if my stop loss is 3% for short-term swing trading then my take profit would be 6% (2 times my stop loss). Similarly, for medium-term swing trading, my take profit stands at 2.5 times my stop loss, whereas for long term swing trading my take profit stands at 3 times my stop loss. After partially booking my profit, I trail the rest.

Additionally, I also look at the slope of the price movement. If it's too steep, i.e., ranges between 60 degrees to 90 degrees, then I book 50%, as it's an unnatural move (recall Figure 5.5).

Complete Exit When Stock Hints Weakness

I completely exit my position as soon as the stock starts showing weakness. I mostly follow the indicator-based exit to confirm the weakness of the stock as mentioned in Table 5.7.

When I opt for the price-based exit, I keep some level below the previous swing low as my trailing stop loss. As soon as the stock touches this level, I consider it as a sign of weakness, and exit the stock.

Keep the Following in Mind When Designing Your Exit Strategy

Trailing stop loss triggers need to be respected, irrespective of your take profit. There will be trades, where you do not get a chance to partially exit as the stock did not show any overbought signs, or your take profit was not achieved. Even in that case you completely exit the stock as per your defined trailing stop loss.

When opting for price-based exits, do not follow the pyramiding concept of capital allocation. In that case, it's best to enter with the full amount that you want to allocate to the stock.

Do not change the stop loss approach after taking the trade. To avoid booking losses, it's very common for novice traders to change the stop loss approach from price-based exits to indicator-based exits. Please do not make such foolish mistakes. The exit strategy needs to be designed in a way that it fits well with your risk management. If you're still figuring it out, then I would suggest trying both systems in different trades, rather than in the same trade, to see what works best for you.

Let's take one of my trades as an example. Though I followed the medium-term swing trading setup, I will discuss all the different setups with you. It was one of my finest trades that helped me generate alpha returns in my portfolio—with BSE Ltd.

Short-Term Swing Trading

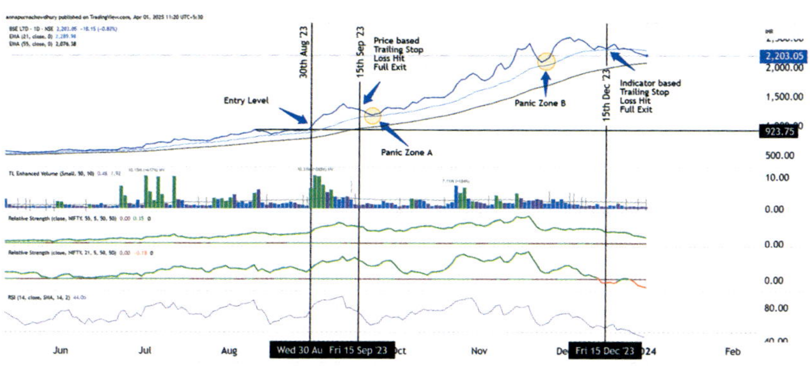

Figure 5.48 Daily chart of BSE Ltd

The entry level as per my mother daughter setup was on 30 August 2023. In the daily chart or the mother setup, the stock was in uptrend along with RS55>0 and RSI 14>50, making me positive on the stock. The daughter setup was aligned too, building my conviction in the stock. As soon as the stock gave a breakout above its previous swing high at the 923 level on the 2-hourly chart or the daughter setup; I entered the stock at the closing of the 2-hourly candle at the 954 level.

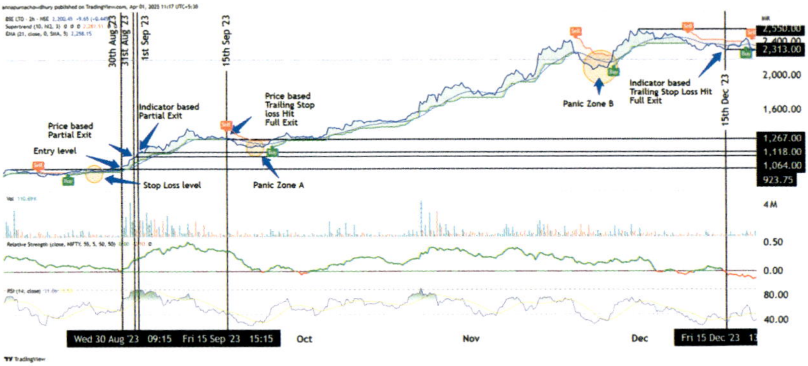

Figure 5.49 2-hourly chart of BSE Ltd

For those who follow the price-based stop loss and exit, stop loss would be 895, i.e., roughly 5% from the entry level, with a take profit of 10%, i.e., at the 1050 level. BSE turned out to be a super stock, giving the 10% return within 1 day. The 2-hourly candle closed at the 1064 level on 31 August 2023. Short swing traders who follow the price-based exit would book 50% at this level and ride the rest 50% till the stock breaks its previous swing low. You can choose which swing low to consider, small swing or large swing. To ride large rallies, it's best to consider a large swing when keeping previous swing low as a trailing stop loss. In this case the stock broke its previous swing low on 15 September 2023 at the 1267 level. Traders who follow the price-based exit would completely exit the stock at this level. The return in this case would be 22.5% within a span of 15 days.

For those who follow indicator-based exit, we would exit partially when the 2-hourly RSI>90. On 1 September 2023 when the stock gave another breakout, RSI touched 91, making it a good point to book 50% at the 1118 level, and riding the stock till the indicators ask me to sell. The stock kept making higher highs supported by both RSI and RS for the next 3 months. On 15 December 2023 in the 2-hourly chart, the stock gave a correction making the supertrend sell, RS55 went below 0, and on the daily chart RS21 (refer to Figure 5.49) too went below 0, making us exit the stock completely at the 2313 level. The returns generated in this case would approximately be 80% in a span of three and a half months.

Observe how on some occasions one or the other indicator was indicating weakness while the other indicators did not follow suit and were still showing strength in the stock. For example, on 25 September 2023, the supertrend became sell and RS55 went below 0 in the 2-hourly chart, although the RS21 on the daily chart was still positive, moreover it was a 14% drop from the top made at 1400 (marked as panic zone A). Tracking such a movement on a real-time basis tends to cause panic among the traders, making them forgo the rule they've set for themselves and take a decision driven by their panic-struck mind. If we sold at this level, we would have missed the next big rally that the stock gave. Observe how the stock reversed after giving a small correction and went up till the 2500 level before making us exit the stock completely. Similarly on 22 November 2023 (marked as panic zone B), the stock went down by 14%, supertrend became sell and even RSI<50, giving weak signals. However, the RS55 was still above 0, hinting that the strength was intact in the stock. Just look how the stock bounced back and made yet another high at the 2550 level. Hence, the confirmation of all the 3 indicators is important before making a decision to exit the stock.

Medium-Term Swing Trading

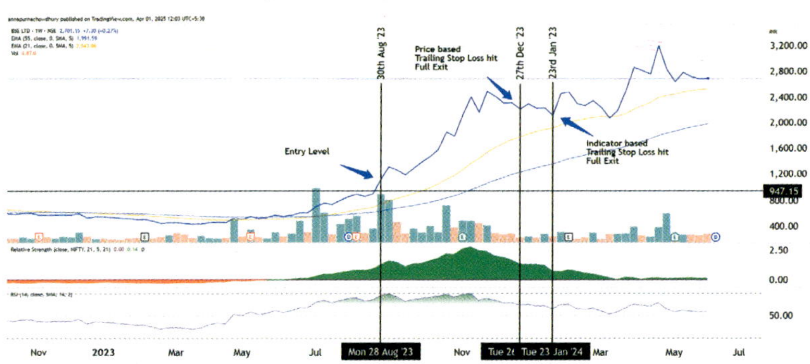

Figure 5.50 Weekly chart of BSE Ltd

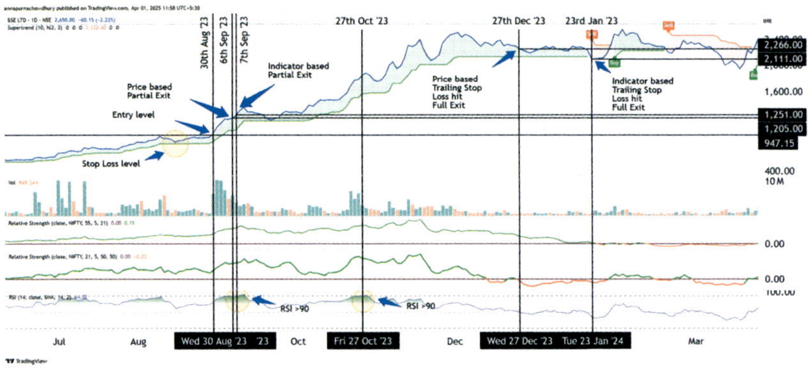

Figure 5.51 Daily chart of BSE Ltd

The stock fulfilled all the criteria for medium-term swing. In the mother setup or the weekly chart, the stock was in uptrend, RSI 14>50, RS21>0, making me bullish on the stock. Coming to the daily chart or the daughter setup, the stock aligned with the mother setup; it was in uptrend, RS55>0, RSI>50, and supertrend was buy. We wait for the stock to give a breakout above previous swing high on the daily chart to enter the stock, which it did on 30 August 2023, with a closing candle at the 967 level. My stop loss in this setup would be 868, roughly 10% from the entry level, making my take profit 1208, 2.5 times of the stop loss.

For those who follow price-based exits, the stock achieved its take profit level on 6 September 2023, making us book partially at the 1205 level. We ride the other half trailing the stop loss to the previous swing low. The stock kept breaking out from previous swing highs, making higher highs and higher lows with each new swing, moving up in a strong uptrend, and largely outperforming the benchmark index. The stop loss trailed from 868 to 1175 on 21 September 2023, to 1280 on 4 October 2023, to 1480 on 17 October 2023, to 1771 on 2 November 2023, to 1963 on 9 November 2023, to 2088 on 22 November 2023, to 2306 on 12 December 2023. The trailing stop loss was triggered on 27 December 2023, when the stock closed at the 2266 level, making us book the rest of the position in the stock. The returns generated in this case was a whopping 80% within a span of 4 months.

For those who follow indicator-based exits, a partial exit was on 7 September 2023 at the 1251 level, when the RSI went above 90 both on the daily chart and weekly chart, indicating that the stock's movement was irrationally high or overbought. Such cases typically lead to some retracement or correction in the stock, which can be seen in the daily chart. After retracing the stock went up to make a higher high and break the previous swing high with a strong upmove. Complete exit from the stock was when supertrend became sell, supported by RS21 going below 0 in the daily chart on 23 January 2024 at the 2111 level. The stock generated roughly 80% return in this case too within a span of 5 months.

An interesting thing to note here is that the RSI crossed 90 again on 27 October 2023 at the 1862 level. Did I partially book again ? No. The first partial booking is done for mental peace that some profit has already been bagged from the trade. Had I partially booked the profits again, then I would have missed the larger rally. Another alternative that I use is to book 20 to 25% of the remaining capital at this level, when I feel restless.

A very common thought that occurs in the mind of beginners is that the stock gave similar returns in both indicator-based exit and price-based exit, moreover the time period in the indicator-based exit was higher with the same return. Remember that price-based exits give an early exit from a strong stock. In some cases, the stock could reverse after making the retail investors exit with price-based stop losses giving larger returns for those following indicator-based exit.

With over twenty years of experience in the market, I am now much more capable of being indifferent to small price fluctuations and hence indicator-based exit suits me as it gives a better opportunity to generate higher returns. *If you have a peaceful sleep following price-based exits, then it is best you follow that since each trader has his own temperament.*

Long-Term Swing Trading/Momentum Investing

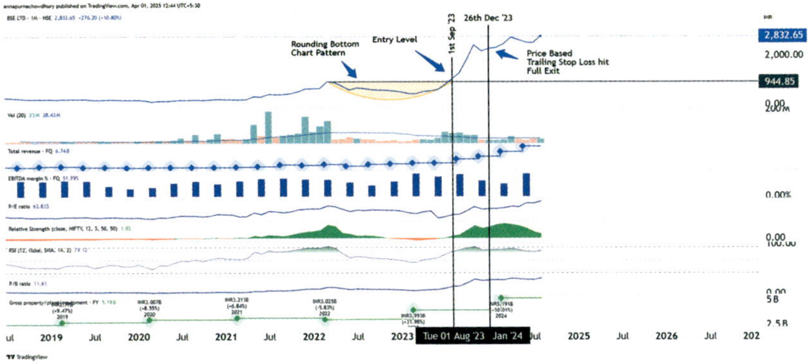

Figure 5.52 Monthly chart of BSE

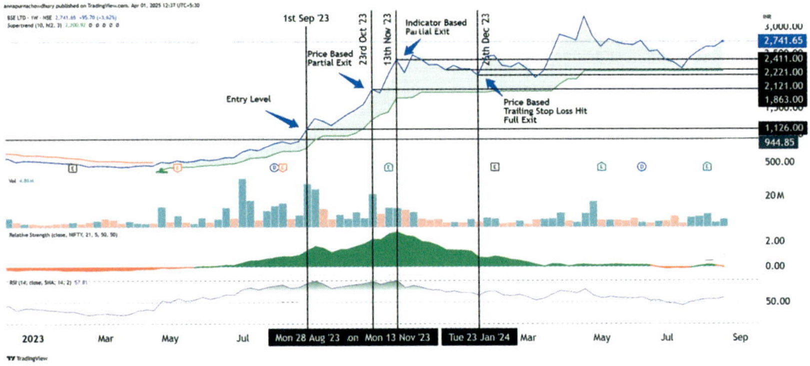

Figure 5.53 Weekly chart of BSE

For long-term swing traders, observe how the fundamentals, namely revenue, EBITDA margins of BSE were improving month on month along with capex growth, making me fundamentally positive about the company. Coming to technicals, the stock seemed to be coming out of correction and transitioning into an uptrend in the mother setup after forming a rounding bottom pattern, supported by RS12>0, and RSI 12>50, making me bullish on the stock. The daughter setup or the weekly chart of the stock was fully aligned with the stock being in uptrend, RS21>0, RSI 14>50. I entered the stock once it confirmed its strength by breaking out of its previous swing high above the 944 level on a closing basis at the 1126 level on 1 September 2023. The stop loss in this case would be 944 roughly 15%, with the take profit being 1667, 3 times of the stop loss.

For those who follow the price-based exit, the stock rallied up and achieved the take profit level of 1667 during the week of 23 October 2023 closing at the 1863 level, making them book partial profits in the stock. With each new breakout, the stop loss was trailed to previous swing low switching from 944 to 1196, to 1799, to 2170, and finally to 2221 during the week of 26 December 2023. This was triggered when the stock broke the 2221 level to close at the 2121 level in the week of 23 January 2024, making them completely exit the stock at that level. The returns achieved was roughly 77% in roughly 4 months.

For those who follow the indicator-based exit; the stock made a steep incline and the RSI of the stock reached around 90 both in weekly and monthly charts during the week of 13 November 2023, making them book partial profits in the stock. When trading in long-term swings, the exit would be when supertrend becomes sell in the weekly chart and the weakness of the stock is confirmed by RS55 going below 0 in the daily chart. In this case, the supertrend of the stock is still buy, even though the RS55 did go below 0 in the daily chart (refer Figure 5.51), as per the rule, the rest of the position should still be intact in the stock.

Strong fundamentals of a company are the basis of long swing trading, and when the fundamentals have changed, and not showing strength anymore, then it's best to square up the trade, because the foundation for entering the stock is no longer supported, no matter what the technical indicators are hinting at. Additionally, when you are in for a longer term, some thematic understanding about the stock is important for you to stay invested in the stock. You would want to understand the fundamental story of the company and the underlying reason for the growth of the company.

Another important thing to note is that both the entry and the exit would be based on the daughter setup; we do refer to other time-frame charts for confirmation of the weakness, but the exit would solely be based as per the chart of the daughter setup in all the trading tenures.

To summarize:

Trading Type	Mother Chart	Daughter Chart (Entry Criteria)	Exit	Take Profit (book 50%)	Complete Exit
Short-term swing	Daily_ RS55>0	2H_RS55>0	Price based	10% to 15%	Price breaking previous swing low
	Daily_RSI 14>50	2H_RSI 14>50	Indicator based	RSI>90	2H_ RS55<0
		Supertrend = Buy			Daily_ RS21<50
		Price breaking previous swing high			Supertrend = Sell
Medium-term swing	Weekly_ RS21>0	Daily_ RS55>0	Price based	20% to 25%	Price breaking previous swing low
	Weekly_ RSI 14>50	Daily_RSI 14>50	Indicator based	RSI>90	Daily_ RS21<50
		Supertrend = Buy			Supertrend = Sell
		Price breaking previous swing high			

Trading Type	Mother Chart	Daughter Chart (Entry Criteria)	Exit	Take Profit (book 50%)	Complete Exit
Long-term swing/ momentum investing	Monthly_ RS12>0	Weekly_ RS21>0	Price based	>=30%	Price breaking previous swing low
	Monthly_ RSI12>50	Weekly_RSI 12>50	Indicator based	RSI>90	Daily_ RS55<0
	Revenue Trend	Supertrend = Buy			Supertrend = Sell
	EBITDA stable/ growing	Price breaking previous swing high			
	PE near long term range				

Table 5.8

The Table 5.8 summarizes the entire trading setup and rules for the different trading tenures in momentum investing.

My journey of momentum investing has been an exciting and rewarding one. With a lot of different trials and errors I've created my own model that works for me, considering my traits and characteristics. I would request you to create your own model; you can choose to build on my model and create your own, but it's important to create a setup that suits you. For example, you can choose to add VWAP, Bollinger Bands, ATR, MACD or any other indicator that you believe works for you to my template and define your own trading style and setup.

A good setup is important; however, patience and resilience to follow the setup is far more important, how a turtle does. Typically, turtles keep moving at a slow pace and follow their natural process until real danger appears. Similarly, in trading, it's crucial to stick to your system and ride the momentum when the market is in your favour. But when conditions shift dramatically or when the market shows signs of extreme danger or unfavourable situations, the wise decision is to retreat, just like the turtle retreating into its shell. By stepping back and protecting your profits, you ensure that you're not exposed to unnecessary risks, maintaining patience and discipline until it's safe to re-enter.

What Should You Be Mindful of as a Momentum Investor?

Each investing/trading type is suited for people with different character traits. You can only be a momentum investor if you have a set of character traits or can adapt to the characteristics needed to become a momentum investor. The following are the things that you would want to keep in mind:

Characteristics of a Momentum Investor

The typical skill set required for a momentum investor would include:

- Ability to understand new emerging business themes and connect the same with price action
- The ability to eliminate noise related to narratives around an opportunity
- Just like swing trading, patience and practice holds the key to momentum investing

A Few Guiding Principles

- Don't add up your position for short-term swing trading
- Don't add to your position when following price-based exits
- Add to your position during medium to long swing and following the indicator-based exit
- A momentum investor does not think about stock being very expensive. They are okay to enter in an expensive stock with a well-defined risk-reward ratio

Things That Could Go Wrong

- Improper risk management
- Poor broader markets
- Trading in highly volatile stocks
- News-based movements and trades
- Trading on important event days

How Do We Get Better Odds

- Be judicious with the number of trades you take. A higher number of trades does not guarantee a success as the chances of success becomes more like coin toss possibility
- The longer chart frames help you in generating higher returns, saves you time from daily trading and mental stress
- Focus on ROTI (return on time invested) and not *ego*.

We should also track the macro markets. If the macros are not in your favour, then the odds of making money goes down significantly.

LEARNER'S CORNER

How do I define my trading tenure?

If you do not know which trading time frame is more suited for you, then ask yourself these questions: How much time can you spend in the market per day, and how frequent do you want to take trades? If you can spend at least 2 hours per day, then you can choose to opt for short-term swing trading or medium-term swing trading. If you cannot spend much time daily but can spend at least 3-4 hours on a weekly basis for analysis and are okay in taking a low number of trades, then you may opt for long-term trading. However, if you're a beginner, then I would suggest you opt for medium-term swing trading to start with.

How many trades should I take initially?

Initially, focus on 10-12 trades to maintain a balanced momentum portfolio. Allocate capital across 3-5 high-performing sectors, and the rest in individual strong stocks. Avoid over-diversification to ensure effective tracking and risk management. Start with smaller positions and scale up as stocks confirm momentum.

How should you understand which breakout is to be ignored due to extended move?

Breakouts occurring after abnormal moves where there are low volumes and are occurring at overbought levels that can be confirmed using indicators are to be avoided or to be traded with very tight stop loss as extended moves tend to give sharp pullbacks as the risk-reward ratio is not favourable.

How should you deal with a false breakout?

Getting stuck in a stock with a false breakout can be very frustrating for a trader. Common mistakes that traders make is not believing it is a false breakout, so they continue holding the position even when the stop loss is triggered. Let's understand one thing: false breakouts are common and even the smartest traders have been trapped in it. The only way to deal with it is to exit when the stop loss is triggered. One way to reduce the frustration is to manage the position sizing at the point of entry. This way, you at least minimize the loss.

How should you understand which trading strategy suits you?

The best trading strategy depends on your risk tolerance and mindset. If you can sleep peacefully holding a position despite market fluctuations, you're likely a long-term investor. For example, if you hold a stock through downturns, believing in its future growth, you align with long-term investing. However, if price swings make you anxious and you frequently buy and sell, a short-term trading strategy may suit you better. Eventually you need to aspire to have a calm mind and a stable strategy in the long term, and evolve to be a momentum investor/value investor.

Does momentum investing work in all market conditions?

The beauty of momentum investing is that we get opportunities only when the stock is showing strength. In a bull market, you will face the problem of plenty as most stocks will look very good to add, with limited capital, we can only trade in select few stocks. Whereas, in a range-bound market, you will still be able to identify select sectors that will demonstrate momentum. However, in the bear market, it's best to stay away, as if the broader markets are not in your favour, then the probability of making money overall decreases significantly. Although there will still be a few stocks that will show strength during that time and tempt you to initiate a trade, yet I would advise you to stay away.

LET'S PRACTICE

This is the final leg. Now I would like you to invest some money in taking the subscription for TradingView and a stock analytics platform and start trading the right way. Try the different approaches, stick to the one that is working for you, and create a trading system for yourself. This will be a perpetual practice if you actually want to trade and make money from the markets.

Macro Analysis

Macro drives micro, and micro drives macro. It's essential to get a 360-degree understanding of current global markets. The Indian financial markets, like that of any other emerging economy, are highly influenced by a variety of macroeconomic factors and global market movements. Very few traders or trainers will talk about this, but I feel it is my responsibility to teach you how to form judgement on the markets, and tracking global markets is a way to do that. I follow the '**CEBC**' framework of tracking the global markets:

1. **C**urrency Markets
   a. Dollar Index
   b. USDINR
2. **E**quity Markets—Global
   a. NASDAQ
   b. S&P 500
   c. Emerging Market Index
3. **B**ond Markets
   a. US Treasury Yield (10 year)
   b. Indian Govt Bond Yield (10-year G-Sec)
4. **C**ommodity Markets
   a. Crude Oil (Brent, WTI)
   b. Gold

Currency Markets

How often have we heard that the INR is becoming weak and is going up against USD. The only thing that comes to the mind of a novice in this case is how the expenses are going to rise once they travel out of India, since most expenses are done in USD. Let's change that perspective now. The reason that even a minute change in Dollar or USDINR becomes a topic of discussion is because of its influence on import costs, export competitiveness and foreign investment flows in the Indian markets. Therefore, tracking the movement of Dollar Index and USDINR becomes crucial for us.

Dollar Index

As we all know, the US Dollar (USD) is one of the most dominant currencies and is widely used in global finance and international trade, with 88% of international trades being done in USD.[7] The dollar index is not the same as the USD. The Dollar Index, commonly known as the DXY, measures the strength of the US dollar against a basket of 6 major world currencies: the Euro (EUR), Japanese Yen (JPY), British Pound (GBP), Canadian Dollar (CAD), Swedish Krona (SEK) and Swiss Franc (CHF). Think of it as a report card that shows how well the US dollar is performing compared to other major currencies. Each currency in this basket has a different weight, with the Euro having the largest influence (about 57.6%). When the DXY strengthens (meaning the US dollar is gaining against other major currencies), the Indian Rupee often depreciates against the dollar. This is because a stronger dollar means investors are pulling money into dollar-denominated assets, which can lead to outflows from emerging markets, including India.

Naturally, a strong DXY leads to a weaker Indian Rupee (INR), which impacts market sentiment negatively. A depreciating rupee increases the cost of imports and puts pressure on companies with foreign debt, affecting corporate earnings and investor confidence. Since India is a net importer country, this plays out negatively for us and the Indian markets.

- **Stronger DXY → Weaker INR → Negative Sentiment on Nifty50**: As the rupee depreciates due to a stronger DXY, import-dependent sectors like oil, chemicals and consumer electronics face higher costs. Companies with significant dollar-denominated debt also suffer, which can impact their stock prices, contributing to negative sentiment on the Nifty50.

- **Weaker DXY → Stronger INR → Positive Sentiment on Nifty50**: A weaker dollar often leads to a stronger rupee, which helps reduce import costs and improves margins for companies reliant on imported goods. This creates a favourable environment for the Nifty50, boosting investor sentiment and driving up the index.

USDINR

The USDINR exchange rate measures the value of the Indian Rupee (INR) against the US Dollar. Apart from the movement in DXY, the monetary policies of the 2 nations are another major driver for the movement of USDINR. Difference in interest rates between the US Federal reserve and the Reserve Bank of India influences the exchange rate. A higher US rate strengthens the Dollar against the Rupee (increasing USDINR). The effect plays out in the Indian markets too, as the returns for Foreign Institutional Investors (FIIs), who are one of the drivers of the Indian markets, diminish in dollar terms with a weakening rupee, making Indian equities less attractive. This often leads to capital outflows putting downward pressure on Nifty50. Similarly, a decreasing USDINR creates positive sentiment and drives the FII inflows in the market.

In brief, Dollar index and Nifty50 typically share an inverse correlation where an upmove in DXY can lead to a downmove in Nifty50 and vice versa. Similarly, USDINR and Nifty50 also share an inverse correlation with each other, where a strengthening dollar and a weakening INR leads to a weakening move in Nifty50 and vice versa.

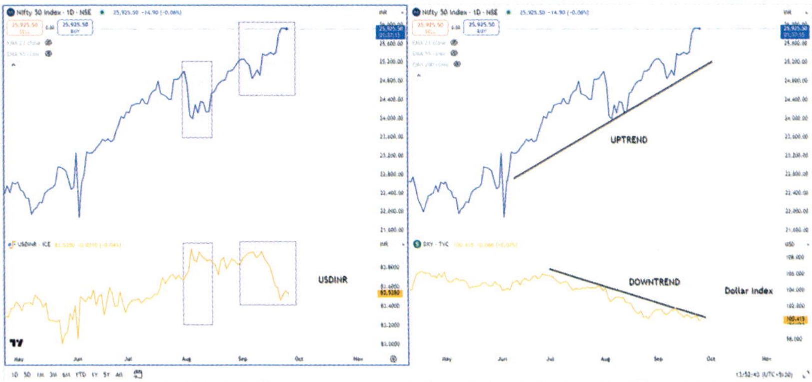

Figure 5.54 Daily chart of Nifty50, USDINR and Dollar Index

In Figure 5.54, we have plotted the movement of USDINR and Dollar Index at the bottom left and bottom right respectively. Observe how the movement of these instruments are almost inversely correlated to each other. Nifty50 was in a strong uptrend while the dollar index was showing weakness. Similarly, every fall or rise of USDINR was followed by a rise or a fall of Nifty50.

Equity Markets–Global

NASDAQ and S&P 500

NASDAQ and S&P 500 are the benchmark indices of the US markets, just as Nifty50 is the benchmark index of India. The performance of US indices in specific is crucial as they often set the tone for the global market sentiment. When the S&P 500 and NASDAQ perform well, it generally signals a risk-on environment globally, encouraging investors to allocate more capital to emerging markets like India. This leads to inflows into the Nifty50, driving the index higher. Conversely, a decline in the S&P 500 or NASDAQ, especially during periods of high volatility, can lead to a risk-off sentiment, causing global investors to pull back from riskier assets, including Indian equities. This can result in selling pressure on the Nifty50. In brief, a strong NASDAQ or S&P 500 typically leads to a strong movement in Nifty50 and vice versa.

Figure 5.55 Daily chart of Nifty50, NASDAQ and S&P 500

In Figure 5.55, observe how Nifty50 has almost been synchronous with the movement of NASDAQ and S&P 500. Some correction was witnessed in the US markets in July 2024. On close observation you will notice that Nifty50 did follow suit and corrected although it was a minor correction relative to the global markets.

Why do you think this happened? In recent times even when the global markets have given a significant correction, Indian markets have stood strong and outperformed the global markets. This hints at trust in the potential growth of the Indian economy and belief in its potential.

Emerging Market Index

India is an emerging market. To track the performance of stocks in developing countries like India, including the economies of China, Brazil and South Africa, an index such as MSCI Emerging Markets Index is formed. It provides a benchmark for the overall performance of emerging market equities.

When the Emerging Market Index performs well, it usually reflects strong foreign investment inflows into emerging markets, including India, boosting the Nifty50. Conversely, if the Emerging Market Index declines due to factors like global economic slowdown, rising US interest rates or geopolitical risks, it often leads to outflows from Indian equities, putting pressure on the Nifty50.

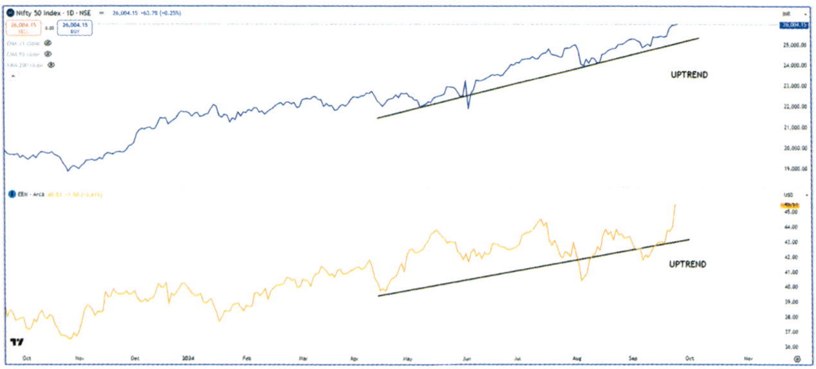

Figure 5.56 Daily chart of Nifty50 and Emerging Markets Index

Observe in Figure 5.56 how the Nifty50 movement is almost synchronous with the Emerging Market Index movement.

Bond Market

The bond market is where debt securities are issued and traded. It impacts the economy and equities by influencing interest rates, borrowing costs and investor sentiment, with rising yields often leading to higher borrowing costs and lower stock valuations.

US 10-Year Bond Yield

The US 10-year bond yield is the interest rate paid by the US government on its 10-year Treasury bonds, which are considered one of the safest investments globally. It reflects investor expectations about future economic conditions, inflation and interest rates. This yield is a key benchmark for borrowing costs across the world and influences everything from mortgage rates in the US to investment flows in global markets, including the Nifty50 in India.

When the 10-year yield rises, US Treasuries become more attractive, often leading to outflows from Indian equities as investors seek safer, higher-yielding assets, which can put downward pressure on the Nifty50. Higher yields also signal tighter global liquidity and risk aversion, negatively affecting market sentiment. Additionally, a rising yield strengthens the US dollar, weakening the Indian Rupee, increasing import costs, and inflation, which can hurt corporate earnings in India. Conversely, a declining 10-year yield boosts the appeal of riskier assets, encouraging inflows into the Nifty50, supporting its performance through improved market sentiment and a more favourable currency environment.

Indian Government Bond Yield (10-year G-Sec)

The Indian 10-year Government Bond Yield (G-Sec) represents the interest rate on long-term government debt, reflecting market expectations for future economic conditions, inflation and monetary policy in India, serving as a benchmark for borrowing costs across the economy.

When the 10-year G-Sec yield rises, it signals higher inflation expectations or potential rate hikes by the Reserve Bank of India (RBI), leading to increased borrowing costs for companies and consumers. This can dampen corporate profitability and reduce market valuations, putting downward pressure on the Nifty50. Conversely, when the 10-year G-Sec yield falls, it reflects lower inflation or expectations of accommodative monetary policy, making borrowing cheaper and boosting corporate earnings and investor confidence, which supports the Nifty50. The yield also guides FII flows, as higher yields attract foreign investment into bonds, potentially leading to equity outflows, while lower yields encourage risk-taking in equities, benefiting the Nifty50.

Figure 5.57 Daily chart of Nifty50, the US 10-year Bond Yield, and India 10-year Govt. Bond Yield

Observe in Figure 5.57, how US 10-year bond yield and India 10-year bond yield share an inverse relationship with Nifty50.

Commodity Markets

Commodity prices, particularly oil, gold and industrial metals, have a profound impact on the Indian economy. India is a major importer of crude oil, and fluctuations in oil prices can significantly affect inflation, trade balance and corporate profitability.

Crude Oil (Brent & WTI)

Crude oil is a critical commodity used globally for producing fuel (such as gasoline, diesel and jet fuel), manufacturing petrochemicals and as a key input in various industries like plastics, pharmaceuticals and fertilizers. Brent and WTI (West Texas Intermediate) are the 2 primary global benchmarks for crude oil pricing, with Brent representing oil extracted from the North Sea and widely used in Europe and Asia, while WTI is sourced in the US and is known for its lighter, sweeter quality, influencing oil prices worldwide. Crude oil prices have a significant impact on Nifty50 due to India's heavy reliance on oil imports. India primarily imports Brent crude oil, as it is the benchmark for the Middle Eastern, African and European oil that makes up the bulk of India's oil imports, aligning with India's geographical trade patterns and refinery preferences.

When crude oil prices rise, it increases input costs for many sectors, particularly in transportation, manufacturing and refining, leading to higher inflation and reduced corporate profitability, which can negatively affect the Nifty50. Conversely, falling crude oil prices lower costs for these industries, ease inflationary pressures, and improve profit margins, supporting better market performance. Additionally, high oil prices can worsen India's trade balance and put pressure on the rupee, further affecting market sentiment and investment flows into the Nifty50.

Gold

Gold typically has an inverse relation with the Dollar Index. When the Dollar Index rises, gold prices often fall because a stronger dollar makes gold more expensive for buyers using other currencies, reducing demand. Conversely, when the Dollar Index weakens, gold prices usually increase as the weaker dollar boosts gold's appeal as a safe-haven asset and hedge against currency devaluation. Since Dollar Index and Nifty also share an inverse relationship, it makes the movement of gold and Nifty50 almost synchronous to each other.

Having said that, it's important to note that the movement of gold prices is a factor of multiple geopolitical reasons too. Gold is considered a safe-haven asset for a reason. Its price typically rises during periods of economic or geopolitical uncertainty, as investors shift away from riskier assets like equities. An example would be when China was aggressively hoarding gold with the People's Bank of China, increasingly from November 2022 onwards, aiming to reduce reliance on the US dollar amid rising global tensions. This coupled with ongoing geopolitical events like the Russia-Ukraine war (since Feb 2022) and renewed conflict in the Middle East, including the Israel-Gaza escalation in October 2023, have fuelled a surge in gold prices, reflecting heightened risk aversion. As a result, equity markets like the Nifty50 often face pressure during such times, as investors seek the safety and stability that gold traditionally offers.

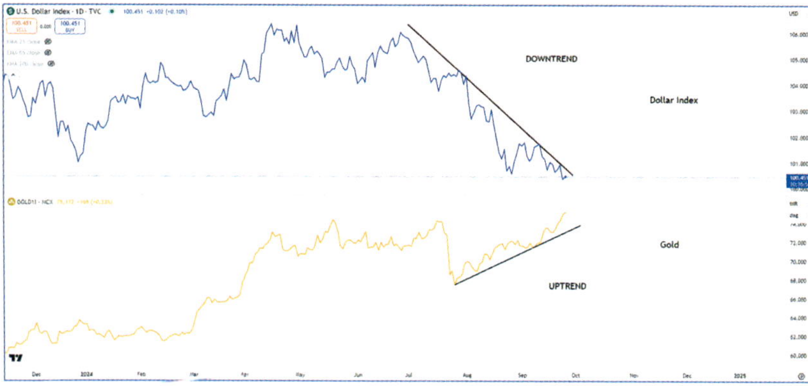

Figure 5.58 Daily chart of Dollar Index and Gold

In Figure 5.58, observe how the gold price increased with a weakening of the Dollar Index, demonstrating an inverse relationship.

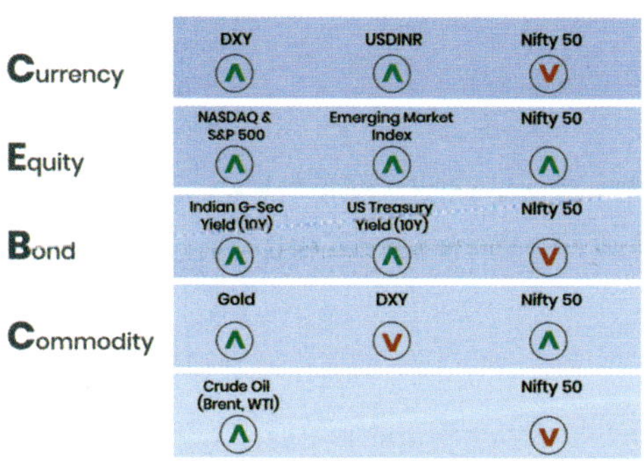

Figure 5.59 Summary of the macro markets and its impact on Nifty

Analysis of Nifty50

After getting a comprehensive view on the global markets, a quick analysis of Nifty is also needed to confirm the judgement in the markets. Two parameters that can help us analyse whether the market movement has been strong or weak are:

Market Breadth

Recall the concept of market breadth. We've used this data earlier to identify sectors where the contribution of market participants is higher and moving the sector. Similarly, an overall market breadth measures the number of advancing stocks versus declining stocks within the Nifty50, offering a clearer picture of overall market sentiment and participation.

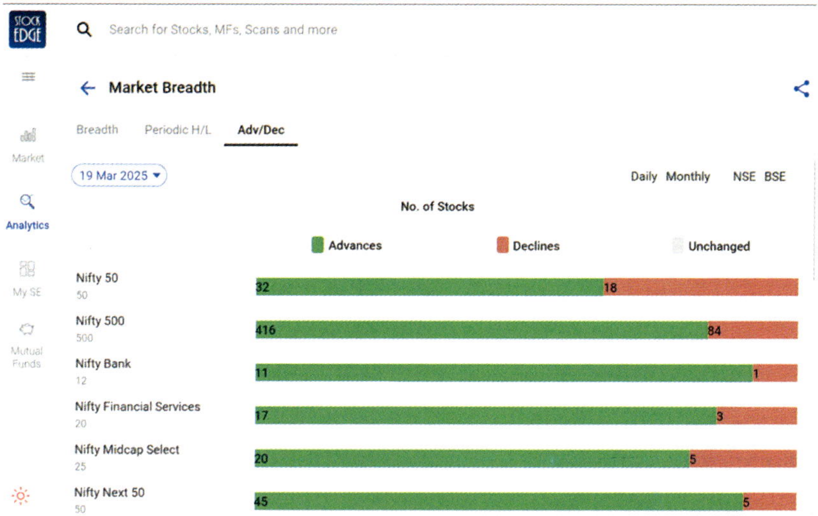

Figure 5.60

In Figure 5.60, observe the advancing and the declining stocks of an index. If more stocks are advancing, then it is a sign of a strong market breadth. Strong market breadth, where most stocks are advancing, suggests broad-based buying interest and a healthy market rally, indicating that the index's gains are well-supported. Conversely, weak market breadth, with few stocks driving the index while the majority decline, signals that the market rally might be unsustainable and vulnerable to reversals. Monitoring market breadth helps to assess the true momentum behind market moves.

Foreign Institutional Investment (FII) flows

FII flows are a direct reflection of foreign investor sentiment towards Indian markets. A consistent inflow indicates positive sentiment, while outflows can signal caution or risk aversion. Monitoring these flows provides insights into how global investors perceive the risk-return profile of Indian assets, influenced by global and domestic economic conditions.

Tracking FII data is crucial for understanding the movement of the Nifty50, as foreign investors hold significant positions in large-cap Indian stocks. For example, in March 2020, during the Covid-19 panic, FIIs pulled out over Rs 60,000 crore from Indian equities, triggering a steep fall in the Nifty50 of nearly 30% in just a few weeks. Their selling created a liquidity crunch and reflected global risk aversion. Conversely, when FIIs turned net buyers later that year, the index surged rapidly. This shows how FII flows can directly influence market direction, volatility and investor sentiment. If we take the most recent example, note how FIIs took out Rs 1,04,251 crores from the market in October 2024. This led to a fall of the index by over 1600 points, or 6.22%, which is a massive fall for an index.

Figure 5.61

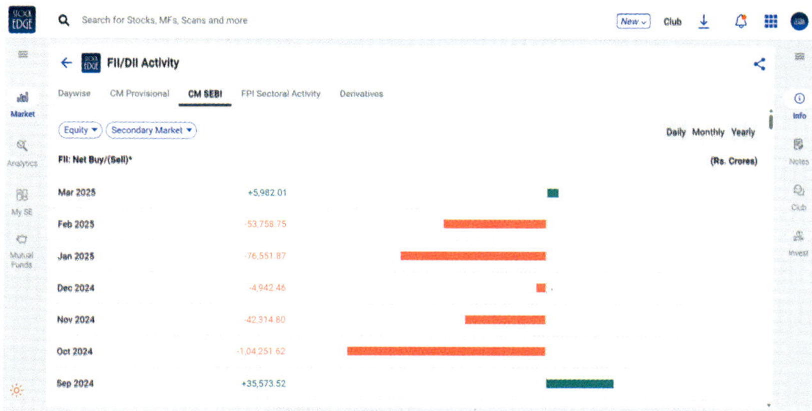

Table 5.9

In brief, if market breadth is strong and FIIs are consistently buying, it's a sign of broad market strength—consider taking long positions. If breadth is weak and FIIs are selling, stay cautious—stay put till the market settles. During mixed signals (e.g., breadth positive but FIIs selling), avoid aggressive trades and stick to high-conviction setups. You would want to focus on capital protection by reducing position sizing in each stock. However, always remember to have a proper risk management in place irrespective of the market conditions.

Having said that, you would want to make the most of the market during the bull run, stay put and protect your capital during a bear market, and be very stock/sector specific during a range-bound market.

Macros Help in Making Informed Judgements

Imagine that you're in a helicopter, starting at a height of 10,000 feet, and slowly descending closer to the ground. As you descend, your view becomes more detailed and focused, just like when analysing the economy, sector and individual stocks. Tracking the global economy is like having a broad view of the landscape from 10,000 ft; tracking the local or the domestic markets is like focusing on specific terrains or cities from 1,000 ft; tracking sector is when your focus sharpens and you get a view of specific neighbourhood or districts from 100 ft; tracking industry is like focusing on specific blocks of a neighbourhood or a district from 10 ft; finally when you have a much more focussed view on individual homes and streets from 1 ft, that's like tracking an individual stock.

Tracking these macro markets and indicators provides a comprehensive view of the factors influencing the Indian financial markets. By understanding the interplay between global equity movements, currency fluctuations, commodity prices, bond yields, domestic economic data and FII flows, traders can make more informed decisions and better anticipate market movements.

The next time when your stocks are not doing well very frequently, check for the movement of the global/macro markets and see if they're all indicating positive sentiment for Nifty50. If the macro markets are not doing well, then do not expect your stocks to do well.

Level	Focus Area	Examples
10,000 ft	Global Economy	Macro trends, geopolitics, currency shifts, inflation, fiscal spending
1,000 ft	Domestic Market	GDP, central bank policy, national inflation, fiscal spending
100 ft	Sector Focus	Tech, energy, banking, sector rotation
10 ft	Industry Insights	Semiconductor demand, fintech disruption, oil refiners vs upstream
1 ft	Individual Stocks	Financials, company-level fundamentals

Table 5.10 Approach to analyse the markets

Moreover, avoid high aggressive trading when there are major events happening globally or in India. For example, the Ukraine-Russia War, the Israel-Gaza war, the Indian Elections and the US Elections all fell at the same time during the years 2024 and 2025. This makes the market very uncertain and highly volatile for you to trade. It's best to avoid trading during such highly volatile markets.

An overall understanding of the macro elements and how they influence Nifty50 and other indices of the Indian market will help us become more confident traders.

SUMMARY

- Macro analysis helps in making a broader judgement on the markets.
- Follow the CEBC framework to track the macro markets:
  - Currency markets
    - Dollar Index & USDINR:
      Stronger DXY → Weaker INR → Negative sentiment on Nifty50 weaker DXY → stronger INR → Positive sentiment on Nifty50
  - Equity markets—Global
    - NASDAQ & S&P 500: Positive US markets hint towards positive movement in the Indian markets
    - Emerging market index: Positive movement in the emerging markets index hints at a positive movement of Nifty50
  - Bond markets
    - US Treasury Yield (10 year) & Indian Govt Bond Yield (10-year G-Sec): Bond market and Nifty50 share an inverse relationship, where increase in the bond yield leads to a down movement of Nifty50
  - Commodity markets
    - Crude oil (Brent, WTI): Increase in crude oil prices impact the movement of Nifty50 negatively
    - Gold: Gold and Dollar Index share an inverse relation, making the movement of gold and Nifty50 synchronous
- Nifty50 analysis: Strong market breadth and high inflow of FIIs indicate a positive sentiment of Nifty50.
- Avoid trading on major events.

Through this book I have brought to you my style of trading. It has taken me years of practice and trial and error to build this, and I am forever grateful to all those who helped in my journey.

If you've started practising the strategy, you will come across with a lot of doubts and queries.

LEARNER'S CORNER

How often do I need to track the macros?

It's best if done daily. Once you get in the habit, it will barely take 15 minutes of your time to quickly track the global markets. However, if not daily, then at least once a week is good to start tracking the macros.

How should you trade in volatile markets?

Beginners should avoid trading during volatile markets as they might not be able to manage their positions. Position sizing and risk management is the key to hail through volatile markets. Reduced position sizing can help a lot in volatile markets. Additionally, the market is typically volatile due to any upcoming event—global or local—or on the day of the event. For example, the market was very volatile during the results of the Indian elections held on 4 June 2024. Moreover, the entire financial year of 2025 was reeking of uncertain events like US elections, trade wars, Russia-Ukraine war, Israel-Gaza war, supply chain disruptions, etc. As traders, you would want to avoid trading on such event days or during such times of uncertainty, as volatile markets are tough to play and the chances of hitting stop loss is higher as compared to normal market conditions.

Daily Affirmations

I want you to take this page and stick it near your trading desk. Chant it out loud to yourself before you start your day.

1. I am grateful for the opportunity to trade and grow each day.
2. I am calm and balanced, regardless of market conditions.
3. I am patient, disciplined and consistent in my actions.
4. I focus on my process, regardless of profit or loss.
5. A stop loss is a stop loss for me, and I cut my losses when it is triggered.
6. I know my limits, and I trade within my limits.
7. I trust my analysis and intuition, and I adapt with the market.
8. I exit from a trade regardless of profit/loss, when my system tells me to.
9. Every successful/failed trade is an opportunity for me to learn and grow.
10. I will stay true to my Karma.

6

The Turtle Mindset: The Right Psychology of Trading

We have in this book already presented a bouquet of technical know-how that you need to start trading. The last chapter took you through my personal journey. This chapter, unlike the rest of the book, is to address something that only comes with experience in the market—attaining the turtle mindset. You have seen it mentioned through the book, but it is time to know how to own it.

Learning hard skills is just a part of the game. We may have the best charts, the best data, the best research—not to undermine their importance here—but if our mindset doesn't allow us to follow through, the market won't reward us. IQ can give us weapons, but it is our EQ that helps us use them wisely.

EQ is what truly sets us apart, and by EQ, I mean our patience, resilience and ability to stay calm through uncertainty. While skills can be learnt and refined over time, a mindset is something that must be built from within. In trading, it's not just what we know, but how we think and react to the information that ultimately determines our success.

Having the turtle mindset is about being someone who doesn't chase every opportunity. Someone who knows when to be active and when to step back. Someone who is not in a hurry to make profits and is not aggressive but clear, composed and consistent. Turtles are calculative. They don't chase every opportunity, but they also don't miss the ones that truly matter. They move with intention at their own pace and in a clear direction. The turtle doesn't get carried away when others are making quick profits. They are in for the long run.

Deciphering: Who Are You?

Know Yourself

Trading is a journey of self-discovery. The more you learn about yourself, the better you become as a trader.

Personal growth and understanding, composure and clarity of thought are the pillars of being a market player. I am an avid follower of the Bhagwat Gita and try to adopt the teachings in my life and trading journey; that helped me build this turtle mindset. I read this wonderful book titled *I Am Gita* by Deep Trivedi, in which he talks about the 3 dimensions of life: mind, brain and ego, symbolized by Krishna, Arjun and Duryodhan respectively. We are all like Arjun—confused, curious and eager to win the battle of the markets.

Our brain executes what our mind commands while our ego obstructs this healthy communication. Overcoming this ego is the ultimate challenge. This stayed with me.

Trivedi says you can only take advantage of the Bhagwat Gita if you know the questions you seek answers to.

Most retail investors enter the market with the same question: How do I make money from the market?

However, I urge you to try to ask yourself: Who am I and what do I seek?

Each one of us is unique and we have different strengths and weaknesses. If we do not play to our strengths and imitate others, it is like going to a war with the wrong weapon. This is as good as accepting defeat. Can you imagine Arjun fighting in the war with the Gada or Bhim with the Gandiv? This applies to life and the markets too. Each trader needs to identify his/her strengths and leverage it to their advantage, rather than blindly following what others are doing.

Being able to follow this through is what the turtle mindset is about. Why do you think a turtle has the capacity to survive adverse conditions? It knows its strengths. When it comes to the markets, the wisdom lies in knowing that it's not about doing more, it's about doing what suits you best—and doing it well. Slow, at times, is an advantage; less, at times, is an edge; while patience, more often than not, is protection. The turtle knows this and that's why it walks slow—but steady. The turtle is about stillness in movement. It is self-aware. My suggestion to you would be to start understanding yourself better, know your strengths and ask yourself questions like:

- What is it that you enjoy more?
- What brings you peace?
- What activities make you feel energized as well as engaged?
- When do you feel most confident and in control?
- What have people often asked you to help them with?
- What are you willing to put in extra effort on?
- What are you most proud of accomplishing?
- What are you most scared of?
- What is that one thing that is holding you back from fulfilling your dreams?
- What are things that you like about yourself?
- What are the things that you don't like about yourself?
- What comes naturally to you that may be tough for others?

Stop. Think. Ponder. Write. Use a pencil. You might not know everything now, but take effort to observe yourself better, and most importantly, be true to yourself. Erase answers and rewrite them to make them closer to who you are. You may feel that the answers sound mundane or are not exciting enough but that's okay—this is for yourself. We do not want to describe who you want to be but who you are. By doing this, you will become more adept at creating your own trading setup and trading system.

Having said this, these answers will also bring out realizations—and there are ways to work towards changing things about yourself and in turn your trading strategies, but that is for a conversation for another time.

My objective is for you to carve your own trading journey, and if my knowledge, experience, learnings and failures can help you do it better, then that will be the true reward for all the efforts made in writing this book. I'm only left to share all that I can about developing a turtle mindset, no matter what your strategy.

Know Your Emotions

> 'The secret to trading success is emotional discipline. If intelligence were the key, there would be a lot more people making money trading.'
>
> —Victor Sperandeo[1]

Let's take another example from the epic Mahabharata. Do you think Duryodhan was not as great a warrior or not strong enough to win the war? He trained with the best of the warriors, he had all the physical strength, and yet he lost. His ego and temperament played a major role in his downfall in the war. Similarly, all your knowledge and analytical skills will be worthless if you're not able to master your own mind and control your emotions. The market will surprise you, shock you, play you and test you time and again. It is in these moments you need to think clearly, without letting your ego come in the way. This may sound simple but is actually really hard to put into practice.

Deep Trivedi—a master of psychology—says ego clouds judgement and distorts perception, making us overly concerned with how we are perceived rather than focusing on genuine self-improvement. It prevents us from accepting our flaws, admitting mistakes or embracing change. This is because acceptance would threaten the ego's constructed image of perfection and superiority. Ego is detrimental to self-realization and personal growth.

What we forget is that nothing is perfect in the world. Always remember that no growth is in the form of a perfect straight line, be it stocks, personal life or professional life. It is always in the form of swings and all you need to ensure is that the long-term growth curve is upward. You try new things, you fail, you learn, you try some more a little differently and this journey continues. This is the story of growth.

This growth story is what helps in developing the turtle mindset. It requires time, relentless practice and discipline. Just like how you need to practice technical analysis daily, you will also need to practice mental exercises every day to be able to look at things objectively.

I have already shared my best practices through this book for trading and will share things that worked for me in this space of self-discovery through the next few pages. With time you will be able to take actions as commanded by Krishna (the mind) rather than Duryodhan (the ego).

Know Your Journey

The shift to rational decision making with the turtle mindset is a gradual one, and very well described in the book *From Strength to Strength* by Arthur C. Brooks.[2] It was a recommendation from one of my mentors, Sandeep Mall, author of *Finding the Oasis*. The following graph from the former book made me more aware about the trajectory of our mind and intelligence. In the book, he referred to Raymond Cattell who classified intelligence into fluid intelligence and crystallized intelligence.

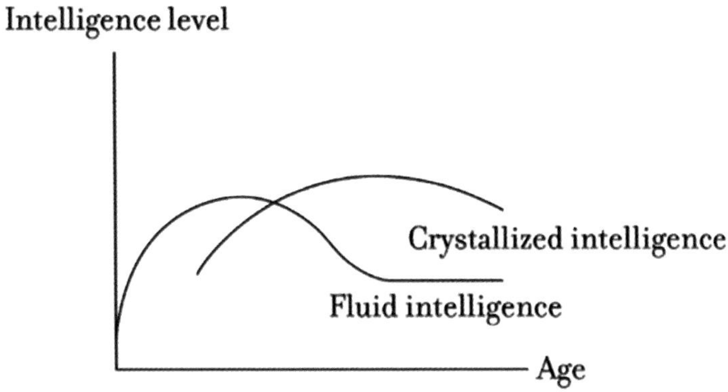

Figure 6.1 Fluid intelligence and crystallized intelligence over the age of a person as shown in the book From Strength to Strength

Fluid intelligence is dynamic and data oriented and is high during ages of learning, where we try our hand at different things, collect information and experiences. Crystallized intelligence, on the other hand, grows as we use our fluid intelligence. It is a collection of our experiences and is wisdom oriented.

Trading, much like life itself, evolves through various stages, where both fluid and crystallized intelligence play crucial roles in shaping our journey. In the early phases of our careers, fluid intelligence reigns supreme. As young traders, we often rely on analytical skills, quick decision-making and the ability to process vast amounts of market data rapidly. We are driven by a thirst for knowledge and an eagerness to understand market mechanics. However, as we mature, our focus shifts towards crystallized intelligence, where experience and wisdom take precedence. With time spent in the markets, we begin to accumulate insights from our successes and failures, learning to interpret market sentiment and recognize patterns that aren't always visible through data alone. This blend of analytical skills and experiential understanding are the steps to making us seasoned traders. This helps us make sharp-witted judgements that align with our market intuition, effectively transforming our trading strategy into a more artful and nuanced practice.

Your ability to understand and appreciate both forms of intelligence will make you better at understanding yourself and thus a better market participant.

What Could Go Wrong?

Even when your fluid intelligence is at play, as beginners you are prone to make mistakes that help you sharpen your skills. Not following your systems and making emotional decisions, rather than data-driven decision making, are a few very common mistakes. I will try to highlight a few common emotions/phases that you may face in the beginning of your trading career and how you can overcome them. If you've already started trading, you will relate to what I'm about to tell you.

Over-Expectations Lead to Downfall

There will always be someone in your vicinity—a neighbour/a relative/a friend—who will talk about their extremely high returns from the market in a short span without actually having or knowing even the basics of technicals. It's common for beginners to set the same expectation, which is also another reason for a lot of us to flock to the market. However, setting the right expectations from the market is absolutely crucial. If we expect to double our money every year, then the profession of trading is not for us. If it was really this simple to get 100% returns from the market in a year, then the richest people in the country would be traders.

As a beginner, the expectations should be to not lose a lot of money in a sideways market and to try to beat the Nifty50 returns in a bull market. Even if Nifty50's returns were 20 to 25% in a year, and you were able to generate 30% in the same year, it is a good start. The underlying logic behind this is that if you can't beat Nifty50, then you are better off investing in Nifty50 and using your time and efforts towards something else.

For mature market participants, a 5% monthly return or 50–60% annually is reasonable, depending on the time and effort you're putting in the markets with the underlying assumption that the broad markets are doing fairly well. If you intend to spend 2 hours weekly in the market, consider index or mutual funds. For 3-4 hours daily, aim higher. Return expectations also depend on capital size, if you have a very small or a very large capital, then please have limited expectations from the market.

Relying on Intuitions Rather Than Formula

> 'The investor's chief problem—and even his worst enemy—is likely to be himself.'
>
> —Benjamin Graham[3]

Our intuitions are manifestations of a combination of cognitive biases and the noises that surround us in our everyday lives. Trusting intuitions is inherent for human beings and comes easily, but these decisions may backfire. Decisions have to be data, logic and process driven however difficult it may be to act on.

There will be times when the market will test your character, making you take intuition-driven actions you regret later. A wise trader with the turtle mindset keeps his/her calm and patience, remaining emotionally unaffected by the market conditions, just like how a turtle keeps walking its path at a steady pace irrespective of its environment. Having said that, knowledge comes from reading or studying, while wisdom comes from experience, and there is no alternative for experience. However prepared we are for the emotions that we would face while making decisions, we will still make that wrong decision, and that is going to be the best teacher. Making a wrong decision once will help make all the right decisions later. Losing some money in the market paves the path to greater profits in the longer run. Don't forget that we're here to finish the longer race that we started.

Wrong Balance between Energy and Emotions

Over time, I've seen this pattern repeat. In myself, in my peers, my colleagues and in my students. It's not always about what strategy we use (trade setup)—it's also about the state we're in when we use it (our mindset). So, I started observing something closely: the interplay between energy and emotions when in the markets. We often make intuitive decisions when we don't know how to balance energy and emotions together. This is where the Market Mindset Matrix comes into play:

Energy × Emotion = Execution

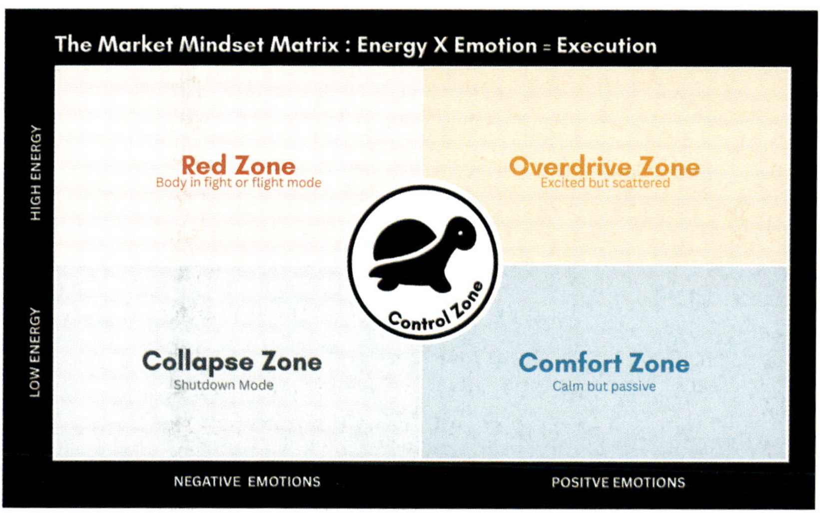

Figure 6.2

Let's break it down:

The Red Zone: Fight or flight

When we enter the Red Zone, we're overwhelmed by high energy and negative emotions—stress, anxiety, frustration or even anger. The urge to act becomes almost overwhelming, and we feel like we have to do something—anything. This is where revenge trading and overtrading happen. We might be chasing a loss or trying to force a win. Emotional clarity is compromised, and we end up making decisions based on a reactive need to act, not on logical analysis. It's a dangerous space to be in because we're not trading with a clear mind—we're simply reacting. A few common mistakes that traders tend to make in this zone are:

1. **Constantly switching strategies**: We jump between different strategies without sticking to one, always second-guessing ourselves.
2. **Averaging down:** We keep adding more to a losing position, hoping to lower our average cost, but it exposes us to more risk.
3. **Revenge trading:** After a loss, we try to make it back by breaking our system and pursuing ego-driven trades.

In the Red Zone, we're driven by the urge to act, but what's missing is emotional clarity and the ability to self-regulate. This is where we need to pause and regain control.

The Collapse Zone: Low Energy, Negative Emotion

In the Collapse Zone, we're exhausted. The market hasn't been kind, and our energy is at a low point. We feel mentally drained, emotionally fatigued and the thought of opening our trading terminal feels overwhelming. We don't feel like participating, and when we do, we're likely to make decisions out of desperation, which often leads to more harm than good. When in this zone, we're likely to:

1. **Doubt ourselves:** We question our strategy because others seem to be doing better or have different results.

2. **Quit after losses:** After a string of losses, we stop trading, losing confidence in ourselves and our strategy.

This is the time to step back. Desperation-based decisions rarely work in the market, and pushing through in this state only leads to more losses. If we're in the Collapse Zone, it's time to rest, recharge and get back to trading with a clearer mind.

The Comfort Zone: Complacency and Lack of Action

This is where things move slowly. We're not excited or energized about our trades, and may even feel a bit bored. There's no real hunger or curiosity to learn and improve, and we end up following the crowd without thinking for ourselves. This is where we might find ourselves acting on tips, following what 'everyone else is doing', or simply buying a stock because someone else made money off it last week. There's no system, no research, just borrowed conviction. A few common mistakes that we tend to make while in this zone are:

1. **Holding on to hope:** We refuse to exit when our stop loss is hit, hoping the stock will turn around, only to see our losses grow.
2. **Following the crowd:** We see someone on social media making huge profits and decide to follow the same path without checking if the setup aligns with our approach.
3. **Trading on tips:** We rely on tips and rumours rather than our own research and strategy.

When we're in this zone, we're not actively engaging with the market. We're drifting, hoping for luck to take over, without any real strategy in place. The Comfort Zone keeps us passive, and it prevents us from building a sound system for long-term success.

The Overdrive Zone: Overconfidence and Reckless Trading

In the Overdrive Zone, the market has been kind and our confidence is soaring. We feel on top of the world, like we've mastered everything.

The market seems to be in our favour, and we start taking trades that normally wouldn't fit your system. We stretch rules, take bigger risks and feel in control. It feels like skill, but more often, it's just luck wearing a suit. A few common mistakes that we tend to make while in this zone are:

1. **Impulsive trading:** We trade just for action, overtrading because we feel the need to do something in the market, even when there's no reason to.
2. **The blowout trade:** Overconfidence from a few wins leads to one big impulsive trade that wipes out all the gains.
3. **Overextending yourself:** We take on bigger positions than we should, thinking we can handle the risk, but it puts unnecessary pressure on our portfolio.
4. **Trade on borrowed money:** Our overconfidence fuels our greed to make more money that overpowers our logical thinking and makes us take debt to increase our capital base.

This is where unintentional errors happen. The rush of dopamine and the low levels of caution can easily lead to impulsive decisions that wipe out previous wins. The Overdrive Zone feels exciting, but it's a dangerous space that can quickly derail progress if we're not careful.

Being in either of the zones could be detrimental to our success in the longer run; they are Danger Zones.

How do we move away when in any zone? We need to gradually work our way into what I call the Control Zone—also known as the turtle mindset—where emotional neutrality meets balanced energy.

It's Not Your Fault, It's In-Built

The mismatch between our emotional and energy state and the reality of the market can lead to poor decisions, and these are just some of the mistakes that beginners are highly prone to. These are driven by the cognitive biases that are inherent in all human beings, even the smartest ones. I will try to outline most of these biases:

a. **Loss aversion:** Humans are built such that they're more distressed by a loss than pleased by a gain of the same size. It is natural for us to cling on to negative emotions or feelings rather than positive ones. From the trading perspective, it is a common trap to hold onto losing stocks, hoping they'll bounce back as the loss is distressing us and weakening our confidence. What we are not realizing is that the money stuck in that trade could be put to better use elsewhere. This bias is very costly.

b. **Herd mentality**: If everyone is doing it, it must be right! This is the mindset of many across all things in life. This is also the mindset that has led to the birth of a lot of historic bubbles for example: the dotcom bubble, the housing bubble, the Japanese bubble economy. Time and experience have taught me to trust my own research and instincts, even when they go against the crowd. It's hard, but it's like tough love—rules and disciplinary actions that parents have for the greater good of their children. These are essential to avoid getting swept away by the tide.

c. **Hindsight bias**: After every market crash or rally, some of us may often think, 'I had seen that coming.' I've caught myself doing this, believing I could have predicted events that, in reality, were far from obvious at the time. This hindsight bias leads to overconfidence, making us think we have predictive powers. It's a humbling reminder that the market is unpredictable. It is always easier to connect the dots after something happens.

d. **Recency effect**: It is human nature to give more importance to recent events like a company merger, instead of considering the data in hand. Recency effect can cloud judgement, causing traders to overlook the data that could be hinting otherwise. I've learned to take a step back and ensure that recent developments don't overshadow data-driven decision making.

e. **Confirmation and cognitive dissonance bias**: Every human is born with an ego and the need to be right. As a result, we only look for information that confirms our pre-existing beliefs and choose to ignore new information which challenge the same. This confirmation bias results in lack of responsiveness and adaptation in trading. Cognitive dissonance has a similar outcome. Humans don't want to go through the psychological distress of dissonance, i.e., lack of alignment by accepting information that proves us wrong.

f. **Endowment bias**: This is when we put more value to something when we own it as compared to when we don't. As a result, we often avoid selling a stock even when your system is suggesting otherwise, either due to emotional attachment with it or the belief that it will provide superior returns (which may or may not be true). This also prevents us from identifying alternative opportunities. It's like marrying your stocks and staying long after the love is gone—clinging to hope when you know deep down it's time to walk away.

We all have fallen prey to biases—top traders, top scientists and mathematicians included, and these biases are what drives us to the danger zones. In one of the most notable instances, Livermore ignored the changing conditions during the 1929 stock market crash. He had become overly confident after his previous successes and failed to adjust his strategy when the market conditions began to shift. He held onto losing positions for far too long, and when the crash came, he lost a significant portion of his wealth. His overconfidence and inability to recognize that the market was changing were influenced by confirmation bias, as he continued to seek patterns that supported his beliefs, rather than objectively reassessing the market environment.

Knowing about these biases is not enough. However, it does help us to pause and reevaluate every decision. It makes us ask questions:

Is this decision data driven?

Is this driven by my biases?

Would I take a different decision if I was in profit?

You can't control the market, but you can control how you react to it.

Wrong Decisions Are the Best Learning Opportunities

> 'You will only fail to learn if you do not learn from failing.'
>
> —Stella Adler

Wrong decisions are not detrimental to your long-term success, but your response towards the wrong decisions is what matters more and defines whether you're in the control zone or one of the danger zones.

Ask Yourself: What Is More Important–Making Money or Being Right?

Take a moment and then read ahead.

No one gets everything right in life. Wisdom is not in always being right but planning for when things go off track. The market rewards those who are prepared, not those who are lucky.

> 'Planning is important, but the most important part of every plan is to plan on the plan not going according to plan.'
>
> —*Psychology of Money* by Morgan Housel

We plan meticulously and with full information but there are so many factors beyond our control that may make our plans fail. Understanding this and letting go of the need to be right, which often makes us hold onto losing trades and refusing to cut losses, is important. Being ready for when the plan is not working or being ready to pivot is essential.

Hoping for a rebound, you may let small losses compound. Stopping losses is as important as riding profits in the long-term large portfolio return matrix. A strong heart, patience and honouring your stop loss is very important.

At the end of the day, our ultimate goal is to make money, not being right. So instead of focusing on that one trade that did not work, we must shift our focus. Trying to channel our energy into the trades that are working, or better yet, into finding new opportunities with potential, is the best way forward. Remember, being a successful trader in the control zone isn't about winning every battle; it's about winning the war. This is the crux of the turtle mindset.

Accepting Mistakes

> 'The elements of good trading are: (1) cutting losses, (2) cutting losses, and (3) cutting losses. If you can follow these three rules, you may have a chance.'
>
> —Ed Seykota[4]

Mistakes can be carried as a burden or used as stepping stones of learning for future decision making. It's perfectly fine to make them—what's not fine is refusing to acknowledge them, failing to learn from them or being unwilling to correct them.

Let me share my experience with you. I entered the financial markets in 2005 when I joined JM Financial as a commodities analyst. This was at a time when commodities were gaining attention, and my job involved analysing gold, silver and crude oil. My predictions in these markets were fairly accurate, which made me overconfident. After a brief stint, I realized that working for a job wasn't fulfilling my entrepreneurial spirit, so I returned to Kolkata in 2006 to start my trading journey.

I entered the market full of optimism in 2006, with a base capital of Rs 10 lakhs, taking actions being in the overdrive zone, but within 6 months, I had lost Rs 2.5 lakhs. This loss wasn't just financial; it was a blow to my confidence. It was difficult for me to accept that someone who was doing so well in the markets with accurate predictions could go so horribly wrong.

I found myself dejected and grappling with self-doubt. Here I was, a well-qualified professional who had returned home to make a mark, and the societal pressure of having left a stable job in Mumbai only added to the weight of this loss. This was my journey from being in the overdrive zone to the collapse zone. However, viewing this setback as a learning cost—an inevitable part of the process of mastering the markets—strengthened my grit. I eventually started taking small steps to get back to trading with a calmer mindset and work towards getting into the control zone.

By now you know about my journey from there on, and this is the power of accepting the lows.

Path to Control Zone: Internal Mastering

बन्धुरात्मात्मनस्तस्य येनात्मैवात्मना जति: |
अनात्मनस्तु शत्रुत्वे वर्तेतात्मैव शत्रुवत् ||

—Bhagavad Gita (Chapter 6, Verse 6)

A beautiful verse from the Gita that translates to: 'For one who has conquered the mind, the mind is the best friend; but for one who has failed to do so, the mind will remain the greatest enemy.'

The market is fundamentally about human psychology, and our subconscious mind plays a crucial role in how we engage with it. While I can help you train your conscious mind, it's up to you to train your subconscious to attain the control zone. This involves not just understanding market dynamics, but also delving into psychology and practicing mindfulness. You are in the control zone when you know your decisions are data-driven and process-driven, and no noise or biases can influence your mind.

Choose Who/What Influences You: Creating Your Circle of Influence

We humans are easily influenced by the people in our surroundings. These influences not only affect our conscious mind but also our subconscious mind and it plays a key role in our decision making. One of the teachings of spiritual guru Sadhguru is that you need to train your conscious mind to filter the commands or information that you send to your subconscious mind. When you're able to do this, you automatically drown out the irrelevant or irrational thoughts and take calculated rational data-driven decisions. This becomes the key for making a gradual shift from one of the danger zones to the control zone. People often ask me how I remain so calm, whether the market is surging or crashing. The truth is, I don't just think with my conscious mind anymore—I think with that deeper, trained mind, making me sustain myself in the control zone. It's taken time and effort to cultivate this mindset, but it has made all the difference.

In today's world, it's easy to get influenced by the noise created by news channels and especially social media. If you've read about how social media maps our minds or watched *The Social Dilemma* on Netflix, you'll understand how dangerous this influence can be. Platforms like Facebook, Instagram and X, and even news channels, are designed to feed our biases. The more we expose ourselves to them, the more they influence our thoughts and decisions.

The recent rise of finfluencers on social media, without any regulations, is catastrophic; numerous retail investors could be trapped due to their advice. Do not mistake good communication skills with good trading skills. Having said that, not all finfluencers are bad, some are doing genuinely good work by propagating the right knowledge. Do your research and follow this filtered list instead. One way that you can differentiate the good from the bad is to check if they're only sharing stock tips, or is it backed by any science or study; assess whether they are only talking about their successful trades or are they also owing up to their failed trades.

Earlier, I talked about the concept of a circle of competence by the great Warren Buffett; now, I'd like to introduce you to the idea of a circle of influence. You need to carefully limit who and what influences you. If you allow too many external voices into your mind, the noise will overwhelm you, making it impossible to train your subconscious effectively. This isn't just crucial for trading; it's vital for every aspect of life. Your goal should be to train your subconscious mind to align with your true intentions and goals to attain the control zone, and cut down the noise in your life.

Resilience: My Backbone

> 'Don't hold back. Be courageous, make mistakes, but never forget to learn from them.'
>
> —Sadhguru

Resilience is perhaps the most critical trait of the control zone that I've developed throughout my trading journey. The market can be unforgiving, but it's in these challenging times that resilience has proven to be my greatest asset. Each setback has been a lesson in disguise, teaching me to adapt, refine my approach and keep moving forward. Whenever I caught myself filled with self-doubt and in the collapse zone, resilience has helped me to take small steps towards the control zone. I've learned that success in trading isn't about avoiding failure; it's about how you respond to it.

It was not an overnight phenomenon. It took some time for me and a few successful trades to gain my confidence back in the markets, but my initial failure matured me as a market participant. Being in the control zone does not mean that I'm devoid of mistakes. I still make mistakes, but rather than just repenting, I analyse them and try to learn and not repeat the same mistake. Every time I've been knocked down, I've made it a point to get back up, stronger and more determined.

Additionally, attaining the control zone once does not guarantee your permanent place in it. There are days I still get dragged in one of the danger zones. However, now it's easier for me to snap back to the control zone through resilience. Resilience has allowed me to weather the storms, maintain focus and continue pursuing my goals, no matter what the market throws my way.

An Unpopular Opinion: Welcome Greed and Fear

Greed and fear have always been considered negative emotions. In my opinion though, without these emotions, one will not be able to take big risks or get out early from failed trades. Both can be destructive if left unchecked and drive you to one of the danger zones, but they can also be powerful tools if you know how to use them wisely, making you attain the control zone.

Greed: I've found greed to actually be a great motivator if kept in check. Greed drives me to aim for higher profits, but I've learned how to not let it overpower me by combining it with a solid exit strategy. Without an exit plan, greed can lead me to overhold, leading to losses and missed opportunities. I have learnt to embrace greed as a part of my trading journey. By setting clear profit targets and sticking to them, I ensure that my greed is a positive catalyst.

Fear: Fear, on the other hand, has often been my biggest challenge. It can paralyse me, preventing me from taking necessary risks or causing me to exit positions prematurely. Fear often stems from the possibility of losing money, and I've found that it becomes particularly acute when I take on positions larger than I can handle. To manage fear, I rely heavily on position sizing and stop-loss orders. By only taking positions that are appropriate to my risk tolerance and setting clear stop-loss levels, I reduce the anxiety associated with potential losses. This approach allows me to stay in the market longer and gives me the confidence to seize profitable opportunities.

Trade Journal: Accountability for the Win

When we were students, periodic grades, tests and worksheets made us accountable to our learning and growth in subjects. As adults, we are not held accountable on a regular basis by anyone else. We have to depend on ourselves and be both our own critic and cheerleader.

When I first started trading, I focused heavily on learning the techniques—how to read charts, analyse trends and execute trades. But what I didn't initially understand was that these techniques are only part of the equation. In fact, they might only account for 20–25% of your success as a trader. The other 75–80% comes from the 'soft aspects' of trading—like discipline, introspection and the ability to learn from your own mistakes. This is where a trade journal becomes invaluable.

A trade journal is more than just a log of your trades; it's a reflection of your thoughts, decisions and emotions. When I trade, I ensure that I document every aspect of my decision-making process.

What was my rationale for entering a trade?

Did I follow my trading plan?

How did I feel about the trade after it was executed?

I've found that maintaining a trade journal allows me to conduct a 'post-mortem' on my trades. This process of reviewing and analysing my trades has been crucial in helping me refine my strategies and improve my discipline. Without this level of introspection, it's easy to repeat the same mistakes or let emotions cloud your judgement.

Creating a trade journal is a straightforward process, but it requires commitment. I recommend starting with a simple spreadsheet—either in Excel or Google Sheets. Here's what I include in my trade journal:

Date	Open/Close	Scrip	Buy/Sell	Qty	Price	Value	Square Off Date	Price	Profit/Loss	%	SL	TP	ORIGINATION LOGIC	COMMENT	KARMA
5Apr2021	0	TATAELXSI	B	2	2820	5640	7Apr2021	2950	260	4.61%	2755	2950	breakout from previous high		1
5Apr2021	1	TATAELXSI	B	2	2820	5640		7965		0.00%	2820	ST	breakout from previous high		-1
9Apr21	0	HINDUNILVR	B	2	2450	4900	13Apr21	2502	104	2.12%	2424	2502	breakout from previous high		1
9Apr21	0	HINDUNILVR	B	2	2450	4900	15Apr21	2450	0	0.00%	2450				1

Table 6.1: Trade Journal

However, I will briefly explain the process of recording each trade.

- Date (Column A):
    - Enter the date of the trade, e.g., 5 April 2021 for when you entered a trade.
- Open/Close Status (Column B):
    - When entering a trade, mark it as 1 (open).
- Once the trade is closed, change it to 0 (close).
    - Scrip Name (Column C):
    - Enter the exact name of the scrip as listed on NSE, e.g., TATAELXSI.
- Buy/Sell (Column D):
    - For a long trade, enter 'B' (Buy).
    - If you are shorting, enter 'S' (Sell).
- Quantity (Column E):
    - Enter the quantity of the stock you're trading, e.g., 2.
- Entry Price (Column F):
    - Record the price at which you entered the trade, e.g., 2820.
- Value (Column G):
    - Multiply the quantity by the entry price to get the total value of your trade.
- Squaring Off Date (Column H):
    - Once you close the trade, enter the date you squared off, e.g., 7 April 2021.

- Exit Price (Column I):
  - Enter the price at which you exited the trade.
- Profit/Loss Amount (Column J):
  - Record the profit or loss amount (Exit Price - Entry Price x Quantity).
- Profit/Loss Percentage (Column K):
  - Calculate the percentage change: ((Exit Price - Entry Price)/ Entry Price) x 100.
- Stop Loss (Column L):
  - Enter the stop loss level set at the time of trade initiation.
- Take Profit (Column M):
  - Record the target exit price or take-profit level.
- Origination Logic (Column N):
  - Write down why you entered the trade, e.g., 'Breakout from previous high.'
- Comments (Column O):
  - Enter any additional notes about the trade. For example, how you felt about it, market conditions, or changes in your strategy.
- Karma Points (Column P). I will come to Karma points a bit later.
- Partial Profits: If you booked partial profits, add a new row below with updated details (quantity remaining and any adjustments). Keep the original trade open until it's fully closed.

By consistently journaling my trades, I've been able to identify patterns—both in the market and in my own behaviour. For example, I've noticed that I tend to make impulsive decisions when a trade isn't going my way, often exiting too early or holding on for too long. Recognizing these tendencies has allowed me to make adjustments, like setting stricter rules for when to exit a trade or being more patient before making a decision. When using multiple different strategies or methods, the trade journal helps to see which strategies work best for different types of trades enabling us to form our own trading system that is data- and process-driven.

Introspection: Counting My Karma Points

> *'कर्मण्येवाधिकारस्ते मा फलेषु कदाचन।*
> *मा कर्मफलहेतुर्भूर्मा ते सङ्गोऽस्त्वकर्मणि॥'*
>
> —Bhagavad Gita (Chapter 2, Verse 47)

A very commonly known and used quote from the Bhagavad Gita that translates to: 'Focus on your action, and duties, without being attached to the outcomes.' A very powerful teaching which is very difficult to adapt. In this era of instant gratification, it becomes even harder to focus your energies only on actions. Very early on in my trading journey, I applied this learning in my trading journal in the form of Karma points, which became a key to attaining the turtle mindset, ensuring that I'm consistent and disciplined.

Karma points have been extremely unique and instrumental for me. I award myself a Karma point for a job well done, i.e., where I was disciplined and not necessarily where I earned a profit, and remove a Karma point if I failed in following my own rules. Your results do not define your Karma, your actions do. The best way to track progress is through introspection, and counting your Karma points is one unique and effective way. Over time, these Karma points continue to give me a clear picture of how disciplined I've been, independent of the financial outcomes.

There have been times when I followed my plan perfectly, but the trade resulted in a loss. Instead of being discouraged, I give myself a positive Karma point because I know that I did everything right according to my strategy. On the other hand, if I deviate from my plan—even if the trade was profitable—I assign a negative Karma point, reminding myself that luck, not discipline, was responsible for the gain. This helps me in rewarding myself for right actions, irrespective of results.

You need to analyse your trades, especially the failed ones. Each failed trade is like a dead body that needs a post-mortem to know what went wrong. This also helps you to assess whether your trades were driven by being in one of the danger zones or the control zone. Profit and loss are not important initially. Please do not get demotivated if you incur a loss. What is important is that you implement your learnings properly month on month and be disciplined.

You can analyse your Karma by giving yourself negative and positive points and at the same time, pat yourself for good Karma and punish yourself for bad Karma. Your confidence will get a big boost on seeing positive Karma even if you've incurred losses, and if your Karma at the end is negative, then you need to analyse what went wrong. It could be 2 things—either improper learning or improper execution. You need to revisit whatever it is that you're lacking and work on it. If your Karma is continuously negative even after proper learning and execution, then maybe there's a problem in my teaching. You need to find a mentor or a guru who can make you focused, help you stay positive and keep you disciplined.

This is a great exercise that you must try for at least 6 months to see the results. Over time, I've learned that real success in trading isn't just about making money—it's about attaining the turtle mindset by becoming more disciplined, more mindful and introspective. The trade journal is a tool for cultivating that discipline. It's a place where you can be honest with yourself, track your progress and continuously improve. By holding yourself accountable and honing each trade skill, you can develop the consistency and discipline (the turtle mindset) needed to thrive in the markets.

I can't stress enough the importance of building this habit early. Trading is a journey, and like any journey, it's the lessons learned along the way that matter the most. The trade journal is where those lessons are recorded, and it's a tool that I believe every trader should use to reach their full potential.

Being a Perpetual Learner: Constant Evolution

Learning never stops in trading. The market evolves, and so should you.

I like to call myself a perpetual learner because I believe that I still have miles to go before I sleep. If I become complacent and get comfortable with what I have now, my growth will be limited. In the fast-paced world of trading, the markets are constantly evolving, driven by new technologies, emerging trends and shifting economic conditions. To stay ahead, constant learning and upskilling are imperative.

The strategies and tools that worked yesterday might not work today, and those who fail to adapt, risk being left behind. By continually expanding our knowledge and honing our skills, we position ourself to identify new opportunities, manage risks more effectively and make informed decisions in an ever-changing landscape.

Enjoying Monotony, Being Calm: The Ultimate Bliss

Process, discipline, learning and journaling can all seem very monotonous when done day after day, but the results that it can reap for you is unparalleled. When you develop the turtle mindset, you start enjoying the routine life; following your own process brings a sense of joy and contentment to your life. Each day in the life of a turtle is pretty much the same—monotonous; however, that's what works the best for them. You need to do monotonous activities to survive in the markets in the longer run. Following a system every day is sometimes boring, but eventually that's what works and helps you sustain yourself in the longer run.

When you attain the turtle mindset, you're devoid of any emotions. A typical day in the life of the turtle involves being very calm and focused, irrespective of the climatic conditions or the surroundings. This is what we need to strive to attain. Being devoid of our gains as well as losses. In this zone, you're neither overly excited nor overly disappointed, but instead, you're present, grounded and alert without restlessness. In this zone, your focus shifts from chasing small wins to playing the larger game. You act when necessary, rest when needed and follow your strengths and systems. You build wealth steadily, allowing success to come as a byproduct. You accept yourself, not seeking to impress anyone or react to FOMO or stress. You simply do what works for you—quietly, consistently and deliberately.

That's the zone the turtle lives in, and that's the zone we should all aim to reach.

The Key to Living a Fulfilled Life: H2O

In conclusion, I would like to highlight a very important framework that has been my key to living a fulfilled life. This is not just about trading. You may be a homemaker, a student who hustles, a trader, an artist or an industrialist. What is important is to have a happy and content life where you look forward to your day. Our days and time are extremely valuable. Let's not waste it on undeserving things or people. Each day needs to be lived like it's our last so that we focus only on things that matter the most. Remember that our journey is more important than our destination.

Life has a way of giving us wake-up calls when we least expect them. For me, it happened during a 10-day period when I was on complete bed rest due to severe back pain. It was a humbling experience that forced me to pause, reflect and reassess the way I was living my life. As I lay there, unable to do the simplest of tasks, I realized that I had been neglecting the most important aspects of my well-being. That's when the idea of the H2O Framework was born—a simple yet profound philosophy centred around Health, Happiness and Optimism.

The Birth of the H2O Framework

During those 10 days of bed rest, I had plenty of time to think. It became clear to me that just as water (H_2O) is essential for life, health, happiness and optimism are essential for a fulfilling life. This realization led me to create a framework that would help me—and hopefully others—live a more balanced and meaningful life. I decided to dedicate myself to this framework for 21 weeks, with the goal of transforming my habits and, ultimately, my life.

Health: The Foundation of Everything

The first pillar of the H2O Framework is health. My back problems were a strong reminder that I had been taking my body for granted.

I realized that good health isn't just about avoiding illness; it's about actively nurturing and maintaining your body. This led me to make several important changes.

1. Food Habits: I became more mindful of what I was eating. I started to see food not just as a source of pleasure, but as fuel for my body. I began paying attention to the quality and quantity of what I consumed, understanding that every bite I took was either contributing to my well-being or detracting from it.
2. Yoga and Exercise: It wasn't until I started practising yoga regularly that I realized how much my body needed it. Yoga became a daily ritual for me, a way to connect with my body and rejuvenate my mind. Each morning, from 6.30 to 7.30, I practice with a teacher who guides me through the exercises. The energy and positivity I feel afterwards are indescribable. I found myself wondering why I hadn't started earlier.
3. Mindfulness and Meditation: Meditation was another practice I introduced into my routine. A dietician suggested that I meditate twice a day for 15 minutes. Initially, I was skeptical, but I decided to give it a try. Now, I meditate at least once a day. Meditation has helped me gain control over my mind and, in turn, my body. It's a practice I now consider essential.
4. Regular Check-ups: I also learned the importance of regular health check-ups. A thorough examination revealed that I had some underlying issues, such as high cholesterol and elevated blood sugar levels. Instead of turning to medication, I decided to tackle these problems by addressing their root causes. This meant making lifestyle changes that would improve my health from the inside out.

Happiness: Cultivating Joy in Everyday Life

The second pillar of the H2O Framework is happiness. I've come to understand that health and happiness are deeply interconnected—

when one thrives, so does the other. But happiness isn't just about feeling good; it's about actively creating joy in your life.

1. Gratitude: One of the most powerful tools for happiness is gratitude. I started keeping a gratitude journal, where I write down 5 things each day that I am thankful for. This simple practice helped shift my focus from what was lacking in my life to what was abundant.
2. Avoiding Negativity: I also made a conscious effort to distance myself from negativity, whether it was from people, situations or even certain activities. Negativity has a way of dragging you down, and I realized that by staying positive and surrounding myself with positive influences, I could create a more joyful and fulfilling life.
3. Acts of Kindness: Another source of happiness has been giving back. Whether it's sharing knowledge through videos or simply helping someone in need, acts of kindness have brought immense satisfaction into my life. There's a unique joy that comes from knowing you've made a positive impact on someone else's life.
4. Celebrating Successes: I've learned to celebrate not just the big wins, but the small successes as well. Whether it's a personal achievement or something as simple as making a friend smile, I've made it a point to acknowledge and celebrate these moments. Sharing these successes with others has also become a source of happiness for me.
5. Appreciating Others: Lastly, I've made it a habit to celebrate the people around me. Recognizing and appreciating others' efforts not only brings joy to them but also reflects back on me, creating a positive and uplifting environment.

Optimism: The Key to a Bright Future

The final pillar of the H2O Framework is optimism. In my experience, optimism is essential for a fulfilling life because it shapes how we view the future and respond to challenges.

1. Drawing Inspiration: I cultivate optimism by reading about the successes of others. Whether it's the story of a visionary like Steve Jobs or the journey of a company like Sony, these stories inspire me to keep pushing forward, no matter the obstacles.
2. Sharing Successes: Just as I celebrate my own successes, I make it a point to share them with others. Whether it's a video that resonated with viewers or a personal milestone, sharing these moments reinforces my belief that the future holds even greater things.
3. Creating a Vision: Optimism also comes from having a clear vision for the future. I've created a roadmap for the next 5 years, setting goals that give me direction and purpose. This clarity helps me stay focused and optimistic, even when faced with uncertainty.
4. Self-Reflection: Writing down my thoughts and experiences, or making videos, has become a valuable tool for self-reflection. It allows me to track my progress, learn from my mistakes and maintain a positive outlook on my journey.
5. Seeking Mentorship: Finally, I've learned the importance of mentorship. Whether it's through books, programs or personal relationships, having mentors has been crucial in guiding me through life's challenges. They provide wisdom, support and perspective, helping me stay optimistic and focused on my goals.

The 21-Week Challenge: A Commitment to Change

After developing the H2O Framework, I decided to put it into practice with a 21-week challenge. For 21 weeks, I committed to following this framework diligently, making small but significant changes in my life. I tracked my progress in an Excel sheet, assigning 'Karma points' to each action I took. If I met my goals for the week, I earned positive points; if I fell short, I recorded a negative point.

This challenge wasn't just about improving my own life—it was about building a community of like-minded individuals who wanted to live better, more fulfilling lives. I invited others to join me, to take the challenge and share their progress. Together, we're working to create a positive, supportive environment where everyone can thrive.

Embracing Change

The H2O Framework has been a transformative force in my life. It has helped me overcome negativity, improve my health and cultivate a more optimistic outlook on life. But more importantly, it has given me the tools I need to live with intention and purpose. I'm excited to continue this journey and to share it with others. If you're ready to make a change, I invite you to join me in embracing the H2O Framework and transforming your life, one step at a time.

Notes

Scan this QR code to access the detailed notes.

About the Author

Vivek Bajaj is a distinguished Indian entrepreneur, market expert and financial educator who has played a significant role in improving stock market awareness in India. With over 20 years of experience in the financial markets, he has dedicated his career to making investing and trading easier to understand for everyday learners.

Vivek is a chartered accountant (CA) and company secretary (CS), and holds an MBA from IIM Indore. He started his career in the financial markets as a commodities analyst and later built one of the largest stock market firms in eastern India.

Among his notable ventures is Kredent, a financial services firm that focuses on trading, advisory and market-related solutions. Another important venture is iRage, a technology-driven platform that provides advanced trading infrastructure and market access to active traders.

In addition to these, Vivek is also the co-founder of Elearnmarkets, a comprehensive financial education portal, and StockEdge, a leading investment analytics platform with millions of users. Through these platforms, he has empowered countless individuals with the knowledge and tools to navigate the complexities of the stock market.

Beyond entrepreneurship, he is an active knowledge contributor across social media platforms in finance, with over a million followers. Through his widely followed *Learn2Trade* series on YouTube, Vivek has guided thousands of beginners step by step through the fundamentals of the stock market. His approachable teaching style and deep market insight have made him one of India's most respected voices in retail investing education.

Vivek Bajaj continues to inspire and mentor aspiring investors with a simple belief—the right knowledge, when shared honestly, has the power to transform lives.

About the Co-author

Annapurna Chowdhury represents the journey of a beginner stepping into the world of the stock market with curiosity and determination. She holds a Bachelor of Commerce (B.Com) degree and a Master of Science (MSc), giving her a strong academic foundation. With a genuine interest in understanding the stock market, Annapurna became part of Vivek Bajaj's *Learn2Trade* series, where she began learning the fundamentals of trading and investing under structured guidance.

Her journey reflects the experience of many first-time investors—starting with basic questions, learning core concepts, and gradually developing clarity through guided learning. Annapurna's progress highlights the importance of the right mentorship and a willingness to learn.

She stands as an example of how with proper guidance, effort, patience and consistency, anyone can begin their journey towards financial understanding.